CW00591449

Mic. osoft
Works Suite 2002
explained

Books Available

By the same authors:

If you would like to purchase a Companion Disc for any of the listed books by the same authors, apart from the ones marked with an asterisk, containing the file/program listings which appear in them, then fill in the form at the back of the book and send it to Phil Oliver at the stipulated address.

Microsoft Works Suite 2002 explained

by

N. Kantaris
and
P.R.M. Oliver

Bernard Babani (publishing) Ltd
The Grampians
Shepherds Bush Road
London W6 7NF
England
www.babanibooks.com

Please Note

Although every care has been taken with the production of this book to ensure that any projects, designs, modifications and/or programs, etc., contained herewith, operate in a correct and safe manner and also that any components specified are normally available in Great Britain, the Publishers and Author(s) do not accept responsibility in any way for the failure (including fault in design) of any project, design, modification or program to work correctly or to cause damage to any equipment that it may be connected to or used in conjunction with, or in respect of any other damage or injury that may be so caused, nor do the Publishers accept responsibility in any way for the failure to obtain specified components.

Notice is also given that if equipment that is still under warranty is modified in any way or used or connected with home-built equipment then that warranty may be void.

© 2002 BERNARD BABANI (publishing) LTD

First published - March 2002
Reprinted - November 2002

British Library Cataloguing in Publication Data:

A catalogue record for this book is available from the
British Library

ISBN 085934 522 X

Cover Design by Gregor Arthur
Printed and Bound in Great Britain by Cox & Wyman Ltd, Reading

About this Book

This book *Microsoft Works Suite 2002 explained* was written to help both the beginner and those transferring from another version of Microsoft Works. The material in the book is presented on the 'what you need to know first, appears first' basis, but you don't have to start at the beginning and go right through to the end. The more experienced user can start from any section, as they have been designed to be self-contained. The book does not, however, describe the workings of Microsoft Windows, or how to set up your computer hardware. If you need to know more about these, then may we suggest that you refer to our other books, also published by BERNARD BABANI (publishing) Ltd, and listed earlier in this book.

The core of Microsoft's Works Suite 2002 is Works 6.0 which makes this book suitable for users of both packages. The main differences are that Works Suite has Word 2002 as its word processor, and comes bundled with other Microsoft goodies such as Money 2002, Picture it! Photo 2002, Encarta Encyclopedia 2002, and AutoRoute Europe 2002. If you have Works Suite, you should ignore the section on the Works 6.0 word processor, and concentrate on the Word 2002 section instead. Other common elements include spreadsheets with graphing, database management with reporting, a calendar, an address book, the Works Portfolio and electronic communications using Outlook Express version 6.0 (version 5.5 for Works 6.0) and Internet Exporer 6.0. The package uses the Task Launcher as a front end and has been designed for 'home users', but it contains all the power that most of us will ever need.

The power and versatility of Works Suite 2002 is evident in its integration which allows data from any module to be quickly and easily transferred into any of the other modules. The package is a powerful one, offering many commands and functions. We found the Works 6.0 word processor which now includes autocorrect, tables that can span pages, and support for hyperlinks, to be almost as powerful as many of the 'stand alone' packages available today. Any missing features are the least used anyway, and probably not used at all by most people.

As is usual now, Microsoft have gone to town regarding the number and quality of Tasks and Wizards supplied with the Works Suite 2002 package. As with previous books, we have not, however, spent much time describing these for two good reasons:

1. They are very user friendly and almost anyone should be able to work through them without too many problems.

2. We feel strongly that you will become more proficient with the Works Suite 2002 program, as a whole, if you build your own applications.

If you want to start off using these 'tailor made' files and documents, have a look through Chapter 14 before getting too much further in the book. However, bear in mind that predefined word processing templates and wizards, such as letters and reports, in the Task Launcher require Word 2002.

This book is intended as a supplement to the on-line Help material, and to the very limited documentation that now seems to come with Microsoft's packages. It will provide the new user with a set of examples that will help with the learning of the most commonly used features of the package, and also help provide the confidence needed to tackle some of the more advanced features later.

About the Authors

Noel Kantaris graduated in Electrical Engineering at Bristol University and after spending three years in the Electronics Industry in London, took up a Tutorship in Physics at the University of Queensland. Research interests in Ionospheric Physics, led to the degrees of M.E. in Electronics and Ph.D. in Physics. On return to the UK, he took up a Post-Doctoral Research Fellowship in Radio Physics at the University of Leicester, and then in 1973 a lecturing position in Engineering at the Camborne School of Mines, Cornwall, (part of Exeter University), where between 1978 and 1997 he was also the CSM Computing Manager. At present he is IT Director of FFC Ltd.

Phil Oliver graduated in Mining Engineering at Camborne School of Mines in 1967 and since then has specialised in most aspects of surface mining technology, with a particular emphasis on computer related techniques. He has worked in Guyana, Canada, several Middle Eastern and Central Asian countries, South Africa and the United Kingdom, on such diverse projects as: the planning and management of bauxite, iron, gold and coal mines; rock excavation contracting in the UK; international mining equipment sales and international mine consulting. In 1988 he took up a lecturing position at Camborne School of Mines (part of Exeter University) in Surface Mining and Management. He retired from full-time lecturing in 1998, to spend more time consulting, writing, and developing Web sites.

Acknowledgements

We would like to thank friends and colleagues, for their helpful tips and suggestions which assisted us in the writing of this book.

Trademarks

Arial and **Times New Roman** are registered trademarks of The Monotype Corporation plc.

HP and LaserJet are registered trademarks of Hewlett Packard Corporation.

IBM is a registered trademark of International Business Machines, Inc.

Intel is a registered trademark of Intel Corporation.

Lotus, 1-2-3 are registered trademarks of Lotus Development Corporation, a subsidiary of IBM.

Microsoft, **Encarta**, **IntelliMouse**, **MS-DOS**, **Windows**, are either registered trademarks or trademarks of Microsoft Corporation.

PostScript is a registered trademark of Adobe Systems Incorporated.

TrueType is a registered trademark of Apple Corporation.

All other brand and product names used in the book are recognised as trademarks, or registered trademarks, of their respective companies.

Contents

1

Package Overview

Microsoft Works Suite 2002 is a collection of powerful, fully featured, programs with a similar look and feel which, with the help of the Task Launcher, are made to work together as if they were a single program. The package was specifically designed for 'home use' to let you work with your data in an easily understood, but powerful, environment which enables you to quickly and efficiently obtain the results you want.

The core of Microsoft Works Suite 2002 is the Works 6.0 package[1] which can be purchased as a separate, cheaper, entity. The main differences between the two packages are:

- Works Suite 2002 has Microsoft Word 2002 as its word processor, not the slightly cut-down word processor that is included with the standard Works 6.0 package.

- Works Suite 2002 comes bundled with other Microsoft goodies, such as Money 2002, AutoRoute 2002, Picture It! Publishing 2002, Encarta Interactive World Atlas 2002, and FoneSync (a program that allows you to synchronise your data with handheld devices).

This book has been written for users of both packages, and as such, it includes an introduction to the Works 6.0 word processor in Chapters 2 and 3, while Word 2002 is covered in Chapters 5, 6 and 7. The other bundled programs in Works Suite 2002 are not covered however, as they are fairly intuitive anyway. All the other sections of the book, on the spreadsheet, database, calendar, address book, and Outlook Express are common to both versions of the package.

[1] Whenever possible, and for the sake of simplicity, we will refer to the core applications of Works Suite 2002 and Works 6.0, as applications of *Microsoft Works*, rather than referring to the individual names of the packages.

If you are new to computing, the various Microsoft Works applications have the following main functions:

Word Processor
Use this to write and enhance text, such as letters and reports and to make simple lists and create mail merge documents.

Spreadsheet
Use this to make a complex list, or to calculate numbers. From a spreadsheet, you can display your information, such as financial projections, in easily viewed charts.

Database
Use this to organise and track collections or other items in detail. A phone directory is a good example of a simple, but usually large, database. You can print reports showing all or part of the items in your database.

Calendar
Use this to keep track of appointments and special events, like an electronic diary.

Outlook Express
Use this to get full e-mail and Internet News features, as long as you have the required access to the Internet.

Address Book
Use this to create and manage a list of addresses, especially for sending e-mails or doing a mail merge.

All of these program functions can be very easily accessed from the Task Launcher, or from the Windows **Start** cascade menu system. The Task Launcher gives you three choices:

- You can tell Microsoft Works what task you want to carry out, and let it select the program and template to use.

- You can select the program you want to work with.

- You can select to open a file or document you have previously worked on.

All the Microsoft Works applications have a built-in consistency and style which makes them easier to use.

Hardware and Software Requirements

If Microsoft Works is already installed on your computer, you can safely skip this and the next section of this chapter.

Microsoft Works 6.0

To install and use the standard Microsoft Works 6.0 package, you need an IBM-compatible PC equipped with a Pentium 90 MHz or higher processor. As is usual these days though, the more powerful the processor the better. In addition, you need the following:

- Windows 98/Me/2000/XP, (or higher) operating system.

- A minimum of 16 MB of random access memory (RAM), although 32 MB is recommended.

- 65 - 165 MB of hard disc space required, depending on what applications you choose to install.

- Quad-speed or faster CD-ROM drive.

- Super VGA, 256-colour or higher resolution monitor.

- A Microsoft Mouse, or compatible pointing device.

- Microsoft Internet Explorer 6.0 browser and Outlook Express 5.5, which are automatically loaded unless you already have a higher version of these.

- For some features you will need a 28,800 baud, or higher, modem and Internet access, which may require payment of a separate fee to an Internet service provider (ISP). To run Microsoft Works 6.0 from a network, you must also have a network compatible with your Windows operating environment, such as Microsoft's Windows 95/98/Me, Windows NT/2000, Windows XP or higher, LAN Manager, etc.

Microsoft Works Suite 2002

Some of the standard requirements for Microsoft Works Suite 2002 are a little higher than the ones for Works 6.0. For this to work properly you will need:

- A PC with a Pentium 166 MHz, or higher, processor.

- At least 32 MB of RAM; 64 MB of RAM recommended.

- 850 MB of available hard-disc space for a typical installation, or up to 1.0 GB of hard-disc space if you install all the applications to run from your hard disc.

- A super VGA, 256-colour monitor supporting 640 x 480 or higher resolution; 800 x 600 recommended.

- Local bus video with 1 MB or more of video memory.

This may all sound a little daunting if you have an older PC, but entry level PCs come far better equipped than this these days. And they are still coming down in price all the time.

Installing Microsoft Works

Installing Microsoft Works on your computer's hard disc is made very easy using the SETUP program, which also configures Works automatically to take advantage of the computer's hardware. Before running SETUP, make sure you have no other programs active, and disable any virus detection utility, or you might get conflicts.

To install Microsoft Works, place the distribution CD in your CD-ROM drive and close it. The auto-start program on the CD should start the SETUP program automatically. If not, click the

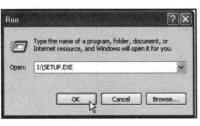

Fig. 1.1 The Run Dialogue Box.

Windows **Start** button, and select the **Run** command which opens the Run dialogue box shown in Fig. 1.1 and type in the **Open** text box the command

        i:\setup

where i: is our CD-ROM drive; yours will probably be different. Clicking the **OK** button, starts the installation of Microsoft Works. Our version of Works displayed the Setup screen in Fig. 1.2.

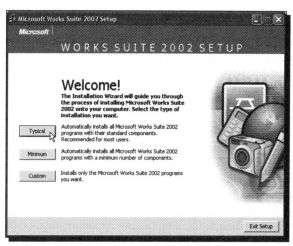

Fig. 1.2 The Microsoft Works Suite 2002 Setup Screen.

Your version may be different, but the basic procedures should be very similar. We suggest that you follow the instructions displayed on the screen. The choice above is between a **Typical**, a **Minimum**, or a **Custom** installation. We will assume you use the **Typical** option, but if there is not enough space on your hard disc drive, you might consider using one of the other options. Clicking the **Typical** option displays the screen in Fig. 1.3.

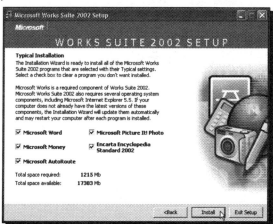

Fig. 1.3 The Microsoft Works Suite 2002 Setup Typical Option Screen.

On this second Setup screen you can select or deselect components of Microsoft Works, and as you are doing so the total hard disc space required is displayed. Clicking the **Install** button starts the file copying process, and gives you some message windows to help pass the time.

Note that if there is enough hard disc space on your C: drive (or the drive on which Windows is installed), Microsoft Works does not give you the option of installing the package on to another drive. Furthermore, the SETUP program automatically installs Internet Explorer 6.0 and Outlook Express 6.0, if earlier versions of these are found on your PC's hard disc.

During the installation process, and depending on your choice of software, you will be asked to insert additional CDs in you CD-ROM drive. If you select all the options shown in Fig. 1.3, you will be asked to insert 4 out of the 5 available CDs. Throughout the installation process the information box shown in Fig. 1.4 keeps you abreast of what is happening. The CDs 4 and 5 will also be required in your CD-ROM drive when you start using the Encarta Encyclopedia 2002 or the AutoRoute Europe 2002 options, respectively.

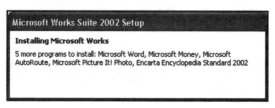

Fig. 1.4 The Information Box Displayed During Installation.

Hopefully you should have a successful installation and after a restart of your system, you will be returned to the Windows desktop which now should have two new shortcut icons, one for MSN and another for Microsoft Money. Also, when you open the cascading **Start** menus there should be several Works entries, similar to the those shown in Fig. 1.5 on the next page. What actually displays on your screen will depend on your version of Microsoft Works and on what applications you installed.

The Works Start Menu Entries

As mentioned previously, when you open the cascading **Start** menus there should be several Works entries, similar to the those shown below.

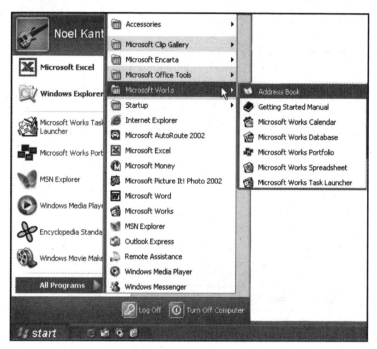

Fig. 1.5 The Microsoft Works Start Menu Entries.

The **Getting Started Manual** option opens a screen version of the short booklet that comes with the Microsoft Works package. Perhaps this would be a good time to take this tour, either on-line, or with the paper version. The choice is yours.

Selecting the Microsoft Works Portfolio from the cascade **Start** menu, displays the utility's icon, shown here in Compact view. There are two other views of this utility which can be accessed when you click the top of the **Portfolio** icon, Docked View and Gallery View. The Docked View is shown in Fig. 1.6, while the Gallery View is shown in Fig. 1.7.

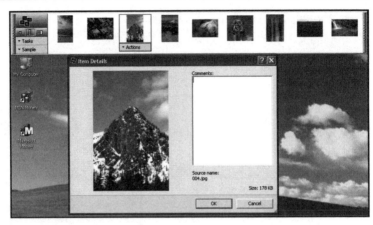

Fig. 1.6 The Microsoft Works Portfolio Opened in Docked View.

Fig. 1.7 The Microsoft Works Portfolio Opened in Gallery View.

Warning: If you have a sizeable number of shortcut icons on your monitor's desktop the Microsoft Works Portfolio can cause a considerable havoc with their positioning on the screen, particularly when displaying in Docked form; it simply pushes your icons out of the way to make room for its display, while the Gallery view slows down your system even if it is minimised on the Task bar. Furthermore, when Portfolio is in Compact view, its window displays on top of all other application windows obscuring parts of their screen. Because of the above reasons, we decided quite early on to dispense with the use of the Works Portfolio. If you also decide to do the same, it can be done quite easily as follows:

- Click the **Tasks** option, then select **Options** from the drop-down menu, as shown in Fig. 1.8 to the right.

- Uncheck the **Start the Works Portfolio every time I start Windows** box in the displayed Option dialogue box and click **OK**, as shown in Fig. 1.9 below.

Fig. 1.8 The Works Portfolio Tasks Menu.

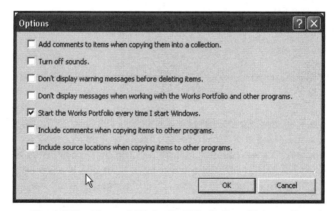

Fig. 1.9 The Microsoft Works Portfolio Options Dialogue Box.

Respond appropriately to the displayed warning boxes, so that next time you start Windows the Works Portfolio is disabled. The Works Portfolio can always be started, when needed, from the **Start** cascade menu as discussed earlier.

The Works Task Launcher

To start the Works program, select the Microsoft Works Task Launcher, shown to the left, from the **Start** cascade menu.

When the program is opened, the following Task Launcher window is displayed.

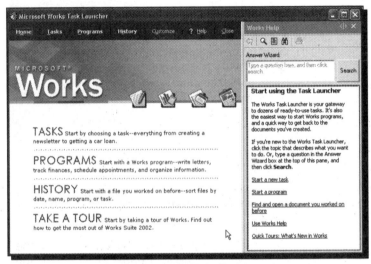

Fig. 1.10 The Microsoft Works Task Launcher.

Note that the **Home** tabbed section at the top of the screen is the active one the first time you use the Task Launcher. As you work with other options, such as **Tasks**, **Programs**, **History**, etc., the Task Launcher remembers your last choice so that the next time you start the Launcher it displays that choice.

Perhaps now is a good time to 'Take a Tour' and find out what is new in Microsoft Works. These tours are pretty short, but you will learn quite a bit if you are a newcomer to Works.

The Task Launcher has six tabbed sections, the first one being **Home**, shown open above, while **Tasks** gives rapid access to all the tasks that come with the package. If you want to use these, fine, but we will first spend some time getting used to the different tools that make up the Works program. For a brief description of using **Tasks** you could look at Chapter 15, otherwise click the **Programs** tab to change the Launcher to that shown in Fig. 1.11 below.

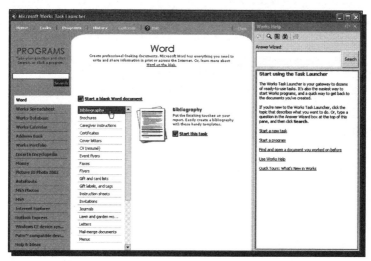

Fig. 1.11 The Programs Screen of the Task Launcher.

We must admit that this is our preferred method of starting the various applications within Works, rather than using the cascade **Start** menu alternative.

This window gives you access to all the programs included in the Works Suite 2002 package with Word (2002) listed as the word processor (to verify the version, start the program and use the **Help**, **About Microsoft Word** menu command). Clicking a button in the list on the left opens a list of the tasks with prepared templates that are available for that application. Those seen above are for the Word 2002 word processor. When you select a task and click its **Start** button, you are usually given a selection of styles to choose from in the Wizard that opens. To simply start an empty Works application, select it in the above left list, and then click the **Start a blank.....** link shown above the task list.

The **History** tab option is used to open files or documents already created in the Microsoft Works applications. A list of previous files (if any!) is displayed and double-clicking on one of them will rapidly open it in the relevant Works tool.

We suggest you experiment with these options and Tasks later, but at the moment simply press the **Start a blank Word document** option in the **Programs** tab Launcher window. This should open the word processor, as shown below.

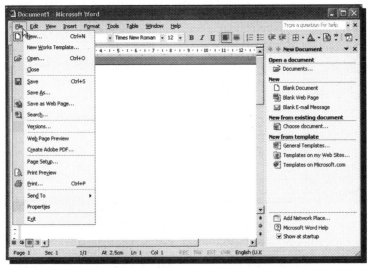

Fig. 1.12 The Shortened and Full File Sub-menu in Word.

In the above composite screen dump we show the drop-down sub-menu of the **File** option, which when it is first activated displays only the most important options of the menu command. A few seconds later, or if you click the double arrow-heads at the bottom of the shortened sub-menu with the mouse pointer, the full sub-menu is displayed. This facility is only available in Word.

The order of the sub-menu options in both the short and the full version of the sub-menu could differ from ours. This is because Word learns from your actions and automatically promotes the items you choose from menu extensions on to the shortened version of the sub-menu.

The Works Menus

The menu bar, as shown in Fig. 1.12, has the item **File** in the menu selected, with its drop-down sub-menu displayed underneath. The drop-down sub-menus associated with the other menu items can be seen by pressing the right arrow key, or by clicking on them with the mouse. Pressing the <Esc> key clears the sub-menus.

To activate the main menu of any Microsoft Works application either use the mouse to point to an item, or press the <Alt> key, which causes the first item of the menu (in this case **File**) to be selected, then use the right and left arrow keys to highlight any of the items in the menu. Pressing either the <Enter> key, or the left mouse button, reveals the drop-down sub-menu of the highlighted menu item.

Menu options can also be activated directly by pressing the <Alt> key followed by the underlined letter of the required option. Thus pressing <Alt+O>, causes the drop-down sub-menu of **Format** to be displayed. You can use the up and down arrow keys to move the highlighted bar up and down a sub-menu, or the right and left arrow keys to move along the options of the main menu. Pressing the <Enter> key selects the highlighted option, or executes the highlighted command. Pressing the <Esc> key returns you to the main menu.

Selection of a sub-menu item can also be achieved by either typing the underlined letter of the required command, or using the mouse to point to the required command and pressing the left mouse button. With a mouse you can select an item from the main menu by pointing to it and pressing the left mouse button; then, with the button depressed, drag the mouse down the revealed sub-menu which highlights each sub-menu item in turn. Once the required item has been highlighted, release the mouse button to select it.

Some sub-menu options have quick keys attached to them, for example pressing the <Ctrl+S> keys together will at any time save the current document, without the menu system even being opened. Throughout this book we use the above convention to encourage you in their use.

Dialogue Boxes

Three periods after a sub-menu option or command, means that a dialogue box will open when the option is selected. A dialogue box lets you enter additional information, such as the name of a file, or lets you change settings.

To illustrate how they work, select the **File**, **Page Setup**, command which will display a tabbed dialogue box shown in Fig. 1.13 below.

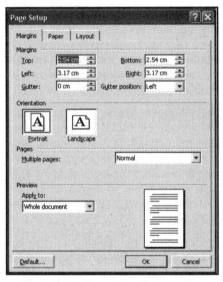

Fig. 1.13 The Page Setup Dialogue Box.

You usually move round a dialogue box with the mouse, but the <Tab> key can be used to move the highlight, or focus to be technical, from one field to the next, (<Shift+Tab> moves the focus backwards) or alternatively you can move directly to a desired field by holding the <Alt> key down and pressing the underlined letter in the field name. Within a group of options you can use the arrow keys to move from one option to another.

Having selected an option or typed in information, you must press a command button such as the **OK** or **Cancel** button, or choose from additional options. To select the **OK** button with the mouse, simply point and click, while with the keyboard, you must first press the <Tab> key until the dotted rectangle, or focus, moves to the required button, and then press the <Enter> key.

Some dialogue boxes contain Combo boxes which show a column of available choices when their right arrow is clicked. If there are more choices than can be seen in the area provided, you use the scroll bars to reveal them. To select a single item from a Combo, or List box, either double-click the item, or use the arrow keys to highlight the item and press <Enter>.

Dialogue boxes may contain Option, or radio, boxes with a list of mutually exclusive items. The default choice is marked with a black dot against its name.

Another type of dialogue box option is the Check box, which can be seen on the **Layout** tab. This offers a list of features you can switch on or off. Selected options show a tick in the box against the option.

If you can't work out the function of something in a dialogue box there is a quick way of getting context sensitive help. Clicking the **?** button, next to the Close button in the top right corner of the box, will add a question mark to the pointer. Click this on the unknown item and an explanation window will open up.

To cancel a dialogue box, either press the **Cancel** button, or press the <Esc> key enough times, to close the dialogue box and then the menu system.

The Works Screen

It is perhaps worth spending some time looking at the various parts that make up the Microsoft Works screen. To illustrate our discussion, click the **Programs** tab in the Task Launcher window and select **Works Spreadsheet**, and click **Start a blank spreadsheet**. Note that the screen window produced now displays a new list of menu names at the top, a Toolbar, a window title (Unsaved Spreadsheet, in this case), an empty worksheet with numbered rows and lettered columns, and a Help window down the right side with its own control buttons.

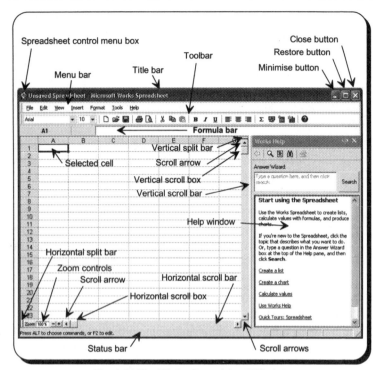

Fig. 1.14 The Works Spreadsheet Window.

The spreadsheet window, as shown in Fig. 1.14, opens in a separate window to the Task Launcher and here takes up the full screen area available. If you click on the restore button, you can make it show in a smaller window. This can be useful when you are working with several sheets, or documents, at the same time and you want to transfer between them with the mouse. Although multiple worksheet, database and document files can be displayed simultaneously in their own windows, you can only enter data into the active window (highlighted at the top). Title bars of non active windows appear in a lighter shade.

The Microsoft Works screen is divided into several areas which have the following functions. These are described from the top of the screen down, working from left to right.

Area	*Function*
Control box	Clicking on the control menu box, which is located in the upper left corner of the window, displays the pull-down Control menu which can be used to control the program window. It includes commands for restoring, re-sizing, moving, maximising, minimising and closing the window.
Title bar	The bar at the top of a window which displays the application name and the name of the current document.
Minimise button	Clicking this reduces the Works application window to an icon on the Taskbar. You click this icon to restore the Works window, which even maintains the cursor position.
Restore button	When clicked on, this button restores the active window to the position and size occupied before being maximised or minimised. The restore button is then replaced by a Maximise button, which is used to set the window to its former size.
Close button	The Windows X button that you click to close an application, or document window.
Menu bar	The bar below the title bar which allows you to choose from several menu options. The names of the main menu commands might be different when using different Works tools.
Toolbar	Displays a set of icons for each tool, which can be clicked to quickly carry out menu commands or functions.
Scroll bars	The areas on the screen (right and bottom of each window) that contain

scroll boxes in vertical and horizontal bars. Clicking on these bars allows you to control the part of a document which is visible on the screen.

Scroll arrows
The arrowheads at each end of each scroll bar which you can click to scroll the screen up and down one line, or left and right one cell, at a time.

Help window
The window that you can open (by clicking the **Help** icon) to display help text alongside your document.

Status bar
The bottom line of the window that displays the current program status and information regarding the present process.

Manipulating Windows

Like all standard Windows programs, Works allows the display of multiple sets of data within a given application tool, or several windows encompassing files from different tools, each within its own window. As with the previous version of Works these all open as completely separate application windows, not as windows within a main Works window.

You will need to manipulate these windows, by selecting which is the active one, moving them so that you can see all the relevant parts of an application, re-sizing them, or indeed closing unwanted windows once you have finished with them. A short discussion follows on how to manipulate windows so that you can get the best of what Works can provide.

In order to illustrate our discussion, use the **File, New** menu command several times and open some more spreadsheet or word processor documents, from the Task Launcher (which opens each time). As each selection is made, a new window is displayed placed on top of any existing ones.

Changing the Active Window

You can select the active window, from amongst those displayed on the screen, by pointing to any part of it, and clicking the left mouse button.

Closing a Window

Any window (provided it is the active window), can be closed at any time, maybe to save screen space and memory. There are several ways to close the active window; the easiest is to click on its Close button (the X button in the top right-hand corner), also you can double click on the **File Control Menu Box** (the icon in the upper-left corner of the window), or press the <Ctrl+F4> keys, or use the **File, Close** command.

If you have made any changes to a file in a window since the last time you saved it, Works will warn you with the appearance of a dialogue box giving you the option to save the file before closing it.

Moving Windows and Dialogue Boxes

When you have multiple windows or dialogue boxes on the screen, you might want to move a particular one to a different part of the screen. You can do this with either the mouse or the keyboard, but not if the window occupies the full screen, for obvious reasons.

To move a window, or a dialogue box, with the mouse, point to the title bar and drag it (press the left button and keep it pressed while moving the mouse) until it is where you want it to be. Then release the mouse button to fix it into its new position.

To move with the keyboard, press <Alt+Spacebar> to reveal the Application Control Menu. Then, press 'M', to select **Move,** which causes a four-headed arrow to appear in the title bar and use the arrow keys to move the shadow border of the window to the required place. Press <Enter> to fix the window to its new position, or <Esc> to cancel the relocation.

Sizing a Window

You can change the size of a window with either the mouse or the keyboard. To size an active window with the mouse, move the window so that the side you want to change is visible, then move the mouse pointer to the edge of the window or corner, so that it changes to a two-headed arrow (see page 24), then drag the two-headed arrow in the direction you want that side or corner to move. Continue dragging until the window is the size you require, then release the mouse button.

To size with the keyboard, press the <Alt+Spacebar> keys to open the Application Control menu, then press 'S' to select **S**ize, which causes the four-headed arrow to appear. Now press the arrow key that corresponds to the edge you want to move, or if a corner, press the two arrow keys (one after the other) corresponding to the particular corner, which causes the pointer to change to a two-headed arrow. Press an appropriate arrow key in the direction you want that side or corner to move and continue to do so until the window is the size you require, then press <Enter> to fix the new window size.

Splitting a Window

The windows of the Works spreadsheet application tool can be split both horizontally and vertically, so that you can see different parts of your work side by side in the same window.

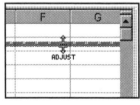

Fig. 1.15 Splitting a Window.

To split a window, move the mouse pointer onto a split bar (the bar either above the top scroll arrow, or to the left of the zoom controls), drag the new pointer shape to the required position as shown in our example in Fig. 1.15, and release the mouse button.

Managing Files

With Works applications you can create, save, open, or generally operate on files, by using the **File** command from the menu bar, by using the toolbar icons, or by using controls in the Open, Save and Save As dialogue boxes.

Saving a File

Once a document has been prepared, under any of the tool 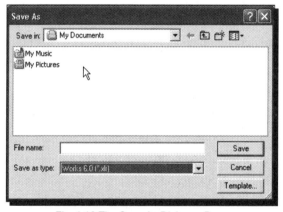 applications, you can save it by using the **File, Save** command, or by clicking the **Save** toolbar icon. The first time you use this command with, say, the spreadsheet, Works opens the Save As dialogue box, shown in Fig. 1.16.

Fig. 1.16 The Save As Dialogue Box.

By default all Microsoft applications use the **My Documents** folder created by Windows itself, within it we have created several sub-folders to hold files of different applications. So unless you want to store your work somewhere else, just select an appropriate sub-folder in the **Save in** text, type a new name without any extension in the **File name** text box and press **Save**, or the <Enter> key, to save your work under the typed filename which now becomes the new document title.

Once a file has been saved, subsequent use of the **File, Save** command, saves the file automatically under that filename, and in the same folder as you first saved your work. If you want to save an already saved file under a different name, then use the **File, Save As** command and type a different name, without an extension (the moment you start typing the new name, the default name vanishes from the display). When you press <Enter>, the program automatically adds the appropriate extension for you and saves the file.

The **Save as type** list box allows you to save the file in any of the formats listed. For example, you would select various Works or Excel versions, or even a Lotus 1-2-3 type, if you wanted to use the file later in that package.

Retrieving a File

To retrieve an already saved document from disc, use the **File, Open** menu command, or click the Open toolbar button, from whatever application you are in. This will bring up the standard Windows Open dialogue box, as shown in Fig. 1.17.

Fig. 1.17 The Open Dialogue Box.

In this case the default 'Works SS (*.xlr;*.wks)' has been selected in the **Files of type** box, so all the Works spreadsheet files in the selected folder are shown. To select a file, double-click at its name with the mouse pointer.

Using the Right-Click Menu

Select

Open
Explore
Search...

Sharing and Security...

Send To ▶

Cut
Copy

Create Shortcut
Delete
Rename

Properties

Fig. 1.18 The Right-
Click Menu.

A very useful Windows feature is the ability to carry out almost any file management functions from either the Open or the Save dialogue boxes. Simply select a file, or files, and click the right mouse button (or the left one if you are using it in left-handed mode!). Options allow you to **Open**, **Explore**, **Search Send To**, **Cut**, **Copy**, **Create Shortcut**, **Delete** or **Rename** a file, as well as open a list of its **Properties**.

The **Sharing and Security** option allows you to share a file or folder with other users of this computer only by dragging the file or folder to the Shared Document folder. It is worth understanding this option, so select it and read the displayed information.

Works File Extensions

With Windows you do not need to get involved with file name extensions, and by default, they do not even display. If you see them in our examples it is because we have changed the default settings. Extensions are used by Windows to determine what application (or Works tool) is needed to work with the file. But all the Windows file manipulation dialogue boxes display icons for the different file types.

To help you determine which type of file is used with the Works Suite 2002 (Works 6.0 word processor in brackets) tools, the filename extensions of the three main application tools are shown with their icons below.

Extension	*Icon*	*Tool*
doc or (wps ; wpt)		Works Word Processor
wlr ; wks		Works Spreadsheet
wdb		Works Database

The Mouse Pointers

With Microsoft Works applications, as with all other graphical based programs, using a mouse makes many operations both easier and more fun to carry out.

Works makes use of the mouse pointers available in Windows, some of the most common of which are illustrated below. When a Works application is initially started up the first you will see is the hourglass, which turns into an upward pointing hollow arrow once the individual application screen appears on your display. Other shapes depend on the type of work you are doing at the time.

     The hourglass which displays when you are waiting while performing a function.

     The arrow which appears when the pointer is placed over menus, scrolling bars, and buttons.

     The I-beam which appears in normal text areas of the screen.

     The 4-headed arrow which appears when you choose to move a table, a chart area, or a frame.

     The double arrows which appear when over the border of a window, used to drag the side and alter the size of the window.

     The Help hand which appears in the Help windows, and is used to access 'hypertext' type links.

Works applications, like other Windows packages, have additional mouse pointers which facilitate the execution of selected commands. Some of these are:

     The vertical pointer which appears when pointing over a column in a table or worksheet, used to select the column.

→ The horizontal pointer which appears when pointing at a row in a table or worksheet, used to select the row.

⇗ The slanted arrow which appears when the pointer is placed in the selection bar area of text or a table.

◄║► The vertical split arrow which appears when pointing over the area separating two columns, used to size a column.

÷ The horizontal split arrow which appears when pointing over the area separating two rows, used to size a row.

+ The cross which you drag to extend or fill a series.

⌀ The draw pointer which appears when you are drawing freehand.

The Microsoft Works Help System

With Microsoft Works by default you get a help window 'permanently' open on the right side of the screen, as shown in Fig. 1.19 on the next page. The contents of this window will depend on the Works application you are using. In our example this is the Works Spreadsheet.

There are several ways of using the Help system. If you can see an underlined item in the pane that seems useful, click it to open more details. A little like using a Web browser to surf the Help pane! You can also use the buttons below to:

◄▷ Control the size of the Help pane; it toggles the pane between full and half size.

✕ Close the Help pane altogether and have much more screen space to work with.

❓ Reopen the Help pane with an initial context sensitive display.

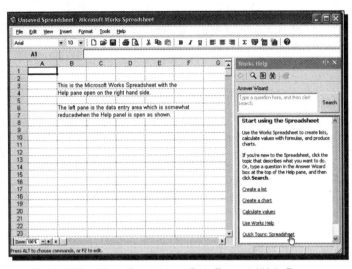

Fig. 1.19 The Works Spreadsheet Data Entry and Help Panes.

You can also type a complete question in the Answer Wizard text box and click the **Search** button, as we have done here.

This produces a list of options based on the keywords you type in. As before, click on one to open it and read its contents.

Fig. 1.20 Using the Answer Wizard.

 Clicking the back button, shown here, takes you back to the previous topic.

 If the text box is not open you can click the Answer Wizard button to make it reappear.

 The Contents button opens a hierarchical list to make it easy to find your way round the current Works application, as shown in Fig. 1.21 on the facing page.

You click on the text of an item to open its contained list. Sometimes you have to go several 'layers' deep, but eventually you will unearth a list with underlined options. Clicking on these will open a page of help information. Unfortunately, if you use the Back button on one of these pages it takes you back to the start of the Contents list. You can use the Related Topics list at the bottom of the pane, but really the whole layout of this section of the Help system is a little amateurish.

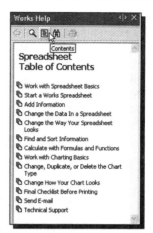

Fig. 1.21 The Help Contents List.

 When you click the Index button, shown here to the left, an alphabetical keyword list is opened, as shown in Fig. 1.22.

Typing a search keyword in the top text box, or double-clicking one in the list, opens a list of topics in the **Topics found** pane. Clicking one of these will open its data page in the main Help pane.

Whatever subject you choose, the Help window gives useful instructions on how to carry out the operation. Remember that when the mouse pointer turns to a hand you can click on the item to open another pane of help information.

Fig. 1.22 The Help Index List.

 Clicking the Print button, when it is available as shown here, opens the Print dialogue box for you to select any options required to send the current Help pane to your printer. Hard copy is sometimes useful for quick reference in the future.

To copy Help information to the Windows clipboard, you should first select it, then click the right mouse button and select **Copy** from the context menu opened, as shown here. You could then paste the text into a word processor file to maybe make your own Help data records.

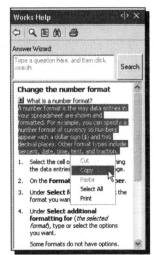

You can also use this method to send selected data only to the printer, using the **Print** menu option.

You should spend some time exploring the Help system; it is quite detailed, which is just as well as it is the only real source of information about Microsoft Works that is provided. Most things are in there, you just have to find them!

Fig. 1.23 Copying Selected Help Topics to the Clipboard.

Exiting Works

Whenever you are ready to leave a Microsoft Works application the procedures are the same whichever tool you are in. You either use the **File**, **Exit** command, click the application's Close button at the top right of the window, or use the <Alt+F4> key strokes. You have to do this with the Task Launcher as well, to completely exit from the Works package.

As long as any open files have been saved since they were last modified, the application will close. If not, you will be given the option to save them, before they are 'lost forever'!

2

Works 6.0 Word Processor

The standard Works 6.0 package comes equipped with an enhanced and quite impressive word processor almost as powerful as most 'stand alone' versions. It has all the normal editing features, including the ability to insert, delete, erase, search for, replace, and drag and drop copy and move.

As you would expect, it also allows you to enhance text and create bold, underlined, italic, strike-through, superscript, subscript and other specially formatted text. Being an integrated package it is easy to embed part of a spreadsheet into a document, carry out a mail merge, or send a document to a distant computer using the communications functions.

Enhanced Features

Enhanced and new features of the word processor include:

Automatic spell checking - the program can find and underline spelling mistakes as you type, and give you options to change the words. It now includes autocorrect.

Improved mail merge - selects names from the Windows Address Book and other data sources and quickly creates envelopes, labels, and form letters.

Easy-to-use tables - rapidly inserts tables to make lists, or to arrange paragraphs of text and pictures. It now supports tables extending over more than one page.

Powerful Undo feature - Undoes up to the last 100 typing or formatting actions you've carried out.

Starting the Word Processor

To access the word processor, as we saw in the last chapter, press the **Start a blank Word Processor document** option in the **Programs** tab window of the Task Launcher. Alternatively you can by-pass the Task Launcher by selecting the **Microsoft Works Word Processor** icon, shown here, from the Windows **Start** cascade menu.

A screen similar to that shown in Fig. 2.1 will appear. Here we have closed the Help window, as it is not very easy to work with it open. But before you do that, make sure you take advantage of what Help has to offer!

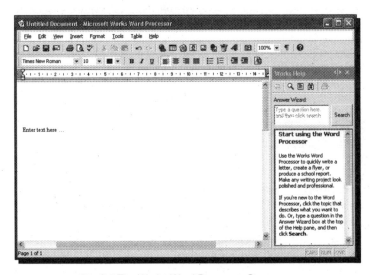

Fig. 2.1 The Works Word Processor Screen.

The Word Processor Screen

At the top of this screen is the Title bar, which shows the document title and the application that is open. Below this is the menu bar, which with the word processor, accesses the following sub menus:

Fig. 2.2 The Works 6.0 Word Processor Menu Bar.

We described in the 'Package Overview' how these are accessed either with the mouse, or by pressing the <Alt> key followed by the underlined letter.

The Toolbars

The Standard and Formatting Toolbars occupy the next lines down. If you use a mouse you will find these a big time saver, once you get in the habit of using them.

Fig. 2.3 The Standard and Formatting Toolbars.

If you prefer, you can turn them off with the **View**, **Toolbars** menu command, as shown in Fig. 2.4. These are toggle commands, when the '√' shows against a sub-menu option that toolbar or other screen feature will display, otherwise it will not. The only advantage to be gained by not showing them is you gain extra screen space.

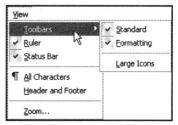

Fig. 2.4 The View Menu Options.

As shown above, you can also choose to have **Large Icons** on your Toolbars, or turn the **Ruler** and **Status Bar** on and off.

When you move the mouse pointer over one of the icons (buttons) on a toolbar, a yellow message box showing its function opens up. To use a toolbar you simply click the mouse on a button, or icon, and either a standard command will be actioned, or a formatting command will affect all text in the document that is highlighted.

The actions of all the toolbar buttons are given below and most are explained in more detail as we get into the book.

The Standard Toolbar

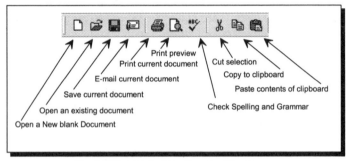

Fig. 2.5 First Half of the Standard Toolbar.

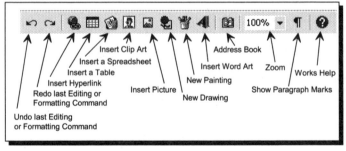

Fig. 2.6 Second Half of the Standard Toolbar.

The Formatting Toolbar

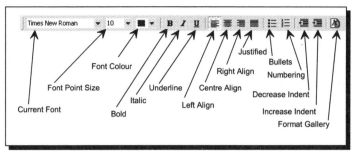

Fig. 2.7 The Formatting Toolbar.

The current font box shows the current typeface. Clicking on the down arrow button to the right of it allows you to change the typeface of any selected text. The font size box shows the size of selected characters which can be changed by clicking on the down arrow button next to it and selecting another size from the displayed list. The font colour button lets you change the colour of selected text

Next, are three character formatting buttons which allow you to enhance selected text by emboldening, italicising, or underlining it. The next four buttons allow you to change the justification of a selected paragraph, and the last four help you set the different types of Bullets, Numbering and Indentation options.

To reposition the Toolbars, click and grab one of the vertical lines on the left end of the tool or menu bars, and drag the bar up or down, as shown here. If your screen is wide enough you can place both Toolbars together to give you more editing space.

If your screen is too narrow to show all the buttons on a bar, small arrow icons will be placed at either end of the bar, as  shown in our example. Clicking one of these arrows will scroll the toolbar buttons through the available space.

The Ruler

Below the Toolbars is the ruler, which appears as a scale across the screen that can be toggled on and off like the Toolbars, with the **View**, **Ruler** command.

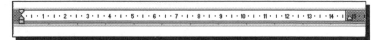

Fig. 2.8 The Horizontal Ruler.

The ruler shows and allows you to change the left and right margin positions and any tab or indent settings active in the paragraph the cursor is in. You change the settings by dragging the markers across the ruler. To add custom tabs to the ruler, you left-click with the mouse pointer to add a left tab and right-click to add a right tab. Double clicking on the ruler opens the Tabs dialogue box which gives you more precise control over the tab settings.

The bottom of the word processing window has a status bar which gives you useful information and shows the status of any keys that are currently locked. This bar can be turned on and off with the **View**, **Status Bar** menu command.

The other scroll bars, boxes and arrows described in the last chapter also surround the working area which makes up the remainder of the screen.

Entering Text

Before going any further, click the mouse in the main text entry area and type the memo text shown in Fig. 2.9, or something else, to get the feel of Works word processing.

When a new file is opened it is ready for you to begin typing in text. Any time you want to force a new line, or paragraph, just press <Enter>, otherwise the program will sort out line lengths automatically which is known as word wrap. So, you can just carry on typing a complete paragraph without having to press any keys to move to a new line.

If you make a mistake at this stage, press <BkSp> enough times to erase the mistake and retype it.

MEMO TO PC USERS

Networked Computers

The microcomputers in the Data Processing room are a mixture of IBM compatible PCs with Pentium processors running at various speeds. They all have 3.5" floppy drives of 1.44MB capacity, and most also have CD-ROM drives. The PCs are connected to various printers via a network; the Laser printers available giving best output.

The computer you are using will have at least a 3.0GB capacity hard disc on which a number of software programs, including the latest version of Windows, have been installed. To make life easier, the hard disc is highly structured with each program installed in a separate folder (directory).

Fig. 2.9 Text to be Typed into the Word Processor.

Now would be a good time to save the document, as described in the previous chapter, press **File, Save As** and type the filename **Memo1** to save in the My Documents folder. Obviously you can change the destination if you want. The program will add the WPS extension for you.

Moving Around a Document

You can move the cursor around a document by clicking the scroll bars and boxes, with the normal direction keys, with the key combinations shown below, or with the **Edit, Go To** command, or press <Ctrl+G>. With the last command you can jump to various document features, or to different page numbers.

To move	*Press*
Left one character	⇐
Right one character	⇒
Up one line	⇑
Down one line	⇓
Left one word	Ctrl+⇐
Right one word	Ctrl+⇒
Up one paragraph	Ctrl+⇑
Down one paragraph	Ctrl+⇓
To beginning of line	Home
To end of line	End
To beginning of file	Ctrl+Home
To end of file	Ctrl+End
Up one window	Pg Up
Down one window	Pg Dn

Document Editing

It will not be long when using the word processor before you will need to edit your screen document. This could be to delete unwanted words, to correct a mistake or to add extra text to the document. Such operations are easy to carry out.

For small deletions, such as letters or words, the easiest method is using the <Del> or <BkSp> keys. With the <Del> key, position the cursor on the first letter to delete and press <Del>; the letter is deleted and the following text moves one space to the left.

With the <BkSp> key, position the cursor immediately to the right of the character to be deleted and press <BkSp>; the cursor moves one space to the left pulling the rest of the line with it and overwriting the character to be deleted.

Word processing is usually carried out in the insert mode. Any characters typed will be inserted at the cursor location and the following text will be pushed to the right, and down, to make room. Pressing the <Ins> key will change you to overstrike mode and the letters 'OVR' will appear on the Status Line. In this mode any text you type will over-write existing text.

To insert blank lines in your text, make sure you are in Insert mode, place the cursor at the beginning of the line where the blank is needed and press <Enter>. The cursor line will move down leaving a blank line. To remove the blank line, position the cursor at its left end and press <Del>.

When larger scale editing is needed, such as using the copy, move and erase operations, the text to be altered must be 'selected', or 'highlighted', before the operation can be carried out. These functions are then available when the **Edit** sub-menu is activated, the toolbar options used, or Drag and Drop is used.

Selecting Text

The procedure in Works, as in all Windows applications, is that before any operation such as formatting or editing can be carried out on text, it must first be selected. Selected text is highlighted on the screen. This can be carried out in several ways.

Using the menu you can select all the contents of a document, with the **Edit**, **Select All** command.

Using the keyboard, position the cursor on the first character to be selected and either:

- Hold down the <Shift> key while using the direction keys to highlight the required text, then release the <Shift> key, or:

- Press <Ctrl+A> to select the whole document.

With the mouse

- Left click at the beginning of the block and drag the cursor across the block so that whole words of the desired text are highlighted, then release the mouse button.

- With the cursor in a word double-click the left mouse button to select that word.

- Position the cursor in the left window margin (where it will change to a right sloping arrow) and then either click the left button to select the current line, or double-click the left button to select the current paragraph, or triple-click to select the entire document.

We suggest you try out all these methods and find which ones you are most comfortable with.

Copying Blocks of Text

Once text has been selected it can be copied to another location in your present document, to another Works document (as long as it is open), to another Works tool, or to another Windows program.

As with most of the editing and formatting operations there are several ways of doing this. One is by using the **Edit, Copy** command sequence from the menu, moving the cursor to the start of where you want the copied text, and use the **Edit**, **Paste** command.

 You can also use toolbar icons, or quick key combinations. Press the **Copy** icon, or <Ctrl+C>, once the text to be copied has been selected, and the **Paste** icon, or <Ctrl+V>, to 'paste' it in the new location. These methods do not require the menu bar to be activated.

To copy the same text again to another location in the document, move the cursor to the new location and Paste it. This operation is called 'pasting' because of the old days (for some of us) with scissors and a glue pot!

When text is copied, or cut, it is actually placed on the Windows clipboard and remains there until replaced by other text.

Moving Blocks of Text

Selected text can be moved to any location in the same document. To do this, 'cut' it to the clipboard by clicking the **Cut** toolbar button, or the **Edit**, **Cut** command, or <Ctrl+X>, and then paste it in the new location by clicking the **Paste** button, with the **Edit**, **Paste** command, or <Ctrl+V>. The moved text will be placed at the cursor location and will force any existing text to make room for it. This operation can be cancelled before the final key command by simply pressing <Esc>.

Drag and Drop Editing

Probably the easiest way to copy and move small blocks of text in a document is with the Drag and Drop feature.

To move a selected block, drag it with the left mouse button depressed and release the button when the vertical bar is in the required new position. To copy it, hold down the <Ctrl> key while you drag, a small '+' is then added to the pointer, as shown above. The new text will insert itself where placed, even if the overstrike mode is active. Text moved, or copied, in this way is not placed on the clipboard, so multiple operations are not possible.

Replacing Blocks of Text

One block of text can be 'replaced' by another using either the cut or copy process. Obviously if cut is used the text at the original location will be removed, but not if the copy command is used. The process is the same as an ordinary copy or move, except that the block of text to be replaced must be selected before the final paste command is made.

Deleting Blocks of Text

When text is cut or deleted it is removed from the document. With Works any selected text can be deleted by pressing the <Del> key, or by selecting the **Edit**, **Clear** menu command. This will not, however, place the deleted text on the Windows clipboard, for possible future use. To do this you must use the **Edit**, **Cut** command, the **Cut** icon, or <Ctrl+X>.

The Undo and Redo Commands

As text is lost with the delete command you should use it with caution, but if you do make a mistake all is not lost as long as you act fairly quickly. Clicking the **Undo** button, or the **Edit**, **Undo..** command reverses your most recent editing or formatting commands. In fact you can undo up to 100 actions this way, heaven forbid! The Undo process works even after Drag and Drop actions.The quick key sequence for the Undo command is <Ctrl+Z>.

After you undo a command or action, the **Edit**, **Redo..** menu command and the **Redo** button, shown here, become active. These both allow you to restore what you've reversed. The quick key sequence for the Redo command is <Ctrl+Y>. Although these are very useful features to use, take care until you become familiar with them; it is sometimes not easy to work out what exactly is going on.

Page Breaks

The program automatically inserts a page break in a document when a page of typed text is full, but there will be places in most multi-page documents where you will want to force a new page to improve the layout. This is done by inserting a manual page break by pressing **Insert**, **Break**, **Page Break**, or just using the key combination <Ctrl+Enter>. Works readjusts all the non-manual page breaks for the remainder of the document. Both types of page break show as a line across the document.

If you use the **View All Characters** command as we have done in Fig. 2.10, it shows the paragraph marks in the document and you can tell the two apart. Both display as the line in Fig. 2.10, but the manual break has the '........ Page Break ....' paragraph mark above it and it does not span the page margins.

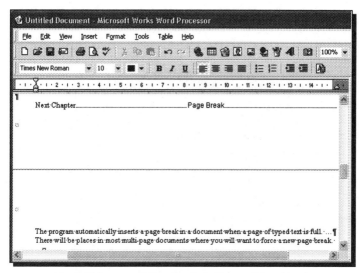

Fig. 2.10 Document Showing Both Types of Page Break.

A manual page break can be deleted by placing the insertion point immediately above it and pressing the <Del> key. An automatic page break cannot be deleted.

Viewing Word Processor Documents

The new Works word processor is fully WYSIWYG (what you see is what you get) with features such as columns, pictures, headers, footers and footnotes appearing in their correct positions. It displays each page in your document as it will look when printed.

The Zoom Command

The Zoom feature allows you to control the amount of the active document that will display on the screen at any time. The zoom size status of a particular document has no effect on the document when it is printed. There are two ways to alter the zoom setting. By clicking the arrow next to the

Zoom toolbar button shown here, or choosing **Zoom** from the **View** menu, and then the size you want from the dialogue box shown in Fig. 2.11.

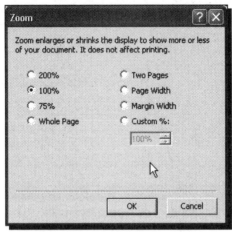

Fig. 2.11 The Zoom Dialogue Box.

In the Zoom box you have a **Custom %** option in which you can specify any magnification between 25% and 500%.

Other Views

Two other document view types are worth mentioning. Clicking the **Print Preview** button, or using the **File**, **Print Preview** command, opens a view of your document on the screen exactly as it will be printed. You can't edit text or make any changes in print preview, but you can also zoom the view in and out, and change the page settings. It is well worth using this feature to check your document every time before you print.

The last view available in the word processor is actioned with the **View**, **Headers and Footers** menu command. This opens the headers area at the top of each page and the footers area at the bottom, so that you can add or edit document headers and footers. Once you have placed either, double-clicking in the header or footer area has the same effect.

Character Enhancement

Another simplistic example will explain the principles of text enhancement. With any word processor it is often easier to type your text in first and worry about the document layout later on. Create a new word processing file and type in the letter text shown in Fig. 2.12 below.

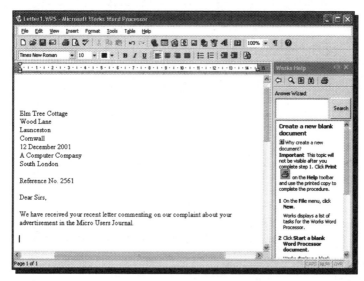

Fig. 2.12 Formatting Text in Works 6.0 Word Processor.

The date on line 5 is not just typed in. A code is embedded so that it will give the current date when the letter is printed. This is generated from the dialogue box opened with the **Insert**, **Date and Time** command. Choose the date format you prefer and select the **Automatically update when printed** option. When you have finished, save the document using the **File**, **Save As** command, calling it **Letter1**.

To improve the layout of the above letter, we will next walk you through the use of some of the commands in the **Format** sub-menu and also some of the toolbar and Quick key options.

First select the top five lines containing the address and date (the easiest way of doing this is to click the mouse alongside line 1, in the left margin, and drag it down to line 5) and then select the F**o**rmat, **P**aragraph command to open the box in Fig. 2.13. In the **Indents and Alignment** tab, select the **Alignment** as **Right** option, as shown, and press **OK**.

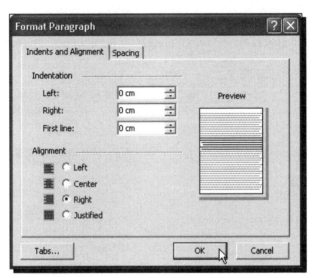

Fig. 2.13 The Format Paragraph Dialogue Box.

The whole block should now be right justified. By default paragraphs are left justified. While the block is still highlighted press the <Ctrl+L> keys and finally click the **Right Align** toolbar icon, shown here. You should now be back with a right justified address.

Then select the Ref... line of text and select **Format**, **Paragraph**, **Indents and Alignment** tab, and click **Center** (or use the quick keys <Ctrl+E>, or the **Center Align** toolbar icon) to centre the line between the left and right margins. While the selection highlight is still active press <Ctrl+U>, or the **Underline** icon on the toolbar, to underline the reference. By now you have probably accepted that the toolbar is by far the most convenient way of carrying out these enhancement functions.

Nevertheless, using a dialogue box usually gives you more options to choose from. With the last 'underline' option, for example, you have 16 different types of underlining to choose from! If you repeat the toolbar click, while the highlight is still active, the feature is turned off again; they act as toggle functions.

B   Next, select the words 'recent letter' and press <Ctrl+B>, or the **Bold** icon, to embolden them. Finally, select the section 'Micro Users Journal' and change them to italics

I   by pressing **Format**, **Font**, **Italic**, or <Ctrl+I>, or the **Italic** icon.

The letter now looks very different and should be similar to our Letter2, shown in Fig. 2.14, where the Help pane has been closed down.

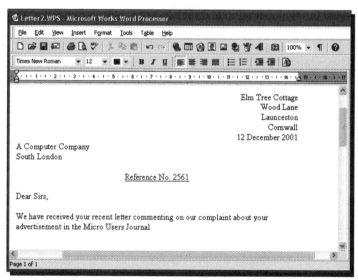

Fig. 2.14 Letter After Applying Formatting Enhancements.

What a difference with only a few keystrokes! Note that when the cursor is in text that has been enhanced, the relevant icon on the toolbar appears 'depressed'. In the above example the **Left Align** icon is selected. These status indicators are useful when the enhancements are not obvious from the screen text.

Fonts

A font is a typeface with a specific design. In Works 6.0 you can work with and print text in any fonts which are supported by your version of Windows. You can also work with any supported colours, but you can obviously only print them if you have a colour printer.

To change the font, size, colour or enhancements of specific text in a document, first select the text. Choose the **Font** command either from the **Format** menu, or from the 'object menu' opened by right-clicking the document edit area, and make selections in the opened dialogue box, as shown in Fig. 2.15.

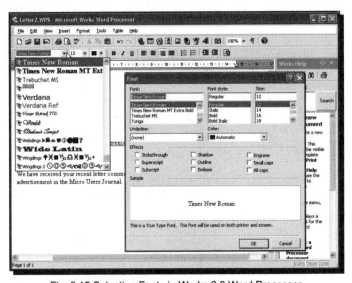

Fig. 2.15 Selecting Fonts in Works 6.0 Word Processor.

You can also, of course, change the font, size and colour of selected text from the **Font**, **Font Size** and **Font Color** toolbar icons. Clicking the arrow alongside each of these opens up a menu of available options.

The composite screen above, shows both methods of changing the font and font size of selected text. You will not be able to get them on the screen at the same time, though, so don't bother trying.

When they are available, the toolbar icons are by far the best option for carrying out these operations.

Works 6.0 word processor measures font sizes in points, where one point is 1/72nd of an inch. You may need to study your printer manual and experiment with these commands to make the most of this Works facility. One thing to remember though is that a printed page usually looks better if you use different fonts and sizes sparingly.

Printing Documents

Printers and Faxes

When Windows was installed on your computer your printers should have been installed as well. Many hundreds of different printers are supported by Windows so, hopefully, you shouldn't have too much trouble getting yours to work. The printer and printing functions are now (under Windows XP) included in a single Printers and Faxes folder, which you can open by double-clicking the above icon in the Control Panel window. Our Printers and Faxes folder, shown in Fig. 2.16, has a list of printers available for use, and an **Add a Printer** option under **Printer Tasks**.

Fig. 2.16 The Printers Dialogue Box.

This screen provides an easy way of adding new printers, configuring existing ones, and managing all your print jobs.

Installing a Printer

To 'manually' install a new printer to your set up, click the **Add a Printer** option under the **Printer Tasks**. This opens the Windows Add Printer Wizard, which really makes the installation procedure much easier than it used to be. As with all Wizards you progress from screen to screen by clicking the **Next** button. The first time you do this, you may have to wait a short time, while the printer driver information database is built.

The dialogue box below lets you choose the make and model of printer you want to install.

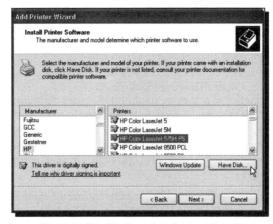

Fig. 2.17 The Windows Add Printer Wizard.

In our case we are setting up a Hewlett Packard (HP in the list) colour model LaserJet 5/5M PS. If you have a disc of drivers that came with the printer, put it in the floppy drive and click the **Have Disk** button.

You are next asked to select the correct Port. This refers to the socket at the back of your PC which is connected to the printer. For a stand alone set-up this would usually be the LPT1 port. (Short for Line Printer No.1). Next you can customise the printer name, maybe on a network, it would be useful to describe where it is actually located. You can also select whether you want the new printer to be your default, in which case all Windows programs will select it by default.

You should then accept **Yes** to have a test print carried out, to check that all is OK with the installation. When you click the **Finish** button a new icon will be placed in your Printers folder and, as long as the printer is switched on, a test page should be produced. Hopefully, this test should give an impressive demonstration of the printer's capabilities and you will be able to answer **Yes** when asked if the test was successful. If not, click the **No** button, and Windows will attempt to sort out the problem for you.

Configuring a Printer

With Windows all configuration for a printer is now consolidated onto a tabbed property sheet that is accessed from its icon in the Printers and Faxes folder. Right clicking a printer icon opens the object menu, shown on the left, which gives control of the printer's operation. If you click the **Properties** option, the dialogue box shown in Fig. 2.18 opens and lets you control all the

printer's parameters, such as the printer port (or network path), paper and graphics options, built-in fonts, and other device options specific to the printer model. All these settings are fairly self explanatory and as they depend on your printer type we will let you work them out for yourselves.

Now your printer is set up you can, at any time, use the **File, Print** command from the Works document menu bar, or <Ctrl+P>, to open the 'Print' box, shown in Fig. 2.19 overleaf.

Fig. 2.18 The Printer Properties Box.

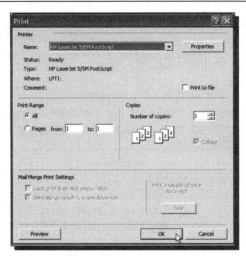

Fig. 2.19 The Print Dialogue Box.

The settings in this box allow you to select which printer is used, the number of copies, and which pages are printed. Finally select **OK**, to send print output from Works to your selected destination, either the printer connected to your computer, or to an encoded file on disc.

 The **Print** icon on the toolbar sends the current document to the printer using the active settings. It does not give you access to the Print box.

Do remember that, whenever you change printers, the appearance of your document may change, as Works uses the fonts available with the newly selected printer. This can affect the line lengths, which in turn will affect both tabulation and pagination of your document.

Page Setup

The next operation, to make sure your printer is happy with your document settings, is to set up Works for the paper and margin layout you want to use. The **File**, **Page Setup** command opens the tabbed dialogue box shown in Fig. 2.20. The settings in the three sections of this box are the UK default.

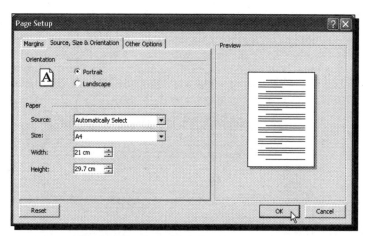

Fig. 2.20 The Page Setup Dialogue Box.

The **Source, Size and Orientation** tab screen, shown above, defaults to A4 size paper (210 x 297 mm). If you want to use a different size paper just select a standard size from the **Size** drop down list, or type in new dimensions for **Width** and **Height**. The default orientation is **Portrait** mode with the height of a page being greater than the width.

The **Margins** section includes settings for **Top, Bottom, Left** and **Right** margins, which are the non-print areas required on each edge of the paper. The **Header** margin is that required between the top of the page and the header line. The **Footer** margin is that between the bottom of the page and the footer line.

The **Other Options** tabbed section gives you control over the **Starting page number** which will normally be '1' unless you break up a piece of work into parts, or chapters, and of the printing of headers and footers, discussed in the next chapter.

Print Preview

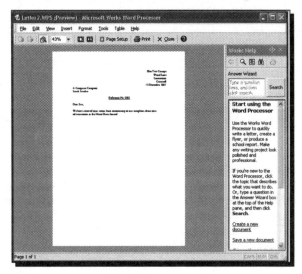

Works gives you an easy way of checking what your printer will produce with the **File**, **Print Preview** command, also actioned by clicking the **Print Preview** toolbar button. It lets you see a screen view of what the printed page should look like, similar to that shown in Fig. 2.21 below.

Fig. 2.21 The Print Preview Screen.

You can zoom in or out with the **Magnifier** button and then click the mouse pointer over a section of the page, to see your work at different magnification levels, and step through a multi-page document with the Previous or Next buttons.

With a long document you can also click the **Multiple Pages** button to get an overview of how the whole file will look when printed. To change page settings, such as margins and paper size as discussed earlier, click the **Page Setup** button.

If you are happy with the preview, press Print to print the document, otherwise press Close to exit Preview. All in all quite an improvement on some older versions of Print Preview.

3

More Advanced WP Features

Paragraph Formatting

Works defines a paragraph, as any text which is followed by a paragraph mark (which appears as a '¶' character on the screen, but only when switched on). So single line titles, as well as long typed text, can form paragraphs. Paragraph markers are not normally shown in Works, but toggling the **View**, **All Characters** command, or the **Show All** toolbar button, will toggle them on and off. The example below shows our file **Memo1** with formatting characters switched on. This facility can be very useful when you are laying out a complicated page of data. Note how blank space characters show as a '·' character.

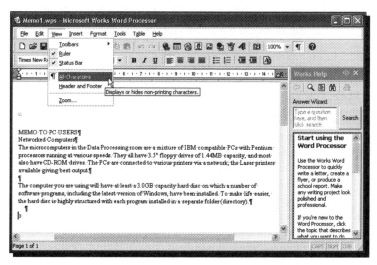

Fig. 3.1 A Memo Displaying Formatting Characters.

A paragraph marker is placed in a document every time <Enter> is pressed. All paragraph formatting, such as alignment, justification, centring, indenting and line spacing, is stored in the marker for the particular paragraph. If this marker is deleted, or moved, the formatting will be deleted or moved with it.

Indenting Text

Most documents with lists, or numbered sections, will require some form of paragraph indenting. An indent is the space between the margin and the edge of the text in the paragraph. This can be on the left or right side of the page.

Retrieve the file **Memo1** and type '1. ' and '2. ' before the first words of the two main text paragraphs. Select the two paragraphs and use the **Format**, **Paragraph** command, then click the **Indents and Alignment** tab to open the dialogue box in Fig. 3.2 below.

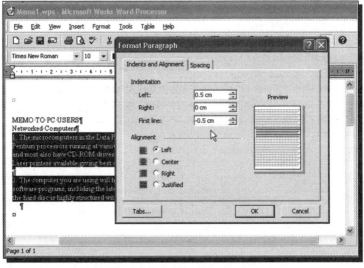

Fig. 3.2 Formatting Paragraphs.

Most of the paragraph formatting operations can either be carried out from the toolbar, the Ruler, or from this box. The alignment box offers:

Left	Smooth left edge, ragged right
Center	Text centred on line
Right	Smooth right edge, ragged left
Justified	Smooth left and right edges

To create left or right indents for the whole paragraph, type the amount of indent in the respective space. If only the first line is to be indented, type the amount needed in the **First Line**, **Indentation** space.

If you select the **Spacing** tab you will find options to fully control the spacing between lines of text and paragraphs. Under **Line Spacing** you can select several spacing options between single and quadruple. The **Lines Before** and **Lines After** options let you control the amount of white space you want above and below a selected paragraph.

Hanging Indents

The dialogue box in Fig. 3.2 is set up to produce hanging indents, so that the paragraph numbers show up clearly at the left of the paragraphs.

To do this you should type the same value in the **First Line** box - with a negative sign in front - as that typed in the **Left**, **Indentations** box. When you have finished, click **OK**, place the cursor in front of the letter 'T' of each numbered paragraph and press the <Tab> key on your keyboard. The memo should now look the same as that shown in Fig. 3.3 below. Save the document as **Memo2**.

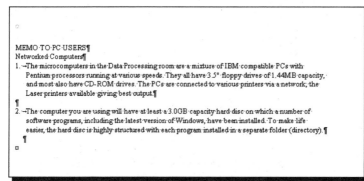

MEMO·TO·PC·USERS¶
Networked·Computers¶
1.·–The·microcomputers·in·the·Data·Processing·room·are·a·mixture·of·IBM·compatible·PCs·with·
    Pentium·processors·running·at·various·speeds.·They·all·have·3.5"·floppy·drives·of·1.44MB·capacity,·
    and·most·also·have·CD-ROM·drives.·The·PCs·are·connected·to·various·printers·via·a·network,·the·
    Laser·printers·available·giving·best·output.¶
¶
2.·–The·computer·you·are·using·will·have·at·least·a·3.0GB·capacity·hard·disc·on·which·a·number·of·
    software·programs,·including·the·latest·version·of·Windows,·have·been·installed.·To·make·life·
    easier,·the·hard·disc·is·highly·structured·with·each·program·installed·in·a·separate·folder·(directory).¶
¶

Fig. 3.3 Formatting Text - Hanging Indents.

Indenting with the Ruler

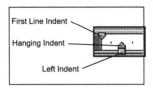

First Line Indent

Hanging Indent

Left Indent

If you look carefully at the Ruler at the top of the screen, after you have placed an indent, you should see that an indent marker has been placed on it. This gives you another way of quickly setting and adjusting indents. You simply drag the marker to the new indent position, as shown by the drop down vertical line, and any selected paragraphs will be indented when you release the mouse button.

Paragraph Borders

As well as the Microsoft Draw and WordArt packages, which are described later, Works 6.0 has the facility to place different types of lines, colours and shading patterns in and around 'selected' paragraphs and pages, with the **Format, Borders and Shading** command. An example of the Borders and Shading box and the results of its settings is shown in Fig. 3.4 below. Try it for yourself, but first refer to the suggestions at the top of the next page.

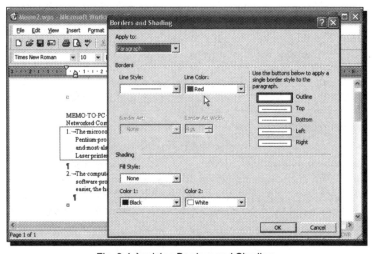

Fig. 3.4 Applying Borders and Shading.

First, select the paragraphs you want to enhance, then in the Borders and Shading box turn on the type of border you want, its **Line Style** and its **Line Color**, and then press <Enter>, or click **OK**. To remove borders you must cancel the selections made in the various boxes.

Even if you do not need these features very often, they are well worth exploring.

Text Enhancement

Tab Settings

The Works 6.0 word processor defaults to left aligned tabs every 1.27cm, or 0.5in, across the page. For most purposes these will be adequate, but if you need to generate lists, or tables, indexes, etc., the custom tab facility could prove useful. You could, of course, use the Table feature for these as well. There are four types of custom tab stops:

Left	Text aligns to the right of tab
Right	Text aligns to the left of tab
Center	Text centres on tab stop
Decimal	Text aligns at a decimal point

Tabs are shown on the ruler at the top of the screen, as can be seen in our example on the next page.

All default tabs to the left of a new custom tab are removed automatically. You can also select one of four types of leader characters to fill the space to the tab spot. This is useful when preparing contents pages.

Our example shows part of a contents page which has two **Left** aligned tabs for the subjects, and a **Right** tab with a dot leader for the page numbers. To set custom tab stops, select the required paragraph, or the whole document, and either double click your mouse on the ruler, or choose **Format, Tabs**. A dialogue box like the one shown in Fig. 3.5 overleaf will open.

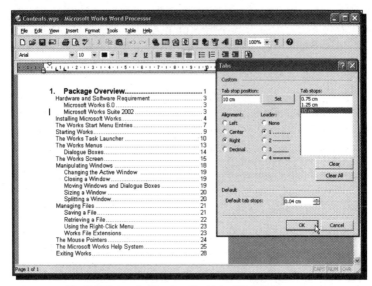

Fig. 3.5 Example Showing the Use of Tab Settings.

If necessary, type the **Tab stop position** in the text box, select the options needed from the **Alignment** and **Leader** boxes and choose **OK** to place the tab on the ruler. This operation can be repeated for as many tabs as are required. Use the **Clear**, or **Clear All** buttons to remove one tab, or all the tabs, from the ruler.

Tables of figures can be created, and adjusted, by the careful use of tab settings. Use decimal, or right aligned tab stops, for columns of figures. It is an easy matter to readjust the width of columns by resetting the tabs, even after the table has been created.

The Tables feature, discussed later in the chapter, is an easier way of creating such tables however.

Headers and Footers

In a printed document a header is text that appears at the top of each page of the document, whilst a footer appears at the bottom. These can be used to add page numbers, titles, dates and times to your documents.

These are easily added in the Works 6.0 word processor by simply typing text, and embedding code, in the WYSIWYG Header and Footer boxes at the top and bottom of the screen page. To place these boxes the first time you need to use the **View**, **Header and Footer** command. Once you have placed one in a document you can double-click in it to access it.

A header is shown in the next example (Fig. 3.6). This can be added to the file **Memo2** as follows.

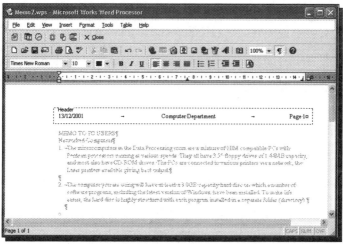

Fig. 3.6 Using Headers and Footers.

To add	Click
A page number	🔢
The date	📅
The time	🕐
Open the **Page Setup** dialog box	🗔
Add the document name to a header or footer	📄
Switch between the header and footer	📧
Close the header and footer areas and toolbar	❌

Use the **View**, **Header and Footer** command to open the Header box and right-click on the right end of the Ruler to place a right custom tab. For some reason this version of the Works word processor does not provide this tab automatically. A new toolbar, as shown in Fig. 3.6 should have been added to the Works window (an explanation of their function is given in the box to the left). Next, move the cursor to the start of the header box and add the date special command by clicking the **Insert Date** button, or typing <Ctrl+D>, or using the **Insert, Date and Time** menu command.

With the latter method you can choose the format of the date. This adds today's date to the screen, but will print the current date on paper when the document is opened at a later date. Press <Tab> and the cursor is automatically centred on the line. Add a title and press <Tab> again to bring the cursor to the right-hand side of the page. Type 'Page' followed by the **Insert**, **Page Numbers** command, or click the **Insert Page Number** button to place the page number, and save as **Memo3**.

Your screen should now look like ours, with the main body of the memo 'greyed out'. Double-clicking there will re-activate the main area and grey out the header box. You could use the **File**, **Print Preview** command to quickly check the printed result. If you want, you can add enhancements, or change the fonts of the header and footer text.

Footnotes

A useful feature in Works is the ability to place reference marks, or numbers, anywhere in a document. Text can be 'attached' to each reference, which will automatically be printed at the end of the relevant page. This operation is carried out with the **Insert**, **Footnote** command.

Footnotes are automatically numbered, and renumbered if edited, but you can also specify other reference marks (such as * or $, for example).

To create a footnote, move the cursor to the position in the document where the reference mark is needed, choose **Insert**, **Footnote,** alter the dialogue box if you want to force a mark instead of a numbered reference, and select **Insert**.

Fig. 3.7 The Footnote and Endnote Box.

If **Autonumber** is selected in the box, the next consecutive footnote number will be placed at the cursor and the footnote pane will be opened at the bottom of the page. You type the reference text here, and format, or enhance it, if required. You move the cursor back to the document with the mouse when you are ready, or double-click on the reference number.

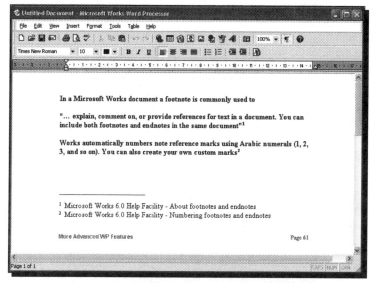

Fig. 3.8 Example Showing the Placement of Footnotes.

Once placed, footnote reference marks are always shown in the document. Footnote text can be edited, the same as any other text and reference marks can also be moved, copied or deleted, with Works looking after the positioning of the attached text.

Endnotes

When you print a document that contains footnotes, they are placed at the bottom of the page holding the reference point. To force your reference text to be printed at the end of the main body of the document text, place them as described above, but click **Endnote** in the Footnotes and Endnotes dialogue box.

Your final printed presentation of these endnotes will be improved if you place blank lines at the end of your document text. Without these the endnote text will be printed immediately under the last line of document text. Any reference heading required should then be placed after these blank lines.

With Works 6.0 you can have footnotes and endnotes in the same document, but only one of them can be automatically numbered.

Searching for and Replacing Text

Works allows you to search for specifically selected text, or character combinations. In the search mode, actioned with the **Edit**, **Find** command, it will highlight each occurrence in turn so that you can carry out some action on it, such as change its font or appearance.

In the **Edit**, **Replace** mode you specify what replacement is to be automatically carried out. For example, in a long book chapter you may decide to replace every occurrence of the word 'programme' with the word 'program'. This is very easy to do.

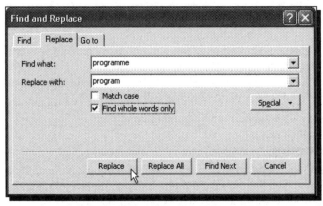

Fig. 3.9 The Find and Replace Dialogue Box.

First go to the beginning of the file, as search only operates in a forward direction, then choose **Edit**, **Replace**. In the **Find what** box, type **programme**, and in the **Replace with** box type **program**. To make sure that part words are not selected, choose the **Find whole words only** option, and then click the **Find Next** button. The first match will be highlighted in the document, then either choose **Replace**, to change once, or **Replace All** for automatic replacement. If you select the **Match case** option, only text with the exactly specified case letters will be selected.

The **Special** button gives options for searching for, and replacing, special characters, or a combination of text and special characters (for example, tab or paragraph marks, or white space). White space is a combination of any number of consecutive spaces and tab marks. A very useful example of this is when you have imported columnar data from another file, and the columns are separated with spaces; you can search for white space, and replace it with a tab, to realign the columns.

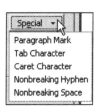

Another example would be searching for a word, which occurs at the beginning of a paragraph, or after a tab. The list below also gives the key combinations of these special characters to enable them to be entered straight into the Find and Replace boxes.

To type the caret (^) character, press <Shift+6>.

To search for, or replace	*Type*
Tab mark	^t
Paragraph mark	^p
Non-breaking space	^s
Non-breaking hyphen	^~
Caret (^)	^^
White space	^w
Any character (wild card)	^?
Any digit	^#
Any letter	^$

Using the Spell Checker

If you have a problem with spelling, the spell checker in the Works 6.0 word processor will be a popular part of the package! As you type text into your document the checker

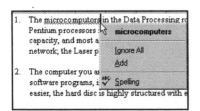

compares every word with the contents of its built-in dictionary. When it finds a word it does not recognise it places a red wavy line under it. If you right-click on such a word, as shown here, you have the choice of accepting a suggested correction, ignoring it, or of adding the word to your dictionary. With the latter option the word will be recognised in the future.

If you select the Spelling option from the above menu, the Spelling and Grammar dialogue box opens, as shown in Fig. 3.10. Here though, we opened it by clicking the **Spelling and Grammar** button on the toolbar, and we could also have used the **Tools**, **Spelling and Grammar** menu command, or the **F7** key.

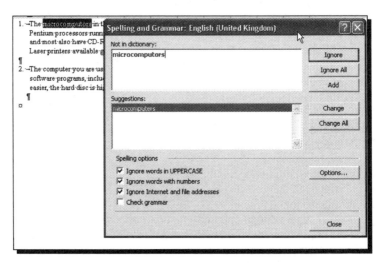

Fig. 3.10 The Spelling and Grammar Dialogue Box.

This is the way to check the spelling of a whole document. It will search for wrongly spelled words, words with incorrect capitalisation, incorrect hyphenation, and repeated words, such as 'if if'. It has a large built-in dictionary, and you can add other words that you may need to check for in the future.

A suspect word will be highlighted in the document, and will also be placed in the **Not in dictionary** box. You have several options now:

a.   To leave the word unchanged choose **Ignore** for this occurrence, or **Ignore All**.

b.   To change the word, edit or re-type it in the box, and choose **Change**, or **Change All** to change all instances of that word in the document.

c.   Choose from the list of **Suggestions**, and then click **Change**.

d.   To add an edited word to the dictionary, choose **Add**.

As long as **Check grammar** is selected in the **Spelling options** list, Works also checks your grammar at the same time. Grammatical errors are highlighted in green. If you do not understand the flagged error, clicking the **Explain Rule** button will open an explanation box.

When you have made your choice, the program continues searching the rest of the document. To leave the checker at any time choose **Close**.

Using the Thesaurus

To help you with composing your documents Works has a built-in thesaurus. With this you should be able to find a synonym, or word with a similar meaning, for most words.

First double-click the word you want to change to select it (we chose 'structured' on the last line of the second paragraph), and use the **Tools**, **Thesaurus** command, or press the <Shift+F7> keys.

This opens the dialogue box shown below in Fig. 3.11.

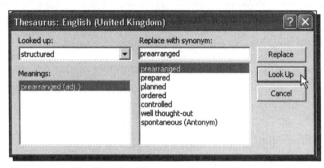

Fig. 3.11 The Thesaurus Dialogue Box.

In the **Meanings** box, on the left, are suggestions of the main meanings of the selected word. Depending on the context in the document, you need to select one of these meanings, and then look in the **Replace with synonym** box for a list of possible replacement words.

In the example shown 'structured' was the word highlighted in the document. The adjective 'prearranged' was listed and selected in the **Meanings** list which produced the six synonyms shown, and an antonym (opposite meaning). If you select one of the synonyms and press **Look Up** you should get more alternatives to look at.

To replace the original word highlighted in your document, select the best alternative and choose **Replace**.

Word Count

Works includes the facility to count the words in a document. This can be useful if you are working on an assignment that requires a specific number of words. The program considers a word to be any text between two space characters.

To carry out a count use the **Tools**, **Word Count** command. The whole document will be counted, with the exception of text in footnotes, headers and footers.

Adding a Table to a Document

The ability to use Tables is built into most top-range word processors these days. This feature in the Works 6.0 word processor has been enhanced from its previous version to cover tables that span more than one page.

Tables are used to create adjacent columns of text and numeric data, a table being simply a grid of columns and rows with the intersection of a column and row forming a rectangular box referred to as a 'cell'. Data is placed into individual cells that are organised into columns and rows. You can modify the appearance of table data by applying text formatting and enhancements.

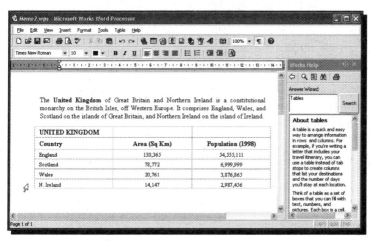

Fig. 3.12 An Example Showing an Inserted Table.

As an example we will step through the process of creating the table shown in Fig. 3.12 above. To build this geographical, but non-political, example place the insertion point after the document body text and use the **Table Insert Table** command, or click the **Insert Table** button.

In the opened dialogue box, shown in Fig. 3.13 on the next page, enter 7 as the **Number of rows** and 3 as the **Number of columns**. There are 17 different table formats to choose from, but we used 'None' as a starter.

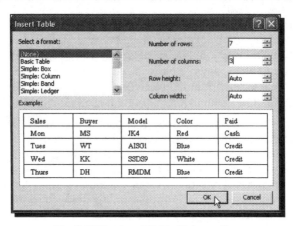

Fig. 3.13 The Insert Table Dialogue Box.

When you are happy with the procedures we suggest you experiment with the other formats. Pressing **OK** returns you to your document in which a full width table has been placed in which you enter the data as shown. To format the column titles you can select the whole of the second row by moving the pointer to the left of it and clicking when it changes to a right sloping arrow. Then click the **Bold** and **Centre Align** toolbar icons.

Format any other data that needs it and finally turn off the grid lines, by selecting the whole table, right-clicking on it, and selecting **Borders and Shading** from the context menu, as shown in Fig. 3.14.

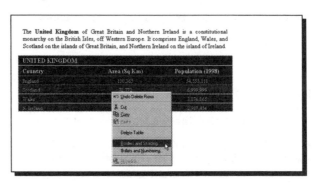

Fig. 3.14 Turning off the Grid Lines of an Inserted Table.

This opens the box shown in Fig. 3.15 below.

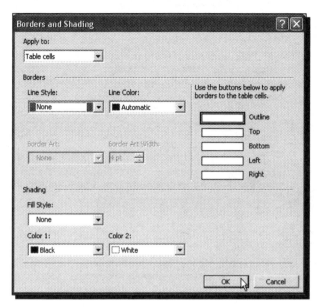

Fig. 3.15 The Borders and Shading Dialogue Box.

Make sure that **Table cells** is selected in the **Apply to** drop-down box, select **None** in the **Line Style** drop-down box, and then click on each of the **Outline**, **Top**, **Bottom**, **Left** and **Right** buttons in turn. We will leave it to you to experiment with the other features in this dialogue box, but try to reproduce the shading on the table as shown below in Fig. 3.16.

The **United Kingdom** of Great Britain and Northern Ireland is a constitutional monarchy on the British Isles, off Western Europe. It comprises England, Wales, and Scotland on the islands of Great Britain, and Northern Ireland on the island of Ireland.

UNITED KINGDOM		
Country	Area (Sq Km)	Population (1998)
England	130,365	54,555,111
Scotland	78,772	6,999,999
Wales	20,761	3,876,865
N. Ireland	14,147	2,987,456

Fig. 3.16 Shading a Table's Contents.

Inserting a Spreadsheet

To embed a spreadsheet into your document, use the **Insert**, **Spreadsheet** menu command, or click the toolbar button shown here. A new, blank spreadsheet appears in the document, as shown in Fig. 3.17. Inserting a spreadsheet gives you access to the functionality of a spreadsheet without leaving the document.

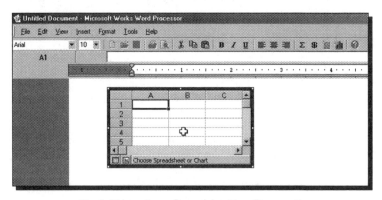

Fig. 3.17 Inserting a Spreadsheet in a Document.

Note that the displayed spreadsheet is automatically 'active' and that its toolbar and menus replace those of the word processor. Next, and before you start typing data in the spreadsheet, increase the size of its window and adjust the size of its columns to suit your needs.

To view the data in a chart, if there is one in the spreadsheet, click Chart at the bottom of the spreadsheet frame. To view the data in the spreadsheet again, click Spreadsheet at the bottom of the frame.

To return to the Word Processor document, click outside the spreadsheet or chart. A useful feature, but you may have to spend some time in the spreadsheet chapters of this book to get the best out of it.

Using a Text Box

A Text Box lets you place text with a different size, orientation, or format anywhere within the body of a document, and have the document text wrap around it, as shown in our example in Fig. 3.18 below.

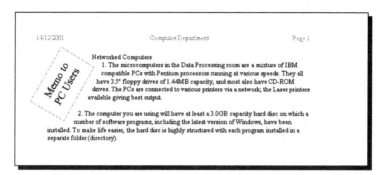

Fig. 3.18 Example Using a Text Box.

Here we have used the **Insert**, **Text Box** command, typed some text into the Text Box, and dragged it to its final position by clicking and dragging it when the mouse pointer changes to that shown here.

The **Format**, **Text Box** command opens a dialogue box which provides three tabbed sheet options giving you complete control on different ways of **Wrapping** text around the Text Box, changing its **Size**, and setting the **Text Box** internal margins and also lets you rotate it (as in our example above). Quite a useful feature.

E-mailing a Document

There are often times when we are creating documents in Works when we reach the stage that we want to send it to someone else, maybe for comment, or approval. This is now very easy to do straight from Works 6.0 word processor itself. With the document open, you simply click the **E-mail** button on the toolbar, or use the **File**,

Send command sequence. These both open your default e-mail program as shown in Fig. 3.19 below.

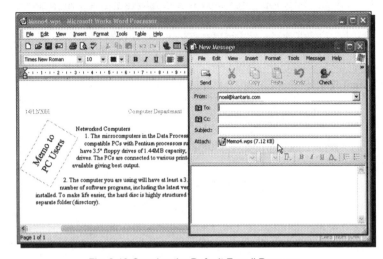

Fig. 3.19 Opening the Default E-mail Program.

Note that the document which was open at the time of clicking the **E-mail** toolbar icon has been entered automatically as an attachment to the new message. Typing the e-mail address of your recipient in the **To** box, a short sentence in the **Subject** box, an explanatory paragraph or two in the main text area of your e-mail program and clicking the **Send** button is all you need to do. This actually sends the document to Outlook Express' Outbox (our default e-mail program). When it is actually transmitted will depend on your type of connection and the settings in Outlook's **Tools**, **Options** dialogue box.

If you want to know more about Outlook Express, please refer to Chapter 13 where not only the program is covered in detail, but also how to connect to your Internet Service Provider (ISP).

Using Hypertext Links

Hypertext links are elements in a document or Web page that you can click with your mouse, to 'jump to' another document. When clicked they actually fetch another file, or part of a file, to your screen, and the link is the address that uniquely identifies the location of the target file, whether it is located on your PC, on an Intranet, or on the Internet itself. This address is known as a Uniform Resource Locator (URL for short). For a link to an Internet file to work you must obviously have access to the Internet from your PC.

Inserting a Hyperlink

If you know the URL address of the link destination, you can simply type it in a Works document and it will be automatically 'formatted' as a hyperlink. This usually means it will change to bright blue underlined text. In Works a hyperlink consists of the text that the user sees that describes the link, (or an image), the URL of the link's target, and a ScreenTip that appears whenever the 'hand' pointer passes over the link on the screen.

To insert a hyperlink into Works, select the display text or image, and either use the **Insert, Hyperlink** command, or click the **Insert Hyperlink** button on the toolbar shown here. Either action opens a dialogue box, shown in Fig. 3.20, which allows you to browse for the destination address.

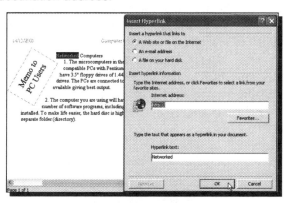

Fig. 3.20 Inserting a Hyperlink.

****

That completes our coverage of the Works 6.0 word processor, but the next chapter on Microsoft's Accessories is equally applicable to this program as well as to Word 2002.

****

4

Microsoft's Accessories

Works installs several accessories which you can use with
either of the word processors provided with its two different
versions. We describe some of these accessories in this
chapter, but you should be aware that they may behave slightly
differently depending on which version of the word processors
you have. In fact, some of these accessories are available to
any program by using its **Insert**, **Object** menu command, but in
our discussions that follow we use the Works 6.0 word
processor to explain them.

Adding a Note to your Document

A very useful facility is the ability to add 'pop-up' notes
anywhere in your documents. To do this, put the cursor where
you want a Note to be placed, use the **Insert**, **Object** command
and select **Microsoft Note-It** from the opened dialogue box, as
shown in Fig. 4.1. This opens the Microsoft Note-It box in Fig.
4.2 on the next page.

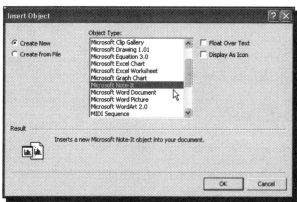

Fig. 4.1 The Insert Object Dialogue Box.

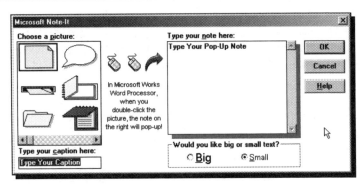

Fig. 4.2 The Microsoft Note-It Dialogue Box.

The **Choose a picture** box gives you the amazing choice of 58 different note types. If it turns you on, you can liven up your document no end! To place a caption under the displayed note, type the required text in the **Type your caption here** text box. The main text to be 'hidden' in the note is typed in the **Type your note here** box. Select the size of Note text you want from the **Big** and **Small** options and finally press **OK** to place your note.

At any time in the future the note text can be read by double clicking on the note, as shown in our example in Fig. 4.3 below.

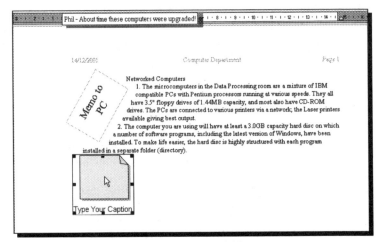

Fig. 4.3 Reading a Note-It Message.

Notes can be very useful if several people are editing a document and they want to make comments for the others to see. Each person would then choose a different shape of note icon, which would be recognisable by the rest of the team.

Adding WordArt to your Document

The WordArt facility lets you easily create quite eye-catching title lines for your documents. To use it, place the insertion point where you want the heading and use the **Insert**, **Object** command and select Microsoft WordArt 2.0 from the display list in the Insert Object Dialogue box, or click the **WordArt** toolbar icon. Type your heading text and note that a new toolbar has been added to the screen, as shown in Fig. 4.4.

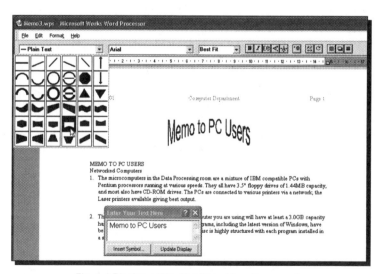

Fig. 4.4 Placing a WordArt Object in a Document.

This also shows the shapes available in the drop down menu opened on the left of the bar. The buttons on the toolbar are used to design the look of your WordArt text, as follows:

Click	*To*
Plain Text ▼	Choose a shape for WordArt
Arial ▼	Change the font
Best Fit ▼	Change the font size
B	Make text bold
I	Make text italic
Ee	Make letters all the same height, regardless of their capitalisation
A	Flip letters on their side
A	Stretch text to the edges of the frame
C≡	Choose how text aligns in a frame
AV	Change the spacing between letters
C	Adjust the shape of the text, or rotate text within a frame
▨	Change the colour or shading of text
▢	Add a shadow to text
≡	Add a border to text

When your heading looks the way you want, simply click the pointer outside the dialogue box to return to your document, which should now have the new heading placed on it. You can edit a WordArt graphic at any time by double-clicking it.

WordArt has its own Help system built in, which is well worth looking into.

Adding Graphics to a Document

It is a very easy matter to add a ClipArt drawing to your documents. Works comes with a folder (or more) of professional graphics for you to use. They are added by clicking the **Insert Clip Art** button, or with the **Insert**, **Picture**, **ClipArt** command, which opens a Microsoft Clip Art dialogue box shown in Fig. 4.5.

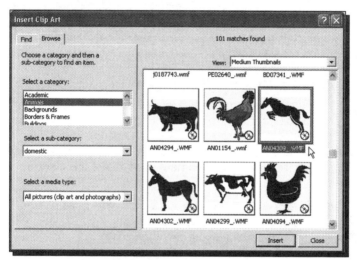

Fig. 4.5 The Insert Clip Art Dialogue Box.

This dialogue box allows you to select a category of Clip Art pictures which then displays various graphics held under this category. We selected 'Animals', then 'Domestic', then the horse, and clicked the **Insert** button which brought the graphic into our document.

The **Format**, **Object**, **Wrapping** commands allow you to select the wrapping style for the inserted object. Once you have done this, the graphic is 'released' and you can then move it, otherwise it remains locked in the inserted position. The display in Fig. 4.6 on the next page shows the result of selecting the **Square** option of wrapping. Pointing to the inserted graphic, changes the mouse pointer to a four-headed arrow which allows you to move the graphic to the required position.

Note that the graphic was inserted in the document without the need for a containing frame, which allows for better wrapping around it.

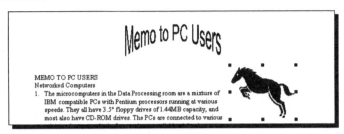

Fig. 4.6 Placing a Clip Art Graphic in a Document.

Inserting a Graphic File Image

If you have a graphic image or photograph saved in file format (maybe from the Internet, a digital camera or scanner) it is easy to add this to a document. Use the **Insert**, **Picture**, **From File** command, or click the **Insert Picture** toolbar button shown here, and select the file from the opened dialogue box.

As with any inserted object in Works, you have to use the **Format**, **Object**, **Wrapping** commands and select either **Square** or **Tight** before you can then move a picture around the page, otherwise it remains locked in the inserted position.

Microsoft Draw

In this version of Works, the method of activating Microsoft Draw and what happens as a result of such an action depends on which word processor you are using. Therefore, we shall cover the two methods separately.

MS Draw in Works 6.0 Word Processor

To create a new drawing in your document, place the insertion point where you want the drawing and use the **Insert**, **Picture**, **New Drawing** command, or click the **New Drawing** toolbar button shown here. Microsoft Draw places a frame in your document for the new drawing, and opens the separate Microsoft Drawing 1.01 screen, as shown in Fig. 4.7. You can then use the Drawing tools to create, or edit, a graphic consisting of lines, arcs, ellipses, rectangles, and even text boxes. These can either exist in their own right, or be additions to a picture or object.

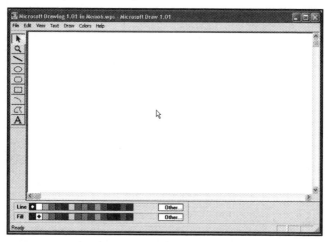

Fig. 4.7 Using Microsoft Drawing in a Document.

The Draw Toolbar

If you action the **Help Index** menu command while Microsoft Draw is in control of your document (or press the **F1** function key), the Help screen in Fig. 4.8 is displayed showing the various buttons on the **Draw** toolbar and giving information on their use by clicking the various hypertext links.

It is perhaps worthwhile spending some time finding your way around this Help screen. Next, click the **Contents** button to display the more detailed Help screen shown in Fig. 4.9.

Fig. 4.8 The MS Draw's Toolbox.

Fig. 4.9 Help Topics in Microsoft Draw.

Creating a Drawing

The effects of the drawing tools can be superimposed either on the document area or on top of a graphic. The result is that you can annotate drawings and pictures to your heart's desire.

To create an object, click on the required **Drawing** button, such as the **Oval** or **Rectangle**, position the mouse pointer where you want to create the object on the screen, and then drag the mouse to draw the object. Hold the <Shift> key while you drag the mouse to create a perfect circle or square. If you do not hold <Shift>, Draw creates an oval or a rectangle.

You can use the menu **Draw** command to select a different **Line Style**, or select a pre-drawn **Pattern**. First click on the desired line or shape, then position the mouse pointer where you want to create the object on the screen and click the left mouse button to fix it in that position.

Editing a Drawing

To select an object, click on it. Draw displays white handles around the object selected.

You can move an object, or multiple objects, within a draw area by selecting them and dragging to the desired position. To copy an object, click at the object, then use the **Edit, Copy** / **Edit, Paste** commands.

To size an object, position the mouse pointer on a white handle and then drag the handle until the object is the desired shape and size.

To delete an object, select it and press the <Del> key. To delete a drawing, hold the <Shift> key down and click each object in turn that makes up the drawing, unless they are grouped or framed, then press <Del>.

Using Layered Drawings

You can select an object, then use the **Edit, Bring to Front** or **Edit, Send to Back** menu options to determine the order of layered drawings. Drawings, or pictures, layered on top of each other can create useful visual effects, provided you remember that the top drawing and/or picture obscures the one below it, as shown in Fig. 4.10.

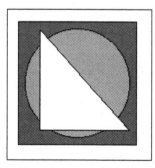

Fig. 4.10 Layered Drawings.

Here we have used Draw's Rectangle, Oval, and Line options to draw the three displayed shapes. The order you draw these is not important as you can use the Bring to Front and Send to Back options to rearrange them to your taste. We then selected each shape in turn, and used the **Fill** palette, shown in Fig. 4.11 overleaf, to give them different shades.

Fig. 4.11 The Fill Palette.

Clicking the **Other...** button, pointed to above, opens up the additional Color box of Fig. 4.12 so you can make additional colour selections.

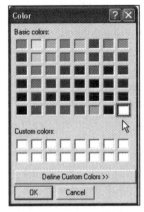

Fig. 4.12 The Color Fill Box.

Finally, select each shape, while holding down the <Shift> key, then use the **Dr̲aw**, **G̲roup** menu command to lock them together, before attempting to move the whole group to a different position within the draw area (you can tell they are grouped because attempting to move them, moves the whole group, which shows with a dotted outline).

Finally, to transfer the finished drawing into your Works 6.0 document, use the **F̲ile**, **U̲pdate** command. We strongly recommend you to experiment with these and other options, like us you will almost certainly surprise yourself with the results.

MS Draw in Works Suite 2002 Word Processor

In Microsoft Word (to be discussed in detail in Chapters 5-7),
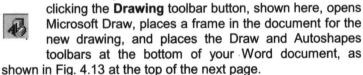 clicking the **Drawing** toolbar button, shown here, opens Microsoft Draw, places a frame in the document for the new drawing, and places the Draw and Autoshapes toolbars at the bottom of your Word document, as shown in Fig. 4.13 at the top of the next page.

To start drawing, all you need to do is click one of the Draw or Autoshape buttons, then use the modified cursor to start drawing in Word's working area. More about this shortly.

Clicking the **Drawing** toolbar button once more, removes the Draw and Autoshapes toolbars from Word's Task bar.

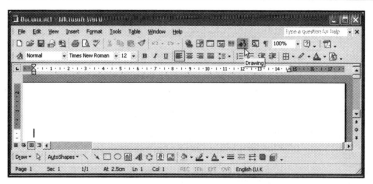

Fig. 4.13 The Drawing Tool Opened in Microsoft Word.

The Drawing Toolbar

The various functions offered by the Drawing toolbar, shown here in Fig. 4.14, are shared by all Office XP applications and give Word a superior graphics capability. Amongst the many features available are:

AutoShapes – the AutoShape categories, such as connectors, block arrows, flowchart symbols, stars and banners, callouts, and action buttons make drawing diagrams much easier.

Bezier curves – used to easily create exact curves with pinpoint precision.

3-D effects – allow you to transform 2-D shapes into realistic 3-D objects with 3-D effects, such as changing the lighting perspective of a 3-D object.

Perspective shadows – allow you to select from a wide range of shadows with perspective, and you can adjust the depth and angle of each shadow to make pictures more realistic.

Fig. 4.14 The Drawing Toolbar.

Arrowhead styles – allow you to change the width and height of arrowheads for maximum effect.

Object alignment – allow you to distribute and space objects evenly, both horizontally and vertically.

Precise line-width control – allows you increased control over the width of lines by selecting pre-set options or customised line widths.

Transparent background – background colours can be turned into transparent areas. These can now be graded with slider controls to give very professional results.

Creating a Drawing

To create an object, click on the required Drawing button, such as the **Oval** or **Rectangle**, position the mouse pointer where you want to create the object on the drawing canvas, and then drag the mouse to draw the object. Hold the <Shift> key while you drag the mouse to create a perfect circle or square. If you do not hold <Shift>, Word creates an oval or a rectangle.

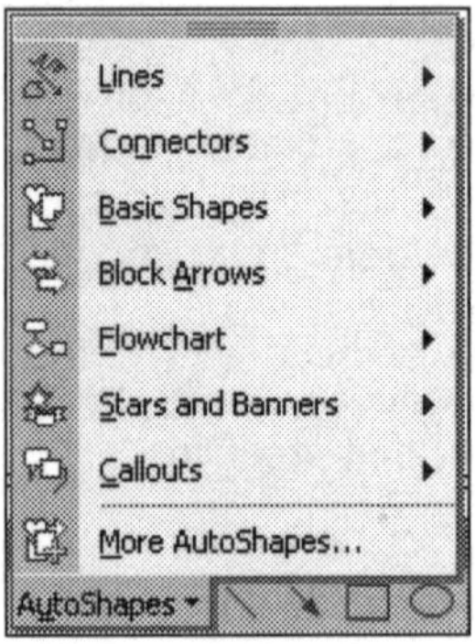

You can use the **AutoShapes** button to select from a variety of pre-drawn **Lines**, **Basic Shapes**, etc., shown in Fig. 4.15. First open the menu bars and click on the desired line or shape, then position the mouse pointer where you want to create the object on the canvas and click the left mouse button to place it.

All of the Autoshape graphical sub-menus can be dragged off the menu and floated on the screen for easy access. Fig. 4.16 is a composite showing all the standard Autoshape options.

Fig. 4.15
Autoshape Options.

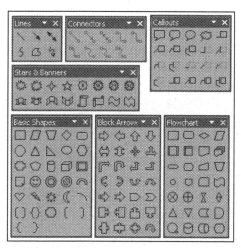

Fig. 4.16 The Seven 'Floating' Autoshape Menus.

Editing a Drawing

To select an object, click on it. Word displays white handles around the object selected. Shapes can be re-sized, rotated, flipped, coloured, and combined to make more complex shapes. Some AutoShapes have a coloured adjustment handle that you can use to change the most prominent feature of a shape — for example, the star overleaf has variable depth rays.

You can move an object, or multiple objects, within the canvas by selecting them and dragging to the desired position. To copy an object, click it, then use the **Edit, Copy** / **Edit, Paste** commands or toolbar buttons.

To size an object, position the mouse pointer on a white handle and then drag the handle until the object is the desired shape and size.

To delete an object, select it and press the <Del> key. To delete a drawing, just delete the canvas.

Placing a Drawing

Once you are happy with your drawing you can use the Drawing Canvas toolbar, shown on Fig. 4.17, to place it at the correct location in your document.

Fig. 4.17 Some Objects Placed on the Drawing Canvas.

Clicking the **Fit** button will shrink the canvas to the size of the drawing. The **Expand** button enlarges the canvas a little, every time it is clicked. Neither of these buttons affect the drawing itself. The **Scale Drawing** button places hollow white handles around the canvas. You drag these in the normal Windows way to enlarge, or shrink, both the canvas and all of the objects on it. This is a very powerful feature.

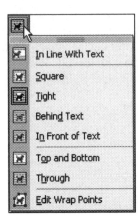

Before you can move the canvas you will need to click the **Text Wrapping** button shown here in Fig. 4.18 with its menu options. By default a canvas is placed **In Line With Text** and will only move when the text around it moves.

Fig. 4.18 Wrapping Options.

In Fig. 4.19 we selected **Tight** wrapping and dragged the canvas to where we wanted it. As can be seen, the surrounding text wraps tightly over the canvas. You can even control how this happens by selecting **Edit Wrap Points**, as shown above, and dragging any of the square points. Do try out some of these effects, they really are fun.

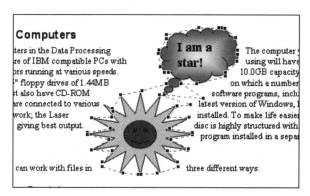

Fig. 4.19 Editing Drawing Canvas Wrapping Points.

We strongly recommend you to experiment with these and other options, like us you will almost certainly surprise yourself with the results.

Note: The help screens you get while drawing when you are using Works Suite 2002 are those of Microsoft Word. To get specific help with drawing you will have to find the appropriate Help Book and browse through its various sections.

Inserting Objects into a Document

You can insert 'Objects' into a Microsoft Word document to include information created in other Office programs or in many other Windows programs. An Object can take the form of a table, chart, graphic, equation, or other type of information. (In case you wondered, Objects created in one application, for example spreadsheets, and linked or embedded in another application are called OLE Objects.)

To insert an Object into a document you use the **Insert, Object** command which opens the dialogue box shown in Fig. 4.20 below. From this, you can choose different 'Object types', from say a Lotus 1-2-3 Worksheet or a WordPad Document.

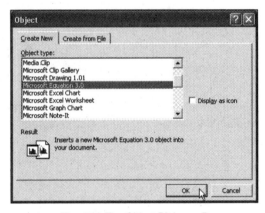

Fig. 4.20 The Object Dialogue Box.

Word may take several seconds to open this box as it scans your system to build the list of Object types you can use, depending on the software that you have installed.

For example, if you select 'Microsoft Equation 3.0' from the **Object type** list, as shown above, Word displays the Equation Editor which allows you to build mathematical equations in your Word document. This should have been installed with Office XP and is, in fact, the same editor that was included in earlier versions of Microsoft Office.

Inserting an Equation

If building equations is not your cup of tea, you can safely skip this section. If, on the other hand, you want to learn how to build equations, activate the Equation Editor from the above box.

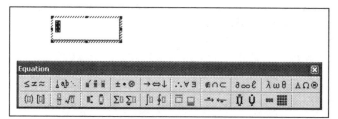

Fig. 4.21 The Microsoft Equation Editor.

This places an equation box at the insertion point and opens the Equation toolbar, as shown in Fig. 4.21. We suggest you first press **F1** to display the Help screen shown in Fig. 4.22.

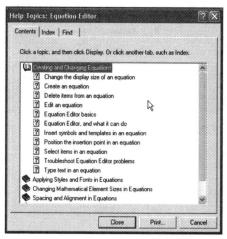

Fig. 4.22 The Equation Editor Help System.

Selecting the first option, reveals a further list of topics under it, as shown. Working through these will give a good introduction and tell you about the Equation toolbar and how you can use it. It is an 'older' Help system though and is not quite as easy to get around as the main Word help.

The top row of the Equation Editor toolbar has buttons for inserting more than 150 mathematical symbols, many of which are not available in the standard Symbol font (to be discussed later).

To insert a symbol in an equation, click a button on the top row of the toolbar, as shown on the composite screen dump in Fig. 4.23 below, and then click the specific symbol from the palette that appears under the button.

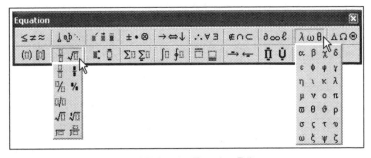

Fig. 4.23 Using the Equation Editor.

The bottom row of the Equation Editor toolbar has buttons for inserting templates or frameworks that contain such symbols as fractions, radicals, summations, integrals, products, matrices, and various fences or matching pairs of symbols such as brackets and braces. There are about 120 templates, grouped on palettes, many of which contain slots - spaces into which you type text and insert symbols. Templates can be nested, by inserting them in the slots of other templates, to build complex hierarchical formulae.

Finally, select the second recommended help topic to find out about spacing and alignment, expanding templates, styles, embellishments, and how to position the insertion pointer so that you can achieve best results.

As an example, we will take you through the steps required, when using the Equation Editor, to construct the equation for the solution of a quadratic equation, as shown here.

$$x = \frac{-b \pm \sqrt{\{b^2 - 4ac\}}}{2a}$$

To construct this equation, place the insertion pointer at the required place in your document, activate the Equation Editor, and follow the steps listed below. The templates and symbols you require from the Equation Editor are shown to the right of the appropriate step.

- Type *x =* followed by selecting the template shown here from the lower second button.

- Type *–b* followed by selecting the ± symbol from the upper fourth button.

- Select the square root template shown here from the lower second button.

- Select the brackets template shown here from the lower first button.

- Type *b* followed by selecting the template from the lower third button.

- Type *2* and re-position the insertion pointer as shown here, and then type *–4ac*.

- Position the insertion pointer at the denominator and type *2a*.

Obviously, the Equation Editor is capable of a lot more than we have covered here, but this simple example should serve to get you started. Try it, it's simpler than it looks.

5

Microsoft Word 2002 Basics

Users of Works Suite 2002 have Microsoft Word 2002 as their word processor. This can be started by clicking the Windows **Start** button, then selecting **All Programs**, **Microsoft Works Task Launcher** and selecting **Word** in the Programs list which opens an extensive list of Tasks that can step you through the process of starting different documents. To open a blank document click the **Start a blank Word document** link located above the Task list, as shown in Fig. 5.1 below.

Fig. 5.1 The Microsoft Works Task Launcher.

Word can also be started by double-clicking a Word document file icon. In the latter case the document will be loaded into Word at the same time.

The Word Screen

The opening 'blank' screen of Word 2002 is shown below. It is perhaps worth spending some time looking at the various parts that make up this screen. Word follows the usual Microsoft Windows conventions and if you are familiar with these you can skip through this section. Otherwise a few minutes might be well spent here.

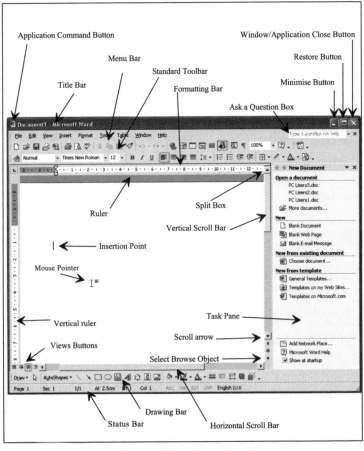

Fig. 5.2 The Word Screen Layout.

The layout as shown is in a window, but if you click on the application restore button, you can make Word take up the full screen area available. Using a window can be useful when you are running several applications at the same time and you want to transfer between them with the mouse.

Note that in this case, the Word window displays an empty document with the title 'Document1', and has a solid 'Title bar', indicating that it is the active application window. Although multiple windows can be displayed simultaneously, you can only enter data into the active window (which will always be displayed on top, unless you view them on a split screen). Title bars of non-active windows appear a lighter shade than that of the active one.

The Word screen is divided into several areas which have the following functions:

Area	*Function*
Command buttons	Clicking on the command button, (see upper-left corner of the Word window), displays a pull-down menu which can be used to control the program window. It allows you to restore, move, size, minimise, maximise, and close the window.
Title Bar	The bar at the top of a window which displays the application name and the name of the current document.
Minimise Button	When clicked on, this button minimises Word to an icon on the Windows Taskbar.
Restore Button	When clicked on, this button restores the active window to the position and size that was occupied before it was maximised. The restore button is then replaced by a Maximise button, as shown here,

	which is used to set the window to full screen size.
Close button	The extreme top right button that you click to close a window.
Menu Bar	The bar below the Title bar which allows you to choose from several menu options. Clicking on a menu item displays the pull-down menu associated with that item.
Ask a Question Box	The text box at the far right of the menu bar. You can type in a help query and press the Return key to get a listing of matching topics.
Standard Toolbar	The bar below the Menu bar which contains buttons that give you mouse click access to the functions most often used in the program.
Formatting Bar	The buttons on the Formatting Bar allow you to change the attributes of a font, such as italic and underline, and also to format text in various ways. The Formatting Bar contains three boxes; a style box, a font box and a size box to give instant access to all the installed styles, fonts and character sizes.
Rulers	The horizontal and vertical bars where you can see and set page margins, tabulation points and indents.
Split Box	The area above the top vertical scroll button which when dragged allows you to split the screen.
Task Pane	A new pane which presents formatting options and other relevant

controls on the right-hand side of the Word screen. It has its own button bar for instant control.

Scroll Bars   The areas on the screen that contain scroll boxes in vertical and horizontal bars. Clicking on these bars allows you to control the part of a document which is visible on the screen.

Scroll Arrows   The arrowheads at each end of each scroll bar which you can click to scroll the screen up and down one line, or left and right 10% of the screen, at a time.

Insertion pointer   The pointer used to indicate where text will be inserted.

Views Buttons   Clicking these buttons changes screen views quickly.

Status Bar   The bottom line of the document window that displays status information.

The Toolbars

There are nineteen different toolbars available in Word 2002. To see the full list you can use the **View**, **Toolbars** menu command, or more easily, right-click in the toolbar area. In this list active bars are shown with a blue tick to their left. Clicking on a list entry will toggle that toolbar on or off. By default, only two bars are active, the Standard and the Formatting toolbars. When Word is first opened these two bars will probably be placed alongside each other, which means that not all the buttons will be visible. To see the other available buttons click the toolbar options button ▓ at the right end of each bar, as shown in Fig. 5.3 on the next page.

Fig. 5.3 Toolbar Options.

Clicking any of the buttons now displayed will action that function. For our screen layout of Fig. 4.3 we have clicked the **Show Buttons on Two Rows** option. We find it easier to work with both toolbars almost fully open. You might feel differently.

To 'complicate' matters further, Word automatically customises both toolbars and menus, based on how often you use their commands. As you work, they adjust so that only the buttons and commands you use most often are shown. Thus your screen may not display the same features as ours.

The Standard Toolbar

As we show it, this is located below the Menu bar at the top of the Word screen and contains command buttons. As you move the mouse pointer over a button it changes to an 'active' blue colour and a banner opens to indicate the button's function. Left-clicking the button will then action that function or command.

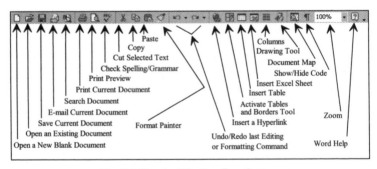

Fig. 5.4 Standard Toolbar Functions.

The use of these Standard toolbar buttons will be discussed in great detail, with worked examples, in the next chapter.

The Formatting Bar

This is located to the right of, or below, the Standard Toolbar, and is divided into sections that contain command buttons, as shown in Fig. 5.5 below.

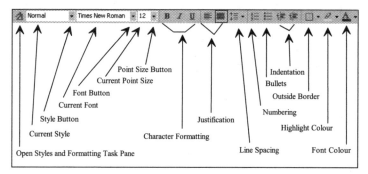

Fig. 5.5 Formatting Toolbar Functions.

The first option displays the name of the current style (Normal) in a box. Clicking the down-arrow against this box, opens up a menu of default paragraph styles with their font sizes. The Current font box shows the current typeface. Clicking on the down-arrow button to the right of it allows you to change the typeface of any selected text. The Current point size box shows the size of selected characters which can be changed by clicking on the down-arrow button next to it and selecting another size from the displayed list.

Next, are three character formatting buttons which allow you to enhance selected text by emboldening, italicising, or underlining it. The next buttons allow you to change the justification of a selected paragraph, control the Line spacing and set the different types of Numbering and Indentation options. The last three buttons allow you to add an Outside Border to selected text or objects, and change the highlight and font colour of selected text.

The Status Bar

This is located at the bottom of the Word window and is used to display statistics about the active document.

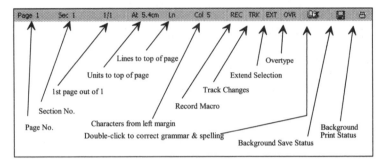

Fig. 5.6 The Word Status Bar.

For example, when a document is being opened, the Status bar displays for a short time its name and length in terms of total number of characters. Once a document is opened, the Status bar displays the statistics of the document at the insertion point; here it is on Page 1, Section 1, and 5 characters from the left margin.

Double-clicking the left of the status bar displays the Find and Replace dialogue box, as shown in Fig. 5.7. This is shown with the **Go To** tab selected. You can choose which page, section line, etc., of the document to go to, or you can use the other tabs to **Find** and **Replace** text (more about this later). Double-clicking the other features on the Status bar will also activate their features.

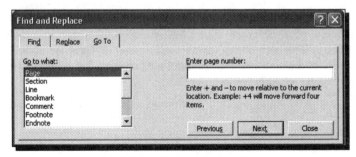

Fig. 5.7 The Find and Replace Box.

The Menu Bar Options

Each menu bar option has associated with it a pull-down sub-menu. To activate the menu, either press the <Alt> key, which causes the first option of the menu (in this case the **File** menu option) to be selected, then use the right and left arrow keys to highlight any of the options in the menu, or use the mouse to point to an option. Pressing either the <Enter> key, or the left mouse button, reveals the pull-down sub-menu of the highlighted menu option. The sub-menu of the **File** option is shown in Fig. 5.8 below.

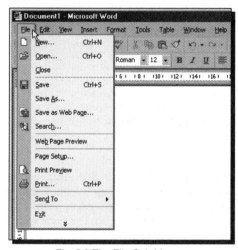

Fig. 5.8 The File Sub Menu.

Note that as in the previous version of Word, the drop-down sub-menu displays only the most important options, but you have the option to view the full sub-menu by highlighting the double arrowheads at the bottom of it, by either pointing to that part of the sub-menu with the mouse or using the down-arrow cursor key to move the highlighted bar down.

The full sub-menu of the **File** menu option is displayed here in Fig. 5.9 on the next page. However, the order of your sub-menu options in both the short and the full version of the sub-menu could differ from ours. This is because Word learns from your actions and automatically promotes the items you choose from menu extensions on to the shortened version of the sub-menu.

Menu options can also be activated directly by pressing the <Alt> key followed by the underlined letter of the required option. Thus, pressing <Alt+F>, opens the pull-down **File** sub-menu. You can use the up and down arrow keys to move the highlighted bar up and down a sub-menu, or the right and left arrow keys to move along the options in the menu bar. Pressing the <Enter> key selects the highlighted option or executes the highlighted command. Pressing the <Esc> key once, closes the pull-down sub-menu, while pressing the <Esc> key for a second time, closes the menu system.

Fig. 5.9 The Full File Sub Menu.

Some of the sub-menu options can be accessed with 'quick key' combinations from the keyboard. Such combinations are shown on the drop-down menus, for example, <Ctrl+S> is the quick key for the **Save** option in the **File** sub-menu. If a sub-menu option is not available at any time, it will display in a grey colour. Some menu options only appear in Word when that tool is being used.

To get more details about any of the above menu options, simply highlight the option and use the <Shift+F1> key combination. This opens a pop-up box like that shown in Fig. 5.10 for the **Tools**, **Options** menu.

Fig. 5.10 The Pop-up Help Box.

Shortcut Menus

Context-sensitive shortcut menus are now one of Windows' most useful features. If you click the right mouse button on any screen feature, or document, a shortcut menu is displayed with the most frequently used commands relating to the type of work you were doing at the time. In this version of Word, Microsoft have also combined 'smart tags' as part of the shortcut menu system. These automatically link related features or data to the situation involved.

The composite screen dump in Fig. 5.11 below shows in turn the shortcut menus that open when selected text, or the Toolbar area is right-clicked. In the first shortcut menu the **Cut** and **Copy** commands only become effective if you have text selected.

Fig. 5.11 Example Shortcut Menus.

So, whatever you are doing in Word, you have rapid access to a menu of relevant functions by right-clicking your mouse. Left-clicking the mouse on an open menu selection will choose that function, while clicking on an area outside the shortcut menu (or pressing the <Esc> key), closes down the shortcut menu. If you are wondering about the smart tags we mentioned, don't worry we will get round to them a little later on.

Task Panes

Some of the common tasks in Word 2002 can now be carried out in new Task Panes that display on the right side of your document. You can quickly create new documents or open files using the Task Pane that appears when you first start the program. The **Search** Task Pane gives you easy access to Word's file search facilities, or you can visually pick from a gallery of items in the Office **Clipboard** Task Pane.

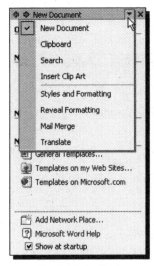

Fig. 5.12 shows the **New Document** Task Pane with its control buttons on top. The left and right arrows let you quickly move between the Task Panes you have open, the down arrow opens a drop-down list of the available tasks, as shown here. The **x** button lets you close the pane. To reopen it you use the **View**, **Task Pane** menu command.

We must admit to having reservations about this new feature of Microsoft Word 2002, but once you get used to the panes, they

Fig. 5.12 The Task Pane List.

'become less of a pain' and at times can make some of Word's features much easier and quicker to access. Each type of pane will be discussed in more detail as they are encountered within the word processing section of the book.

Getting Help in Word 2002

No matter how experienced you are, there will always be times when you need help to find out how to do something in Word 2002. Word is after all a very large and powerful application with a multitude of features. As we shall see, there are several ways to get help now, including the Office Assistant, or Clippy as he is called by Microsoft, although by default it is switched off.

Ask a Question Box

To quickly access Help, you can use the Ask a Question box on

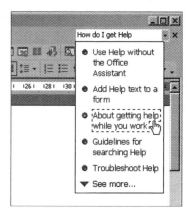

Fig. 5.13 The Ask a Question Box.

the menu bar. You type a question in this box, as we show in Fig. 5.13, and press the <Enter> key.

A list of help topics is then displayed, as shown here. To see more topics, left-click the small triangle at the bottom of the list with the caption 'See more'. Once you select an option from the list and click on it, the Help system is opened and you should quickly be able to find the answers you need. In fact it works the

same way as the Assistant, but without the constant 'distractions'.

It seems to be better to type a full question in the Ask a Question box, rather than just a keyword. The options presented can then be more relevant. When you use the feature several times, the previous questions can be accessed by clicking the down-arrow to the right of the text box. However, the list is cleared whenever you exit the Office application you are using at the time.

The Office Assistant

The Office Assistant is turned off by default in this version of

Office and may not even be installed unless you specifically request it. When activated, it first appears as we show on the left, and automatically provides Help topics and tips on tasks you perform as you work. To find out how it works, start an Office application (we used Word) and use the **Help**, **Show the Office Assistant** menu command to open Clippy. Now left-click him to open the 'What would you like to do?' box, shown in Fig. 5.14.

To get help you simply type your query here and click the **Search** button. From then on the procedure is the same as with the Ask a Question box.

If you like, you can customise the Assistant, and decide if you want it to automatically display tips, messages, and alerts, make sounds, move when it's in the way, and guess a Help topic that it thinks you may need.

Fig. 5.14 Using the Office Assistant.

You can also switch it off once you have mastered a particular Office application, or cannot cope with its intrusions any more! All of these features are controlled from the box shown in Fig. 5.15 which is opened by clicking the **Options** button shown in Fig. 5.14.

To change the shape of your Office Assistant (there are eight

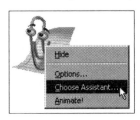

shapes to choose from), either left-click the Gallery tab of the dialogue box shown in Fig. 5.15, or right-click the Office Assistant and select the **Choose Assistant** option from the displayed menu, as shown here to the left.

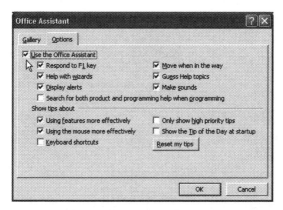

Fig. 5.15 The Office Assistant Options Box.

Either of these actions displays the following dialogue box (Fig. 5.16) in which you can select your preferred Assistant shape by left-clicking the **Next** button.

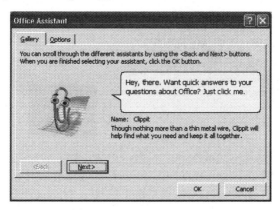

Fig. 5.16 The Office Assistant Gallery Box.

The eight shapes of the available Assistants are shown in Fig. 5.17 on the next page. We find the Office Assistant's animated characters to be very clever and amusing, but must admit that like most people we prefer to work with the facility turned off. To do this, make sure the **Use the Office Assistant** option is not selected in the Options box shown in Fig. 5.15.

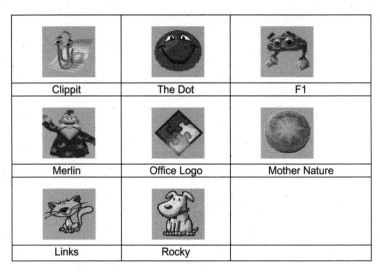

Clippit	The Dot	F1
Merlin	Office Logo	Mother Nature
Links	Rocky	

Fig. 5.17 The Office Assistant Shapes.

The Main Help System

If you turn the Office Assistant completely off (as described on the previous page) and press the **F1** function key, or click the
 Help toolbar button shown here, or use the **Help**, **Microsoft Word Help** menu command, Help will be accessed directly through the Help window. This is the way we prefer to use it.

When first opened, the Microsoft Word Help Center will be displayed in the right-hand pane as shown in Fig. 5.18 on the next page. This gives a quick way to get information on **What's New** with Word 2002, the **Microsoft Office Web Site** and about **Getting Help** itself. Each of these has a very colourful button you can press.

In Fig. 5.18 there is a listing of 'hypertext links' to some of the help topics Microsoft thought you were most likely to use first. Clicking any of these opens the relevant Help page, without you having to look for the item itself.

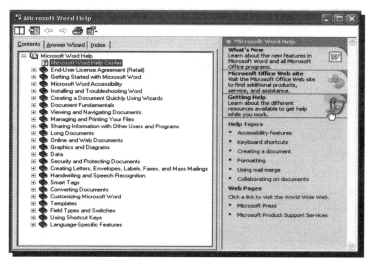

Fig. 5.18 Microsoft Word Help.

As can be seen here, the left pane of the Help window has three tabbed sections.

Fig. 5.19 Help Contents List.

The **Contents** tab of the Help screen opens up an impressive list of topics relating to the Word 2002 program. Clicking a '+' at the left of an item, or double-clicking a closed book icon, opens a sub-list; clicking a '-', or double-clicking an open book icon, will close it again. Clicking a list item, with the ? mark as shown, opens the help text in the right-hand pane.

To type a question in the Help window, you click the **Answer Wizard** tab. When you want to search for specific words or phrases, you click the **Index** tab. For example, click the **Answer Wizard** tab, and type the text *How do I open a document* in the **What would you like to do?** text box. Then click the **Search** button and you should see something like the screen in Fig. 5.20 on the next page.

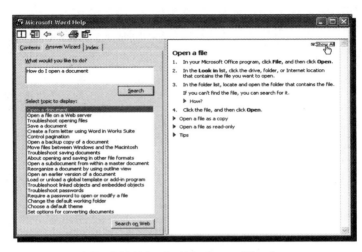

Fig. 5.20 Using the Help Answer Wizard.

Clicking an item in the list of topics opens the relevant Help page in the right pane. A new feature with Office XP is that the Help pages are opened in an 'outline' view. Clicking a blue link item with a ▶ symbol to its left, opens up more detail, whereas clicking the ▼ **Show All** link in the top-right corner will fully expand the page. This is very useful if you want to print or copy the Help information.

The Help Toolbar

Note the Web browser type buttons at the top of the Help screen. These allow you to carry out the following functions:

⊞	**Auto Tile** - click this button to tile the Help window on the screen next to the main Word window.
⊞	**Show** - click this button to display the help screen tabs which allow you to access Help's Contents, Answer Wizard, and Index.
⇦	**Back** - if more than one help screen has been opened, click this button to go back to the previously opened help screen.

	Forward - if you have moved back to a previous help screen, click this button to move forward through opened help screens.
	Print - click this button to print the contents of the current help screen.
	Options - click this button to open up a menu of options which control all of the above facilities plus the ability to select the Internet Options dialogue box.

The Word Help system is very comprehensive but it is not always easy to find the information you are looking for. It usually pays to select the feature, or object, you want details on before accessing Help, you may then get exactly the right information straight off. Do spend some time here to learn, particularly what is new in the Office application you are using. Other topics can always be explored later.

ScreenTips

If you want to know what a menu command or button does, or if you want to know more about an option in a dialogue box, you can also get ScreenTips help. These can be accessed in three ways:

- For help with a menu command, toolbar button, or a screen region, click **What's This?** on the **Help** menu, or <Shift+F1>, and then click the feature you want help on.

- In a dialogue box, click the Help button 🕮 in the top right corner of the box, and then click the option.

- To see the name of a toolbar button, rest the pointer over the button and its name will appear.

Help on the Internet

If all else fails, you can connect to several Microsoft Web sites with the **Help**, **Office on the Web** menu command. You must obviously have an Internet connection for this to work, though!

6

Creating Word Documents

When the program is first used, all Word's features default to those shown in Fig. 5.2 on page 96. It is quite possible to use Word in this mode, without changing any main settings, but it is also possible to customise the package to your needs.

Entering Text

In order to illustrate some of Word's capabilities, you need to have a short text at hand. We suggest you type the memo displayed in Fig. 5.13 below into a new document. At this stage, don't worry if the length of the lines below differ from those on your display.

As you type in text, any time you want to force a new line, or paragraph, just press <Enter>. While typing within a paragraph, Word sorts out line lengths automatically (known as 'word wrap'), without you having to press any keys to move to a new line. If you make a mistake while typing, press the <BkSp> key enough times to erase the mistake and start again.

MEMO TO PC USERS
Networked Computers
The microcomputers in the Data Processing room are a mixture of IBM compatible PCs with Pentium processors running at various speeds. They all have 3.5" floppy drives of 1.44MB capacity, and most also have CD-ROM drives. The PCs are connected to various printers via a network; the Laser printers available giving best output.

The computer you are using will have at least a 3.0GB capacity hard disc on which a number of software programs, including the latest version of Windows, have been installed. To make life easier, the hard disc is highly structured with each program installed in a separate folder (directory).

Moving Around a Document

You can move the cursor around a document with the normal direction keys, and with the key combinations listed below.

To move	*Press*
Left one character	⇐
Right one character	⇒
Up one line	⇧
Down one line	⇩
Left one word	Ctrl+ ⇐
Right one word	Ctrl+ ⇒
To beginning of line	Home
To end of line	End
To paragraph beginning	Ctrl+ ⇧
To paragraph end	Ctrl+ ⇩
Up one screen	PgUp
Down one screen	PgDn
To top of previous page	Ctrl+PgUp
To top of next page	Ctrl+PgDn
To beginning of file	Ctrl+Home
To end of file	Ctrl+End

Fig. 6.1 Page
Change Controls.

To move to a specified page number in a multi-page document, either drag the vertical scroll bar up or down until the required page number is shown, as in Fig. 6.1, or use the **Edit**, **Go To** command (or <Ctrl+G>), as described on page 102.

To easily step from page to page you can also click the **Previous Page** ▓ and **Next Page** ▓ buttons, shown in Fig. 6.1.

Obviously, you need to become familiar with these methods of moving the cursor around a document, particularly if you spot an error in a document which needs to be corrected, which is the subject of the latter half of this chapter.

Templates and Paragraph Styles

As we saw under the Formatting Bar section earlier, when you start Word for the first time, the Style box contains the word **Normal**. This means that all the text you have entered, at the moment, is shown in the Normal paragraph style which is one of the styles available in the NORMAL template. Every document produced by Word has to use a template, and NORMAL is the default. A template contains both the document page settings and a set of formatting instructions which can be applied to text.

Changing Paragraph Styles

To change the style of a paragraph, first open the **Styles and Formatting** Task Pane by clicking its toolbar button, as shown here. Place the cursor in the paragraph in question, say the title line and select the **Heading 1** style from the **Pick formatting to apply** list in the Task Pane. The selected paragraph reformats instantly in bold, and in Arial typeface of point size 16.

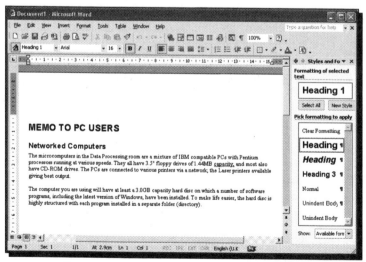

Fig. 6.2 Using the Styles and Formatting Task Pane.

Now with the cursor in the second line of text, select **Heading 3** which reformats the line in Arial 13. Your memo should now look presentable, and be similar to Fig. 6.2 on the previous page.

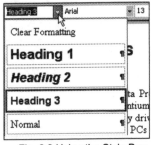

Fig. 6.3 Using the Style Box.

The other way of setting these styles is from the Style box on the Word Formatting toolbar, as shown here in Fig. 6.3. This was the usual way in the previous version of Word, which did not have Task Panes.

If you try both methods you will find that in the long run the Task Pane method is better. As we shall see later, you can carry out most, if not all, of your style format work from the Task Pane without having to resort to dialogue boxes. Microsoft have included Task Panes to make the features of Word more accessible, and this is a good example.

Document Screen Displays

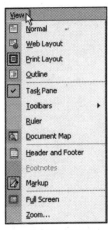

Fig. 6.4 View Menu.

Word provides four display views, **Normal**, **Web Layout**, **Print Layout**, and **Outline**, as well as the options to view your documents in a whole range of screen enlargements by selecting **Zoom**. You control all these viewing options with the **View** sub-menu, shown here, and when a document is displayed you can switch freely between them. When first loaded the screen displays in Print Layout view.

The main view options have the following effect, and can also be accessed by clicking the **Views** buttons on the left of the Status bar.

Normal Layout

A view that simplifies the layout of the page so that you can type, edit and format text quickly. In normal view, page boundaries, headers and footers, backgrounds, drawing objects, and pictures that do not have the **'In line with text'** wrapping style do not appear.

Web Layout

A view that optimises the layout of a document to make online reading easier. Use this layout view when you are creating a Web page or a document that is viewed on the screen. In Web layout view, you can see backgrounds, text is wrapped to fit the window, and graphics are positioned just as they are in a Web browser.

Print Layout

Provides a WYSIWYG (what you see is what you get) view of a document. The text displays in the typefaces and point sizes you specify, and with the selected attributes.

This view is useful for editing headers and footers, for adjusting margins, and for working with columns and drawing objects. All text boxes or frames, tables, graphics, headers, footers, and footnotes appear on the screen as they will in the final printout.

Outline Layout

Provides a collapsible view of a document, which enables you to see its organisation at a glance. You can display all the text in a file, or just the text that uses the paragraph styles you specify. Using this mode, allows you to quickly rearrange large sections of text. Some people like to create an outline of their document first, consisting of all the headings, then to sort out the document structure and finally fill in the text.

With large documents, you can create what is known as a master document by starting with an Outline View, and then designate headings in the outline as sub-documents. When you save the master document, Word assigns names to each sub-document based on the text you use in the outline headings.

Document Map

This view displays a separate pane with a list of document headings. You can quickly navigate through the document, when you click a heading Word jumps to that place in the document and displays the heading at the top of the window.

Full Screen

Selecting the **View, Full Screen** command, displays a clean, uncluttered screen; the Toolbars, Ruler, Scroll bars, and Status bar are removed. To return to the usual screen, click the **Close Full Screen** button on the icon which appears at the bottom of your screen when in this mode.

Zoom

The **Zoom** command opens the Zoom dialogue box, in which you can change the screen viewing magnification factor from its default value of 100%.

Changing Word's Default Options

Modifying Margins

It is easy to change the standard page margins for your entire document from the cursor position onward, or for selected text (more about this later).

Select the **File, Page Setup** command, click the left mouse button on the **Margins** tab of the displayed dialogue box, shown in Fig. 6.5 below, and change any of the margin or gutter settings in the **Margins** boxes.

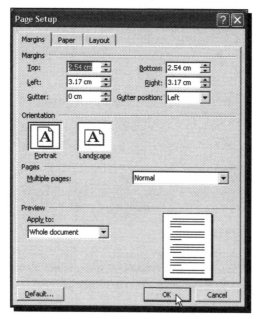

Fig. 6.5 Margins Sheet of the Page Setup Box.

The **Preview** page at the bottom of the box shows how your changes will look on a real page. The orientation of the printed page is normally **Portrait** where text prints across the page width, but you can change this to **Landscape** which prints across the page length, if you prefer.

Changing the Default Paper Settings

To change the default paper settings from those set during installation you do the following.

As before, select the **File, Page Setup** command, but click the **Paper** tab on the Page Setup dialogue box. Click the down-arrow against the **Paper size** box to reveal the list of available paper sizes, as shown in Fig. 6.6. Change the page size to your new choice.

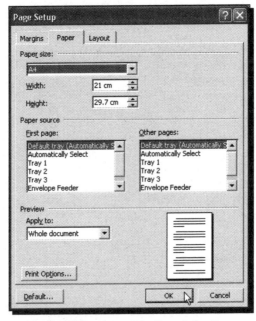

Fig. 6.6 Paper Sheet of the Page Setup Box.

Any changes you can make to your document from the Page Setup dialogue box can be applied to either the whole document or to the rest of the document starting from the current position of the insertion pointer. To set this, click the down-arrow button against the **Apply to** box and choose from the drop-down list. To make any of the new settings you make 'permanent', press the **Default** button and confirm that you wish this change to affect all new documents based on the Normal template.

The Paper source section of the Page Setup box lets you set where your printer takes its paper from. You might have a printer that holds paper in trays, in which case you might want to specify that the **First page** (headed paper perhaps), should be taken from one tray, while **Other pages** should be taken from a different tray.

Modifying the Page Layout

Clicking the last Page Setup tab displays the Layout box, part of which is shown here. From this dialogue box you can set options for headers and footers, section breaks, vertical alignment and whether to add line numbers or borders.

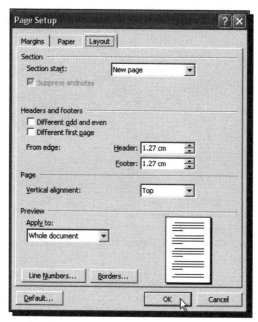

Fig. 6.7 Layout Sheet of the Page Setup Box.

The default for **Section Start** is 'New Page' which allows the section to start at the top of the next page. Pressing the down arrow against this option, allows you to change this choice.

In the Headers and Footers section of the dialogue box, you can specify whether you want one header or footer for even-numbered pages and a different header or footer for odd-numbered pages. You can further specify if you want a different header or footer on the first page from the header or footer used for the rest of the document. Word aligns the top line with the 'Top' margin, but this can be changed with the **Vertical alignment** option.

Changing Other Default Options

You can also change the other default options available to you in Word 2002, by selecting the **Tools, Options** command. This opens the Options dialogue box displayed in Fig. 6.8 below.

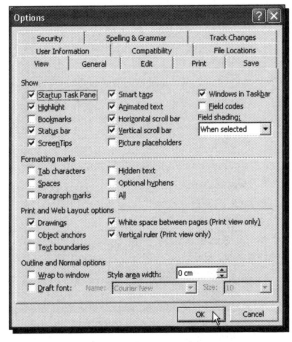

Fig. 6.8 The Word Options Dialogue Box.

As can be seen, this box has eleven tabbed sheets which give you control of most of the program's settings.

You can, amongst other things, do the following:

- Specify the default **View** options. For example, you can select whether non-printing formatting characters, such as Tabs, Spaces, and Paragraph marks, are shown or not.

- Adjust the **General** Word settings, such as background re-pagination, display of the recently used file-list, and selection of units of measurement.

- Adjust the **Print** settings, such as allowing background printing, reverse print order, or choose to print comments with documents.

- Change the **Save** options, such as selecting to always create a backup copy of your work.

Saving to a File

To save a document to disc, use either of the commands:

- **File, Save** (or click the **Save** toolbar button) which is used when a document has previously been saved to disc in a named file; using this command saves your work under the existing filename automatically without prompting you.

- **File, Save As** command which is used when you want to save your document with a different name from the one you gave it already.

Using the **File, Save As** command (or with the very first time you use the **File, Save** command when a document has no name), opens the dialogue box shown in Fig. 6.9 on the next page.

Note that the first 255 characters of the first paragraph of a new document are placed and highlighted in the **File name** field box, with the program waiting for you to over-type a new name.

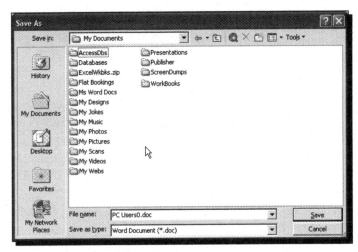

Fig. 6.9 The File Save As Box.

Any name you type must have less than 255 characters and will replace the existing name. Filenames cannot include any of the following keyboard characters: /, \, >, <, *, ?, ", |, :, or ;. Word adds the file extension **.doc** automatically and uses it to identify its documents.

You can select a drive other than the one displayed, by clicking the down arrow against the **Save in** text box at the top of the Save As dialogue box. You can also select a folder in which to save your work. The large buttons on the left of the box give rapid access to five possible saving locations. If you do not have a suitably named folder, then you can create one using the **Create New Folder** button, as shown in Fig. 6.10.

Fig. 6.10 Creating a New Folder.

We used this facility to create a folder called **Word Docs** within the **Documents** folder. To save our work currently in memory, we selected this folder in the **Save in** field of the Save As dialogue box, then moved the cursor into the **File name** box, and typed **PC Users1**. We suggest you do the same.

By clicking the **Save as type** button at the bottom of the Save As dialogue box, you can save the Document Template, or the Text Only parts of your work, or you can save your document in a variety of 29 formats, including Rich Text, and several Web Page options.

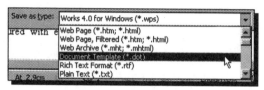

Fig. 6.11 Saving a Document as a Different File Type.

Selecting File Location

You can select where Word automatically looks for your document files when you first choose to open or save a document, by selecting the **Tools, Options** command, click the File Locations tab of the displayed Options dialogue box, (Fig. 6.8), and modify the location of the document files, as shown on the next page in Fig. 6.12.

As you can see, the default location of other types of files is also given in this dialogue box.

Microsoft suggests that you store documents, worksheets, presentations, databases, and other files you are currently working on, in the **My Documents** folder, which is easily accessed from the Desktop by clicking the special **Documents** button. This, of course, is a matter of preference, so we leave it to you to decide. We prefer to create sub-folders within **My Documents** to group our files more closely.

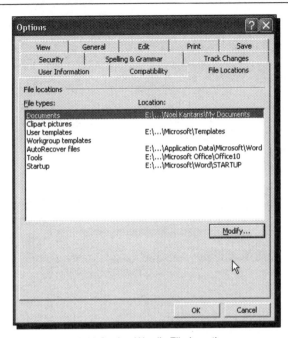

Fig. 6.12 Setting Word's File Locations.

To change the default folder for any of the file types listed above, simply select the type and click the **Modify** button. This opens a dialogue box very similar to the Save As box for you to locate or even create the folder you want to select.

Fig. 6.13 A File
Right-click Menu.

While any of the file opening, saving and location dialogue boxes are open you can use them to generally manage your files and folders. You do this by right-clicking on the name of a file or folder you want to manipulate. A context sensitive menu is opened like ours in Fig. 6.13. All of these options may not be available on your system, but the common ones of Open, New, Print, Cut, Copy, Create Shortcut, Delete, Rename and Properties should always be there.

Document Properties

A useful feature in Word is the facility to add document properties to every file by selecting the **File, Properties** command. A Properties box, as shown in Fig. 6.14 below, opens for you to type additional information about your document.

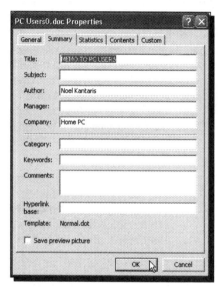

Fig. 6.14 The Document Properties Box.

One of the most useful features in this box is the Statistics tabbed page.

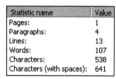

Fig. 6.15 Document Statistics.

As we show in Fig. 6.15, this gives a listing of the document statistics, including the number of pages, paragraphs, lines, words and even characters. Very useful for writing papers and reports, where the size is important.

To use this feature on a more regular basis, make sure that the **Prompt for document properties** box appears ticked on the Save tabbed sheet of the Options dialogue box (use the **Tools, Options** command and click the Save tab).

Closing a Document

There are several ways to close a document in Word. Once you have saved it you can click its **x** close button, or double-click on the **Document Control** button at the left end of the menu bar, or use the **File, Close** menu command.

If the document (or file) has changed since the last time it was saved, you will be given the option to save it before it is removed from memory.

If a document is not closed before a new document is opened, then both documents will be held in memory, but only one will be the current document. To find out which documents are held in memory, look at the Windows Taskbar, (see note below) or use the **Window** command to reveal the menu options shown in Fig. 6.16.

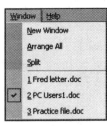

Fig. 6.16 Window Menu.

In this case, the second document in the list is the current document, and to make another document the current one, either type the document number, or point at its name and click the left mouse button.

To close a document which is not the current document, use the **Window** command, make it current, and close it with one of the above methods.

Note - With Word 2002 it is now possible to limit what is shown on the Taskbar. By default all your open Word windows (or documents) will each have an entry on the Taskbar. But you can change this so that only the current, or active, document is shown there. This can be useful to save clutter if you have several programs open at the same time.

To do this, open the View tab sheet of the **Tools, Options** dialogue box, shown in Fig. 6.8, and uncheck the **Windows in Taskbar** option.

Opening a Document

 You can use the Open dialogue box in Word, shown in Fig. 6.17 below, to open documents that might be located in different locations. As we saw earlier, this is opened by clicking the **Open** toolbar button, or with the **File**, **Open** command, or the <Ctrl+O> keystrokes.

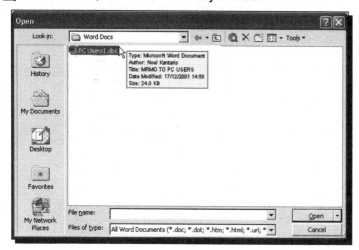

Fig. 6.17 The File Open Box.

For example, you can open a document which might be on your computer's hard disc, or on a network drive that you have a connection to. To locate other drives and folders, simply click the **Up One Level** button pointed to in Fig. 6.18 below.

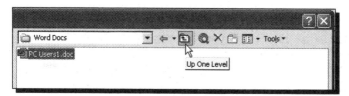

Fig. 6.18 The Up One Level Button.

Having selected a drive, you can then select the folder within which your document was saved, select its filename and click the **Open** button on the dialogue box.

As in older versions of Word, the last few files you worked on are also listed at the bottom of the **File** menu, as shown in Fig. 6.19 below. Selecting one of these will reopen that file.

If you do not have any past files displayed, as described above, open the General tab sheet of the **Tools**, **Options** dialogue box, and make sure the **Recently used file list** option is checked. In the **entries** box next to it you can choose to have up to the last nine files listed. The default is four, which is probably plenty for most people.

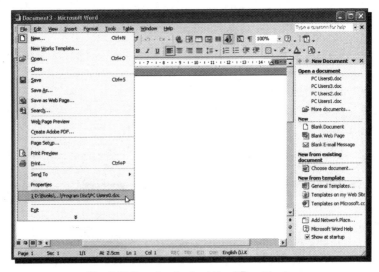

Fig. 6.19 Opening the Last Used Documents.

The New Document Task Pane

The **New document** Task Pane, shown above, is another way of opening both new and recently used documents. If it is not open, simply use the **View**, **Task Pane** command.

The **Open a document** section at the top, lists the last few files you have used. Simply clicking on one will open it. The More documents option displays the Open dialogue box, seen in Fig. 6.17, for you to find and select an existing file to open.

The **New** section offers several options for opening new documents of different kinds. **Blank Document** opens a new empty document using the Normal template (the same as clicking the **New** toolbar button). **Blank Web Page** opens a blank page in Web layout view, for you to build a Web page. The **Blank E-mail Message** option lets you use Word to write an e-mail which you can then send using Outlook.

The **New from existing document** section is a very welcome new feature which lets you create a document based on the features of an existing one. You can click **Choose document** to open an existing file, maybe a letter with all your address and salutation details, and make any changes you want to it. When you click the **Save** toolbar button, however, the Save As dialogue box is opened with a new filename suggested. It was so easy before this to overwrite the old file accidentally during the saving process.

The last section **New from Template** lets you open a template to use for your document. Microsoft have produced 'hundreds' of templates for particular types of documents. These make it very easy for a 'newish' user to produce very professional documents. Once opened you just change the existing text to your own, print it and wait for the admiring comments - maybe. The **General Templates** option accesses those that came with Word, as shown in Fig. 6.20.

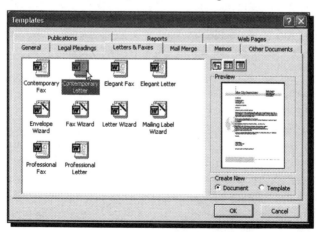

Fig. 6.20 Some of the Templates Available in Word.

These templates are well worth exploring as you may save yourself an awful lot of work. In the example below (Fig 6.21) we opened a new document with the Contemporary Letter template from the Letters & Faxes sheet.

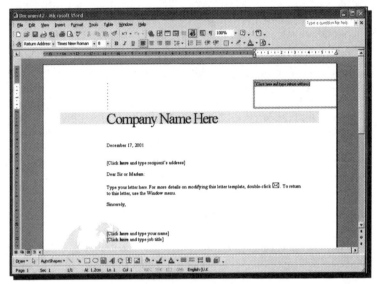

Fig. 6.21 Using a Microsoft Template.

This letter has instructions in it that tell you what to customise and how. Once you have entered your name and address it is a good idea to save the document again, but as a template, so that you can use it again in the future. To do this, select Document Template in the **Save as type** box of the Save As dialogue box and rename the document. It will then be available in the General tabbed section of the Templates box, for you to use again and again.

The other two template options on the **New Document** Task Pane let you access templates from your own Web space, maybe a company intranet, or from Microsoft's own Web sites. That should keep you busy for a while!

As long as the **Show at startup** option is checked at the bottom of the pane, this list should always be available whenever you start up Word.

7

Editing Word Documents

Microsoft have built some very clever editing facilities into Word 2002, and we will introduce some of them here. When you enter text you will notice that some basic errors are automatically corrected and that misspelled words are unobtrusively underlined in a red wavy line and ungrammatical phrases are similarly underlined in green.

AutoCorrect

To demonstrate these, use the **File, New** command (or click ⬜) to create a new file, and type the words 'teh computor is brukn', exactly as misspelled here.

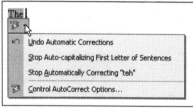

Fig. 7.1 The AutoCorrect Option Button.

As soon as you press the space bar after entering the first 'word', it will be changed to 'The', as shown in Fig. 7.1. This is the **AutoCorrect** feature at work, which will automatically detect and correct typing errors, misspelled words, and incorrect capitalisation. If you agree with the change made, as in our example, all is well. If not, you can move the pointer over the corrected word until a blue box is shown below it. This changes to the **AutoCorrect Options** button when you point to it, and clicking it opens the menu shown above.

Selecting the first menu option **Undo Automatic Corrections** will cancel the correction for you. The other options give you control of how the feature works in the future.

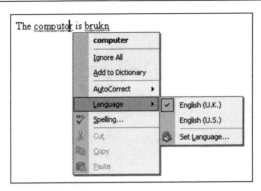

Fig. 7.2 Correcting Spelling Mistakes.

What should appear on your screen is shown in Fig. 7.2, with the two misspelled words underlined in a red wavy line.

Right-clicking the first misspelled word allows you to correct it, as shown above. To do this, left-click the **Computer** menu option. You even have a choice of **Language** to use. This is possibly the most timesaving enhancement in editing misspelled words as you type.

During this process the status bar will indicate your 'state of play'. As shown in Fig. 7.3, the active language is displayed, English (UK) in our case. To the right of this, the small 'book' icon has three forms. In Fig. 7.3 it is ticked to indicate

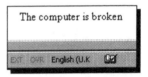

Fig. 7.3 The Status Bar.

that spell checking is completed. If there are errors to correct, it has a red cross on it, and during the actual checking process it displays an active pencil as shown here to the left. If you double-click this icon when it displays a cross, the full spell and grammar checker is opened which will be discussed later in more detail.

If you really have a problem spelling particular words you can add them to the AutoCorrect list yourself. To do this, select the **AutoCorrect** option from the menu in Fig. 7.2 (or the **Tools**, **AutoCorrect Options** menu command) to open the AutoCorrect box shown in Fig. 7.4 on the next page.

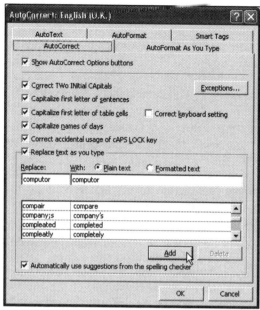
Fig. 7.4 Controlling AutoCorrections.

This dialogue box lets you control all of Word's automatic text, formatting and correction features, as well as the new Smart Tags feature we will encounter later on. Make sure the AutoCorrect tabbed sheet is active, as shown above, and have a good look at the ways you can control how it works for you. We suggest you scroll through the very long list of common misspellings at the bottom to see which ones will automatically be corrected.

In our example we have chosen to have the program always **Replace** the word 'computor' **With** the correct spelling of 'computer' as soon as we type the word. Clicking the **Add** button will add these to the AutoCorrect list.

The top fifteen options on the list are not corrections, but give you a rapid way to enter some common symbol characters by typing in a series of keyboard strokes. For example, if you type the three characters '(c)' AutoCorrect will change them to the copyright symbol '©'.

Editing Text

Other editing could include deleting unwanted words or adding extra text in the document. All these operations are very easy to carry out. For small deletions, such as letters or words, the easiest method is to use the <Del> or <BkSp> keys.

With the <Del> key, position the cursor on the left of the first letter you want to delete and press <Del>. With the <BkSp> key, position the cursor immediately to the right of the character to be deleted and press <BkSp>. In both cases the rest of the line moves to the left to take up the space created by the deleting process.

Word processing is usually carried out in the insert mode. Any characters typed will be inserted at the cursor location (insertion point) and the following text will be pushed to the right, and down, to make room. To insert blank lines in your text, place the cursor at the beginning of the line where the blank line is needed and press <Enter>. To remove the blank line, position the cursor on it and press <Del>.

When larger scale editing is needed you have several alternatives. You could first 'select' the text to be altered, then use the **Cut, Copy** and **Paste** operations available in the **Edit** sub-menu, or more easily, click on their Toolbar button alternatives shown here.

Another method of copying or moving text is to use the 'drag and drop' facility which requires you to highlight a word, grab it with the left mouse button depressed, and drop it in the required place in your text.

These operations will be discussed shortly in more detail.

Selecting Text

The procedure in Word, as with most Windows based applications, is first to select the text to be altered before any operation, such as formatting or editing, can be carried out on it. Selected text is highlighted on the screen. This can be carried out in two main ways:

A. Using the keyboard, to select:

• A block of text.	Position the cursor on the first character to be selected and hold down the <Shift> key while using the arrow keys to highlight the required text, then release the <Shift> key.
• From the present position to the end of the line.	Use <Shift+End>.
• From the present cursor position to the beginning of the line.	Use <Shift+Home>.
• From the present cursor position to the end of the document.	Use <Shift+Ctrl+End>.
• From the present cursor position to the beginning of the document.	Use <Shift+Ctrl+Home>.
• Select the whole document.	Use <Ctrl A>

B. *With the mouse, to select:*

• A block of text.	Press down the left mouse button at the beginning of the block and while holding it pressed, drag the cursor across the block so that the desired text is highlighted, then release the mouse button.
• A word.	Double-click within the word.
• A line.	Place the mouse pointer in the selection bar (just to the left of the line, when it changes to an arrow ⇗) click once. For multiple lines, drag this pointer down.
• A sentence.	Hold the <Ctrl> key down and click in the sentence.
• A paragraph.	Place the mouse pointer in the selection bar and double-click (for multiple paragraphs, after selecting the first paragraph, drag the pointer in the selection bar) or triple-click in the paragraph.
• The whole document.	Place the mouse pointer in the selection bar, hold the <Ctrl> key down and click once.

With Word 2002 you can now select non-contiguous text and graphics (ones that aren't next to each other), by selecting the first item you want, such as a word, sentence or paragraph, holding down the <Ctrl> key and selecting any other items from anywhere in the document. You can only select text, or graphics in this way, not both at the same time.

Copying Blocks of Text

Once text has been selected it can be copied to another location in your present document, to another Word document, or to another Windows application, via the system clipboard. As with most of the editing and formatting operations there are several alternative ways of doing this, as follows:

- Use the **Edit, Copy** command sequence from the menu, to copy the selected text to the clipboard, moving the cursor to the start of where you want the copied text to be placed, and using the **Edit, Paste** command.

- Use the quick key combinations, <Ctrl+C> (or <Ctrl+Ins>) to copy and <Ctrl+V> (or <Shift+Ins>) to paste. This does not require the menu bar to be activated.

- Use the **Copy** and **Paste** Standard Toolbar buttons; you can of course only use this method with a mouse.

To copy the same text again to another location, or to any open document window or application, move the cursor to the new location and paste it there with any of these methods.

The above operations use the system clipboard which only holds the last item cut or copied. Microsoft Office XP comes with a new extra clipboard in which you can store 24 cut or copied items until they are needed. Each item is displayed as a thumbnail on the new **Clipboard** Task Pane as shown in Fig. 7.5 on the next page.

The Clipboard Task Pane

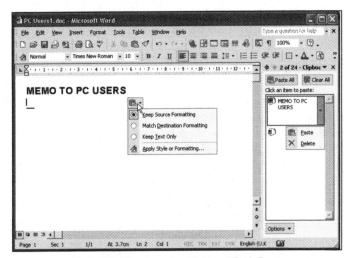

Fig. 7.5 Pasting from the Clipboard Task Pane.

The **Clipboard** Task Pane opens automatically in Word when you cut or copy for the second time, otherwise you can open it with the **Edit**, **Office Clipboard** command.

Fig. 7.5 is actually a composite, showing the **Clipboard** Task Pane on the right with two text items and a picture. The bottom item (with the selection square around it) was clicked to paste the text at the insertion point location in the main document to the left.

This also shows another new Office XP feature, a **Smart Tag** button. By default, one of these is always placed just under newly pasted text in Word 2002. Clicking this button, as shown above, opens a menu which lets you control the style and formatting of the pasted text. If you don't want to make any formatting changes to the text, just carry on and the smart tag will 'go away'.

While the **Clipboard** Task Pane is active in any Office program an icon like the one shown here is placed on the Windows Taskbar. This lets you easily access the pane, and also flags up how many items it contains.

Moving Blocks of Text

Selected text can be moved to any location in the same document by either of the following:

- Using the **Edit, Cut,** command or <Ctrl+X> (or <Shift+Del>).

- Clicking the **Cut** Toolbar button, shown here.

Next, move the cursor to the required new location and use any of the previously described procedures to paste the text where you want it.

The moved text will be placed at the cursor location and will force any existing text to make room for it. This operation can be cancelled by simply pressing <Esc>. Once moved, multiple copies of the same text can be produced by other **Paste** operations.

Drag and Drop Operations

 Selected text, or graphics, can be **copied** by holding the <Ctrl> key depressed and dragging the mouse with the left button held down. The drag pointer is an arrow with two attached squares, as shown here - the vertical dotted line showing the point of insertion. The new text will insert itself where placed, even if the overstrike mode is in operation. Text copied by this method is not placed on the clipboard, so multiple copies are not possible as with other methods.

 Selected text can be **moved** by dragging the mouse with the left button held down. The drag pointer is an arrow with an attached square - the vertical dotted line showing the point of insertion.

Deleting Blocks of Text

When text is 'cut' with the **Edit, Cut** command, or by clicking the **Cut** toolbar button, it is removed from the document, but placed on the clipboard. When the <Del> or <BkSp> keys are used, however, the text is not put on the clipboard.

The Undo Command

As text is lost with the delete command, you should use it with caution, but if you do make a mistake all is not lost as long as you act promptly. The **Edit, Undo** command or <Ctrl+Z> reverses your most recent editing or formatting commands.

Fig. 7.6 The Undo
Cascade Menu.

You can also use the **Undo** Standard Toolbar button, shown here, to undo one of several editing or formatting mistakes (press the down arrow to the right of the button to see a list of your recent changes, as shown here).

Undo does not reverse any action once editing changes have been saved to file. Only editing done since the last save can be reversed.

Finding and Changing Text

As in previous versions, Word 2002 allows you to search for specifically selected text, or character combinations with the **Find** or the **Replace** options on the **Edit** command sub-menu.

Using the **Find** option (<Ctrl+F>), will highlight each occurrence of the supplied text in turn so that you can carry out some action on it, such as change its font or appearance.

Using the **Replace** option (<Ctrl+H>), allows you to specify what replacement is to be automatically carried out. For example, in a long article you may decide to replace every occurrence of the word 'microcomputers' with the word 'PCs'.

To illustrate the **Replace** procedure, either select the option from the **Edit** sub-menu or use the quick key combination <Ctrl+H>. This opens the Find and Replace dialogue box shown on the next page with the **More** button clicked.

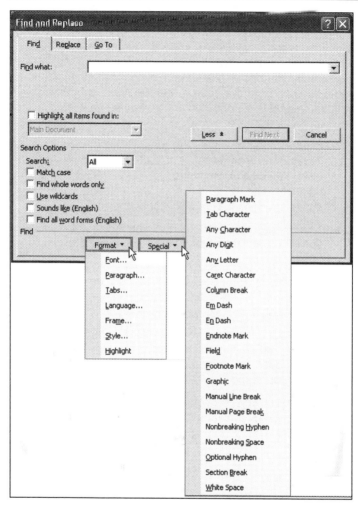

Fig. 7.7 A Composite of the Find and Replace Box.

Towards the bottom of the dialogue box, there are five check boxes; the first two can be used to match the case of letters in the search string, and/or a whole word, while the last three are used for wildcard, 'sounds like' or 'word forms' matching.

The two buttons, **Format** and **Special**, situated at the bottom of the dialogue box, let you control how the search is carried out. The lists of available options, when either of these buttons is pressed, are displayed in Fig. 7.7. You will of course only see one or the other, but not both as shown here. You can force both the search and the replace operations to work with exact text attributes. For example, selecting:

* The **Font** option from the list under **Format**, displays a dialogue box in which you select a font (such as Arial, Times New Roman, etc.); a font-style (such as regular, bold, italic, etc.); an underline option (such as single, double, etc.); and special effects (such as strike-through, superscript, subscript, etc.).

* The **Paragraph** option, lets you control indentation, spacing (before and after), and alignment.

* The **Style** option, allows you to search for, or replace, different paragraph styles. This can be useful if you develop a new style and want to change all the text of another style in a document to use your preferred style.

Using the **Special** button, you can search for, and replace, various specified document marks, tabs, hard returns, etc., or a combination of both these and text, as listed in the previous screen dump.

Below we list only two of the many key combinations of special characters that could be typed into the **Find what** and **Replace with** boxes when the **Use wildcards** box is checked.

Type	*To find or replace*
?	Any single character within a pattern. For example, searching for nec?, will find <u>neck</u>, con<u>nect</u>, etc.
*	Any string of characters. For example, searching for c*r, will find such words as <u>cellar</u>, <u>chillier</u>, etc., also parts of words such as <u>character</u>, and combinations of words such as <u>connect, cellar</u>.

A very useful new feature on the Find and Replace box is the **Highlight all items found in** option. If you tick this, your search will select all the matching words in your document at the same time. Any editing you then carry out will affect all of the selected text. This is a very rapid way of making global changes of font, size or style, etc.

The Search Task Pane

 Clicking the **Search** toolbar button, shown here, opens the new **Search** Task Pane, shown in Fig. 7.8 on the right. This is really to help you locate particular files or text on your computer, but the **Find in this document** option at the bottom opens the Search and Replace dialogue box we have just looked at.

With the default **Basic Search** option this pane lets you search for files on your hard disc by name.

The **Advanced Search** option lets you search your files for particular text, particular authors, or for files with specific creation dates.

Fig. 7.8 The Search Task Pane.

If you want more help on searching for files we suggest you click the **Search Tips** option, which opens the Word Help system at the relevant page.

Page Breaks

The program automatically inserts a 'soft' page break in a document when a page of typed text is full. To force a

manual, or hard page break, either use the <Ctrl+Enter> keystrokes, or use the **Insert**, **Break** command and select **Page break** in the dialogue box, shown in Fig. 7.9.

Pressing **OK** places a series of dots across the page to indicate the page break (this can only be seen in Normal View), as shown in Fig. 7.10 below. If you are in Print Layout View, the second paragraph below appears on the next page. To delete manual

Fig. 7.9 Break Box.

page breaks place the cursor on the line of dots, and press the <Del> key. In Print Layout View, place the cursor at the beginning of the second page and press the <BkSp> key.

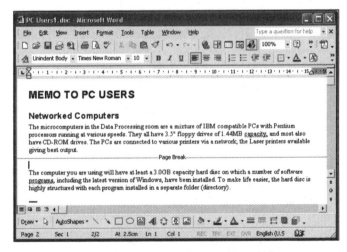

Fig. 7.10 A Hard Page Break in Normal View.

Soft page breaks which are automatically entered by the program at the end of pages, cannot be deleted.

Using the Spell Checker

The package has a very comprehensive spell checker which whenever it thinks it has found a misspelled word, underlines it with a red wavy line. To correct your document, right-click such words for alternatives, as we saw earlier.

 However, the spell checker can also be used in another way. To spell check your document, either click the Spelling and **Grammar Toolbar** button, shown here, or use the **Tools**, **Spelling and Grammar** command (or **F7**) to open the dialogue box shown in Fig. 7.11 below.

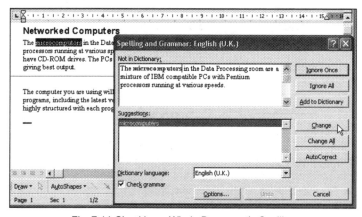

Fig. 7.11 Checking a Whole Document's Spelling.

Make sure you are using the correct dictionary by checking in the **Dictionary language** box. With us this gave an enormous list of English, French and Spanish speaking country options. If you want to check a word or paragraph only, highlight it first. Once Word has found a misspelled word, you can either correct it in the **Not in Dictionary:** box, or select a word from the **Suggestions** list.

The main dictionary cannot be edited, but you can add specialised and personal dictionaries with the facility to customise and edit them. If you choose **Add**, the specified word is added to a custom dictionary.

Using the Thesaurus

If you are not sure of the meaning of a word, or you want to use an alternative word in your document, then the thesaurus is an indispensable tool. To use the thesaurus, simply place the cursor on the word you want to look up and select the **Tools, Language, Thesaurus** command, or use the <Shift+F7> key combination. As long as the word is recognised, the following dialogue box will open.

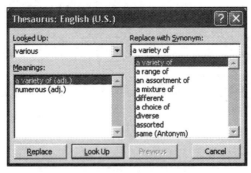

Fig. 7.12 The Thesaurus.

This is a very powerful tool; you can see information about an item in the **Meanings** list, or you can look up a synonym in the **Replace with Synonym** list. To change the word in the **Looked Up** text box, select an offered word in either the **Meanings** or the **Replace with Synonym** list box, or type a word directly into the **Replace with Synonym** box, and press the **Replace** button.

You can use the thesaurus like a simple dictionary by typing any word into the **Replace with Synonym** box and clicking the **Look Up** button. If the word is recognised, lists of its meaning variations and synonyms will be displayed. Pressing the **Replace** button will place the word into the document.

A quick way to get a list of alternatives to a word in your document is to right-click it and select **Synonyms** from the drop-down menu. If you select one from the list it will replace the original word.

Printing Documents

When Windows was first installed on your computer the printers you intend to use should have been selected, and the SETUP program should have installed the appropriate printer drivers. Before printing for the first time, it may be a good idea to check that your printer is in fact properly installed. To do this, click the Windows **Start** button (at the left end of the Taskbar) then click the **Printers and Faxes** menu option to open the Printers and Faxes window shown in Fig. 7.13 below.

Fig. 7.13 The Windows Printers and Faxes Folder.

Here, several printer drivers have been installed with the HP LaserJet 5/5M PostScript as the 'default' printer and an Acrobat Distiller 'printer' which we often use. In our case the HP LaserJet is configured to output to the printer via the parallel port LPT1 - yours may well be via a USB port. LPT1 is short for Line Printer 1 and refers to the socket at the back of your PC which is connected to your printer. Similarly, a USB port is also a socket to be found at the back of your PC.

To see how a printer is configured (whether to print to a printer port or to a file), select it by clicking its icon, use the **File, Properties** command and click the Device Settings tab of the displayed dialogue box.

Next, return to or reactivate Word and, if the document you want to print is not in memory, either click the **Open** button on the Toolbar, or use the **File, Open** command, to display the Open dialogue box described in the previous chapter. Use this dialogue box to locate the file, or document, you want to print, which will be found on the drive and folder on which you saved it originally.

To print your document, do one of the following:

- Click the **Print** button on the Standard Toolbar, shown here, which prints the document using the default printer and current settings.

- Use the **File, Print** command which opens the Print box, shown in Fig. 7.14 below.

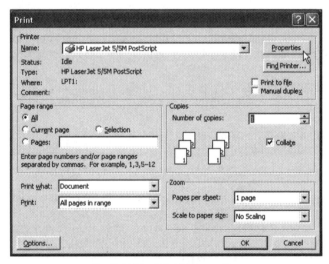

Fig. 7.14 The Print Dialogue Box.

The settings in the Print dialogue box allow you to select the number of copies, and which pages, you want printed. You can also select to print the document, the summary information relating to that document, comments, styles, etc., in the **Print what** drop-down list.

You can even change the selected printer by clicking the down arrow against the **Name** box which displays the available printers on your system.

Clicking the **Properties** button on the Print dialogue box, displays the Properties dialogue box for the selected printer, shown here, which allows you

Fig. 7.15 A Printer Properties Box.

to select the paper size, orientation needed, paper source, etc.

The **Options** button on the Print dialogue box, gives you access to some more advanced print options, such as printing in reverse order, with or without comments, print hidden text or field codes, etc., as shown in Fig. 7.16 below.

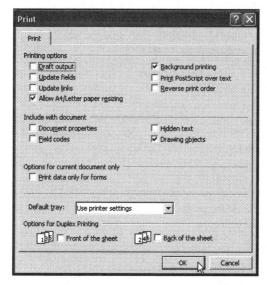

Fig. 7.16 Some Advanced Print Options.

Clicking the **OK** button on these various multilevel dialogue boxes, causes Word to accept your selections and return you to the previous level dialogue box, until the Print dialogue box is reached. Selecting **OK** on this first level dialogue box, sends print output from Word to your selection, either the printer connected to your computer, or to an encoded file on disc. Selecting **Cancel** or **Close** on any level dialogue box, aborts the selections made at that level.

Do remember that, whenever you change printers, the appearance of your document may change, as Word uses the fonts available with the newly selected printer. This can affect the line lengths, which in turn will affect both the tabulation and pagination of your document.

Print Preview

Before printing your document to paper, click the Print **Preview** button on the Standard Toolbar, or use the **File**, **Print Preview** command, to see what your print output will look like, and how much of your document will fit on your selected page size. This depends very much on the chosen font. The **Print Preview** command could save a few trees and equally important to you, a lot of frustration and wear and tear on your printer.

The print Preview window has its own toolbar with options for magnification and number of pages actually viewed. You can even edit your document, if you want to make any last minute changes. To print the document simply click the **Print** button, or to return to your working document from a print preview display, click the **Close** button on its menu bar.

Other enhancements of your document, such as selection of fonts, formatting of text, and pagination, will be discussed in the next chapter.

8

Formatting Word Documents

Formatting involves the appearance of individual words or even characters, the line spacing and alignment of paragraphs, and the overall page layout of the entire document. These functions are carried out in Word in several different ways.

Primary page layout is included in a document's Template and text formatting in a Template's styles. Within any document, however, you can override Paragraph Style formats by applying text formatting and enhancements manually to selected text. To immediately cancel manual formatting, select the text and use the **Edit, Undo** command, or (<Ctrl+Z>). The selected text reverts to its original format. In the long term, you can cancel manual formatting by selecting the text and using the <Shift+Ctrl+N> key stroke. The text then reverts to its style format.

Formatting Text

If you use TrueType fonts, which are automatically installed when you set up Windows, Word uses the same font to display text on the screen and to print on paper. The screen fonts provide a very close approximation of printed characters. TrueType font names are preceded by ⊤ in the Font box on the Formatting Bar.

If you use non-TrueType fonts, then use a screen font that matches your printer font. If a matching font is not available, or if your printer driver does not provide screen font information, Windows chooses the screen font that most closely resembles the printer font.

Originally, the title and subtitle of the **PC Users1** memo, were selected from the default Normal style as 'Heading 1' and 'Heading 3', which were in the 16 and 13 point size Arial typeface, respectively, while the main text was typed in 10 point size Times New Roman.

To change this memo into what appears on the screen dump displayed below, first select the title of the memo and format it to italics, 18 point size Arial and centre it between the margins, then select the subtitle and format it to 14 point size Arial. Both title and subtitle are in bold as part of the definition of their respective paragraph style. Finally select each paragraph of the main body of the memo in turn, and format it to 12 point size Times New Roman. Notice in each case that the Style details in the Style box on the Formatting Toolbar is changed to show the manual formatting that was added. This shows as 'Normal + 12pt' in Fig. 8.1 below.

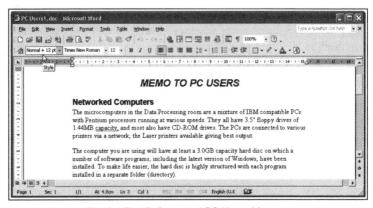

Fig. 8.1 The Reformatted PC Users Memo.

All of this formatting can be achieved by using the buttons on the Formatting Bar (see also the section entitled 'Paragraph Alignment'). Save the result under the new filename **PC Users2**, using the **File, Save As** command.

In all our screen dumps so far we show the Formatting Bar moved from its default position (to the right of the Standard Toolbar) to just below it. Although this takes up more screen space, we have done this to show more buttons on both the Toolbars.

Moving Toolbars

As we have seen, the default buttons appearing on the two Toolbars below the Menu Bar have distinctive functions. By default, the one to the left is the Standard Toolbar, while the one to the right is the Formatting Bar. Each of these two Toolbars is preceded by a vertical handle. Moving the mouse

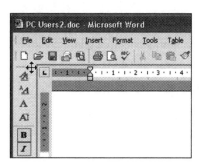

pointer onto such a handle, changes it into a four-headed 'moving' pointer, as shown here in Fig. 8.2. With the left mouse button held down you can then drag the toolbar around the screen.

Fig. 8.2 Moving a Toolbar.

As we show here, it is possible to move Toolbars to any part of the screen, and also change the buttons contained in each (see Fig. 5.3 on page 100). Through this section of the book we have moved the Formatting Bar and placed it below the Standard Toolbar. This gives a good compromise between screen space taken up by the bars and the number of buttons displayed.

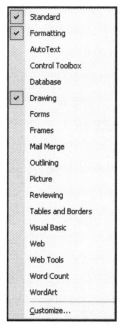

To see additional sets of Toolbars, use the **View, Toolbars** command to open up a menu of options, as shown in Fig. 8.3. You can toggle these on and off by clicking on their names. Be careful, however, how many of these you activate, as they take valuable screen space.

Fig. 8.3 The View Toolbars Menu.

Text Enhancements

In Word all manual formatting, including the selection of font, point size, style (bold, italic, highlight, strike-through, hidden and capitals), colour, super/subscript, spacing and various underlines, are carried out by first selecting the text and then executing the formatting command.

With some actions the easiest way of activating the formatting commands is from the Formatting Bar. With others you have to use the **Format**, **Font** menu command, and select options from the dialogue box in Fig. 8.4 below.

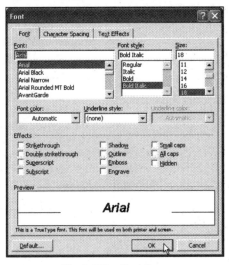

Fig. 8.4 The Font Box.

Yet another method is by using quick keys, some of which are listed below:

To Format	Type
Bold	Ctrl+B
Italic	Ctrl+I
Underline	Ctrl+U
Word underline	Ctrl+Shift+W

There are quick keys to do almost anything, but the ones listed here are the most useful and the easiest to remember.

Paragraph Alignment

Word defines a paragraph, as any text which is followed by a paragraph mark, which is created by pressing the <Enter> key. So single line titles, as well as sections of long typed text, can form paragraphs.

 The paragraph symbol, shown here, is only visible in your text if you have selected **Show/Hide ¶** button from the Standard Toolbar, or used <Ctrl+*>.

Word allows you to align a paragraph at the left margin (the default), at the right margin, centred between both margins, or justified between both margins. As with most operations there are several ways to perform alignment in Word. Three such methods are:

• Using buttons on the **Formatting Bar**.

• Using keyboard short cuts.

• Using the **Format**, **Paragraph** menu command.

The table below describes the buttons on the Formatting Bar and their keystroke shortcuts.

Buttons on Formatting Bar	Paragraph Alignment	Keystrokes
	Left	<Ctrl+L>
	Centred	<Ctrl+E>
	Right	<Ctrl+R>
	Justified	<Ctrl+J>

Fig. 8.5 below shows the dialogue box resulting from using the **Format**, **Paragraph** command in which you can specify any **Left, Right**, or **Special** indentation required.

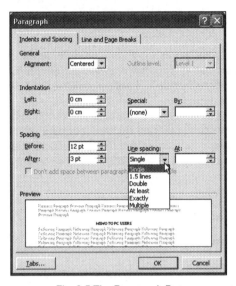

Fig. 8.5 The Paragraph Box.

Paragraph Spacing

The settings in this box will affect the current paragraph (with the insertion point in it), or any selected paragraphs. The above Paragraph dialogue box can also be used to set your paragraph line spacing to single-line, 1½-line, or double-line spacing. You can even set the spacing to any value you want by using the **At Least** option, as shown on the above screen dump, then specify what interval you want.

The available shortcut keys for paragraph spacing are as follows:

To Format	*Type*
Single-spaced lines	Ctrl+1
One-and-a-half-spaced lines	Ctrl+5
Double-spaced lines	Ctrl+2

Whichever of the above methods is used, formatting can take place either before or after the text is entered. If formatting is selected first, then text will type in the chosen format until a further formatting command is given. If, on the other hand, you choose to enter text and then format it afterwards, you must first select the text to be formatted, then activate the formatting.

Word gives you the choice of 5 units to work with, inches, centimetres, millimetres, points or picas. These can be selected by using the **Tools**, **Options** command, choosing the

General tab of the displayed Options dialogue box, and clicking the down arrow against the **Measurement units** list box, shown open here, which is to be found at the bottom of the dialogue box. We have selected to work in the default centimetres.

Indenting Text

Most documents will require some form of paragraph indenting. An indent is the space between the margin and the edge of the text in the paragraph. When an indent is set (on the left or right side of the page), any justification on that side of the page sets at the indent, not the page border.

To illustrate indentation, open the file **PC Users2**, select the first paragraph, and then choose the **Format**, **Paragraph** command. In the **Indentation** field, select 2.5 cm for both **Left** and **Right**, as shown on the next page. On clicking **OK**, the first selected paragraph is displayed indented. Our screen dump shows the result of the indentation as well as the settings on the Paragraph dialogue box which caused it.

You can also use the Formatting Bar buttons, shown below, to decrease or increase the indent of selected text.

 Use this button to decrease indent.

 Use this button to increase indent.

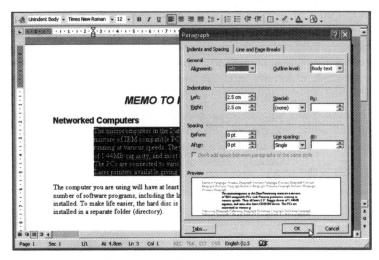

Fig. 8.6 Setting Paragraph Indentation.

The **Indentation** option in the Paragraph dialogue box, can be used to create 'hanging' indents, where all the lines in a paragraph, including any text on the first line that follows a tab, are indented by a specified amount. This is often used in lists to emphasise certain points.

To illustrate the method, use the **PC Users1** file and add at the end of it the text shown below. After you have typed the text in, save the enlarged memo as **PC Users3**, before going on with formatting the new text.

In Windows you can work with files in three different ways:

Name Description

My Computer Use the My Computer utility which Microsoft has spent much time and effort making as intuitive as possible.

Explorer Use the Windows Explorer, a much-improved version of the older File Manager.

MS-DOS Use an MS-DOS Prompt window if you prefer to and are an expert with the DOS commands.

Saving the work at this stage is done as a precaution in case anything goes wrong with the formatting - it is sometimes much easier to reload a saved file, than it is to try to unscramble a wrongly formatted document!

Next, highlight the last 4 paragraphs above, use the **Format**, **Paragraph** command, and select 'Hanging' under **Special** and 3 cm under **By**. On clicking the **OK** button, the text formats as shown in the composite screen dump below, but it is still highlighted. To remove the highlighting, click the mouse button anywhere on the page. The second and following lines of the selected paragraphs, should be indented 3 cm from the left margin.

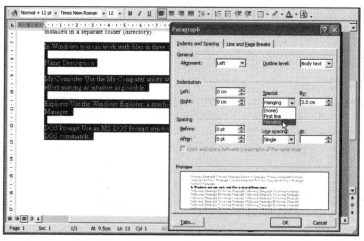

Fig. 8.7 Setting Hanging Indents Manually.

This is still not very inspiring, so to complete the effect we will edit the first lines of each paragraph as follows:

Place the cursor in front of the word 'Description' and press the <Tab> key once. This places the start of the word in the same column as the indented text of the other paragraphs. To complete the effect place tabs before the words 'Use' in the next three paragraphs, until your hanging indents are correct, as shown in Fig. 8.8 on the next page.

In Windows you can work with files in three different ways:

Name	Description
My Computer	Use the My Computer utility which Microsoft have spent much time and effort making as intuitive as possible.
Explorer	Use the Windows Explorer, a much-improved version of the older File Manager.
MS-DOS	Use an MS-DOS Prompt window if you prefer to and are an expert with the DOS commands.

Fig. 8.8 The Result of Using Hanging Indents.

This may seem like a complicated rigmarole to go through each time you want the hanging indent effect, but with Word you will eventually set up all your indents, etc., as styles in templates. Then all you do is click in a paragraph to produce them.

Adding a Drop Capital

A nother text feature that you may want to use at times is to make the first letter of a paragraph a large dropped initial capital letter, as shown here.

With Word that is ridiculously easy. Just place the insertion point at the beginning of the existing paragraph and action the **Format**, **Drop Cap** menu command. This opens the Drop Cap dialogue box, shown in our composite Fig. 8.8. As is often the case, this gives the settings needed to produce the result shown. You would not normally see them both together.

You can choose between **Dropped** and **In margin** for the position of the initial capital letter, change the **Font** (as we have done) and select how many **Lines to drop**.

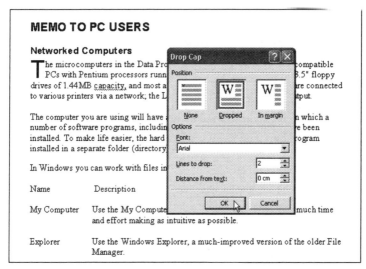

MEMO TO PC USERS

Networked Computers

The microcomputers in the Data Pro[...] ompatible PCs with Pentium processors runn[...] .5" floppy drives of 1.44MB capacity, and most a[...] re connected to various printers via a network; the L[...] tput.

The computer you are using will have [...] which a number of software programs, includin[...] e been installed. To make life easier, the hard [...] ogram installed in a separate folder (directory[...]

In Windows you can work with files in [...]

Name   Description

My Computer Use the My Compute[...] much time and effort making as intuitive as possible.

Explorer   Use the Windows Explorer, a much-improved version of the older File Manager.

Fig. 8.9 Setting a Dropped Capital Letter.

The new first letter is actually a graphic image now. To remove the effect if you decide you don't want it, select the image by clicking it, open the dialogue box with the **Format**, **Drop Cap** command and select **None**.

 When you finish formatting the document, save it under its current filename either with the **File, Save** command (<Ctrl+S>), or by clicking the **Save** button. This command does not display a dialogue box, so you use it when you do not need to make any changes during the saving operation.

Inserting Bullets

Bullets are small characters you can insert, anywhere you like, in the text of your document to improve visual impact. In Word there are several choices for displaying lists with bullets or numbers. As well as the two Formatting Bar buttons, others are made available through the **Format, Bullets and Numbering** command, which displays the following dialogue box.

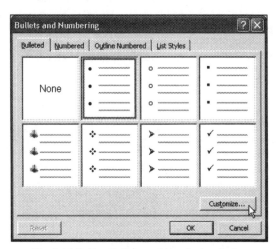

Fig. 8.10 Setting Bullets and Numbering Styles.

You can select any of the bullets shown here, or you could click the **Customize** button to change the shape, font and size of the bullet, choose a character, and set the indentation in the Customize Bulleted List box shown on the left in Fig. 8.11 on the next page.

Further, by pressing the **Picture** button on the Customized Bulleted List dialogue box you can select from an enormous number of bullet pictures, as shown on the right of Fig. 8.11. If none of these images suit, you can even **Import** a graphic image yourself to use as bullets. Very comprehensive.

If you select the **Numbered** or **Outline Numbered** tabs, shown in Fig. 8.10, similar dialogue boxes are displayed, giving you a choice of several numbering or outline (multilevel) systems.

Once inserted, you can copy, move or cut a bulleted paragraph in the same way as any other text. However, you can not delete a bullet with the <BkSp> or <Del> keys. To do this, you need to place the insertion point in the line and click the **Bullets** Toolbar button, shown here. Once you have set up a customised bullet, clicking this button in a paragraph will use it.

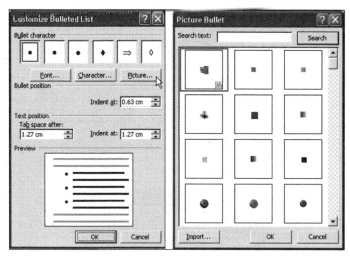

Fig. 8.11 Choosing Custom Bullet Pictures.

Inserting Date and Time

You can insert today's date, the date the current document was created or was last revised, or a date or time that reflects the current system date and time into a document. Therefore, the date can be a date that changes, or a date that always stays the same. In either case, the date is inserted in a date field.

To insert a date field in your document, place the cursor where you want to insert the date, select the **Insert**, **Date and Time** command and choose one of the displayed date formats which suits you from the dialogue box shown in Fig. 8.12 on the next page.

Highlighting '18 December, 2001' (or whatever date is current), and pressing **OK**, inserts the date in your document at the chosen position.

As before, the screen in Fig. 8.12 on the next page is a composite of the operation required and the result of that operation.

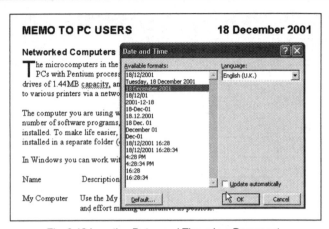

Fig. 8.12 Inserting Dates and Times in a Document.

If you save a document with a date field in it and you open it a few days later, the date shown on it will be the original date the document was created. Most of the time this will probably be what you want, but should you want the displayed date to always update to the current date whenever the document is opened, check the **Update automatically** box, pointed to in Fig. 8.11, and then click the **OK** button.

You may have noticed that many of Word's dialogue boxes have a **Default** button on them, as above. If you click this button you will make the settings active in the box at the time the default ones in any future documents opened with the Normal template. In our case the date would always be presented in the above format.

Comments and Tracked Changes

Another powerful feature of Word is the facility to add comments and to track changes made to a document. Comments are notes, or annotations, that an author or reviewer adds to a document and in Word 2002 they are displayed in balloons in the margin of the document or in the Reviewing Pane, as shown in Fig. 8.13 on the next page. A tracked change is a mark that shows where a deletion, insertion, or other editing change has been made in a document.

To quickly display or hide tracked changes or comments (known as mark-up) use the **View**, **Markup** menu command.

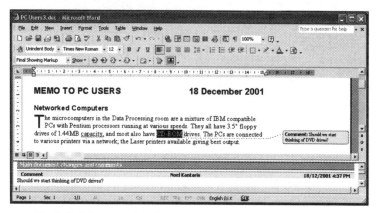

Fig. 8.13 A Comment in a Document with the Reviewing Pane Open.

To add a comment, place the pointer in the correct location, use the **Insert**, **Comment** command, and type the comment into the balloon that opens. If the Reviewing toolbar shown above is hidden, simply right-click any toolbar, and then click Reviewing on the shortcut menu. To open the reviewing pane, as shown above, use the **Show**, **Reviewing Pane** command from the Reviewing toolbar.

You can print a document with mark-up to keep a record of any changes made. If you want to see comments and tracked changes in balloons you must be in Print Layout or Web Layout view.

Formatting with Page Tabs

You can format text in columns by using tab stops. Word 2002 has default left tab stops every 3 ch from the left margin. We do not know what dimension the 'ch' is but the default tabs line up almost exactly at the old 1.27 cm intervals. By default the symbol for a left tab appears in the tab type button at left edge of the ruler as shown in Fig 8.14 on the next page.

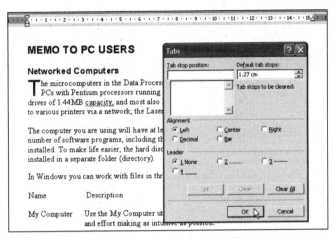

Fig. 8.14 The Tabs Dialogue Box.

To set tabs, use either the **Format**, **Tabs** command which opens the Tabs dialogue box shown above, or click on the tab type button (which cycles through the available tab stops) until the type you want is showing and then click the required position on the lower half of the ruler. To remove an added tab, just drag it off the ruler.

To clear the ruler of tab settings press the **Clear All** button in the Tabs dialogue box. When you set a tab stop on the ruler, all default tab stops to the left of the one you are setting are removed. Tab stops apply either to the paragraph containing the cursor, or to any selected paragraphs.

The tab stop types available have the following functions:

Button	Name	Effect
L	**Left**	Left aligns text after the tab stop.
⊥	**Centre**	Centres text on tab stop.
⅃	**Right**	Right aligns text after the tab stop.
⊥·	**Decimal**	Aligns decimal point with tab stop.
I	**Bar**	Inserts a vertical line at the tab stop.

The tab type button actually cycles through two more types, first line indent and hanging indent. This gives you a quick way of adding these indents to the ruler.

If you want tabular text to be separated by characters instead of by spaces, select one of the three available characters from the **Leader** box in the Tabs dialogue box. The options are none (the default), dotted, dashed, or underline. The Contents pages of this book are set with right tabs and dotted leader characters.

Note: As all paragraph formatting, such as tab stops, is placed at the end of a paragraph, if you want to carry the formatting of the current paragraph to the next, press <Enter>. If you don't want formatting to carry on, press the down arrow key instead.

Formatting with Styles

We saw earlier on page 117, how you can format your work using Paragraph Styles, but we confined ourselves to using the default **Normal** styles only. In this section we will get to grips with how to create, modify, use, and manage styles.

As mentioned previously, a Paragraph Style is a set of formatting instructions which you save so that you can use it repeatedly within a document or in different documents. A collection of Paragraph Styles can be placed in a Template which could be appropriate for, say, all your memos, so it can be used to preserve uniformity. It maintains consistency and saves time by not having to format each paragraph individually.

Further, should you decide to change a style, all the paragraphs associated with that style reformat automatically. Finally, if you want to provide a pattern for shaping a final document, then you use what is known as a Template. All documents which have not been assigned a document template, use the **Normal.dot** global template, by default.

Paragraph Styles

Paragraph Styles contain paragraph and character formats and a name can be attached to these formatting instructions. From then on, applying the style name is the same as formatting that paragraph with the same instructions.

With Word 2002 you create your styles by example using the new **Styles and Formatting** Task Pane, as we show in Fig. 8.15 below.

Creating a New Paragraph Style: Previously, we spent some time manually creating some hanging indents in the last few paragraphs of the **PC Users3** document. Open that document and display the **Styles and Formatting** Task Pane by clicking its toolbar button, as shown here. Place the insertion pointer in one of the previously created hanging indent paragraphs, say, in the 'Name Description' line.

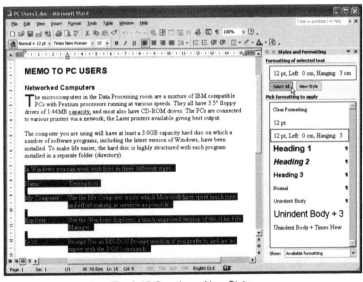

Fig. 8.15 Creating a New Style.

Notice that the selected item in the **Pick formatting to apply** list in the Task Pane has a rectangular selection marker around it. This in fact represents an unnamed style with the formatting we used to create the hanging indents. If you click the **Select All** button in the Task Pane all of our paragraphs with this formatting are highlighted in the main document.

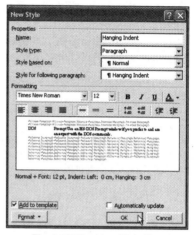

Next click the **New Style** button in the Task Pane to open the New Style box shown in Fig. 8.16. Type the new style name you want to create in the **Name** text box, say, 'Hanging Indent'. Lastly select the **Add to template** option at the bottom of the box and click **OK** to accept your changes.

Fig. 8.16 The New Style Box.

Finally, one by one, highlight the other three paragraphs with hanging indents and change their style to the new 'Hanging Indent', by clicking the mouse in the **Style** box button on the Formatting Toolbar and selecting the new style from the displayed list, as shown in Fig. 8.17 below.

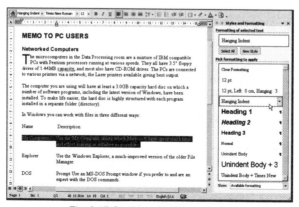

Fig. 8.17 Our New Style in Action.

It would have been nice if this last step could be carried out in the **Styles and Formatting** Task Pane, but the older Style box still seems to be necessary. Once this is done, however, our new style functions exactly the same in the Task Pane as the other ones.

Save the result as **PC Users4**, and make yourself a cup of coffee, or chocolate, or whatever turns you on.

You could also have a look at Word's built-in styles by selecting **St̲yle Gallery** from the **F̲ormat, T̲heme** menu. There are over sixty available styles, one of which might suit your type of document. Try them with the **PC Users4** file open, as it reformats your document on a viewing pane. Some of them may need installing though, but it will carry this out for you without too much trouble.

Document Templates

A document template provides the overall pattern of your final document. It can contain:

- Styles to control your paragraph and formats.

- Page set-up options.

- Boilerplate text, which is text that remains the same in every document.

- AutoText, which is standard text and graphics that you could insert in a document by typing the name of the AutoText entry.

- Macros, which are programs that can change the menus and key assignments to comply with the type of document you are creating.

- Customised shortcuts, toolbars and menus.

If you don't assign a template to a document, then the default **Normal.dot** template is used by Word. To create a new document template, you either modify an existing one, create one from scratch, or create one based on the formatting of an existing document.

Creating a Document Template

To illustrate the last point above, we will create a simple document template, which we will call **PC User**, based on the formatting of the **PC Users4** document. But first, make sure you have defined the 'Hanging Indent' style as explained earlier.

To create a template based on an existing document do the following:

* Open the existing document.

* Select the **File, Save As** command which displays the Save As dialogue box, shown in Fig. 8.18 below.

* In the **Save as type** box, select Document Template.

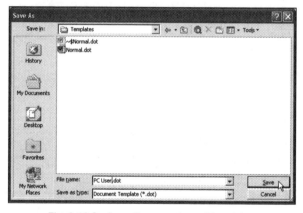

Fig. 8.18 Saving a Document as a Template.

* In the **Save in** box, use the Templates folder which should have opened for you.

* In the **File name** box, type the name of the new template (PC User in our example).

* Press the **Save** button, which opens the template file **PC User.dot** in the Word working area.

* Add the text and graphics you want to appear in all new documents that you base on this template, and *delete* any items (including text) you do not want to appear.

In our example, we deleted everything in the document, bar the heading, and added the words 'PC User Group' using **Insert, Picture, WordArt**, to obtain:

MEMO TO PC USERS

Fig. 8.19 Artwork and Text in our New Template.

- Click the **Save** button on the Toolbar, and close the document.

To use the new template, do the following:

- Use the **File**, **New** command which opens the **New Document** Task Pane. Select **General Templates** from the **New from template** section of the pane. The General tabbed sheet of the Templates box is opened, as shown in Fig. 8.20 below.

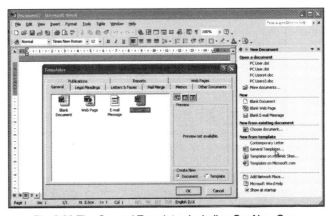

Fig. 8.20 The General Templates Including Our New One.

- Select the name of the template you want to use from the displayed list. This would be PCUsers.dot in our case.

- Make sure that the radio button **Document** is selected, and click the **OK** button.

The new document will be using the selected template.

Templates can also contain Macros as well as AutoText; macros allow you to automate Word keystroke actions only, while AutoText speeds up the addition of boilerplate text and graphics into your document. However, the design of these features is beyond the scope of this book.

Don't forget that Word has a series of built-in templates to suit 'every occasion' as we touched on in page 133.

The Default Character Format

As we have seen, for all new documents Word uses the Times New Roman type font with a 12 points size as the default for the Normal style, which is contained in the Normal template. If the majority of your work demands some different font style or size, then you can change these defaults.

To change the default character formatting, use the **Format**, **Font** command, select the new defaults you want to use, and press the **Default** button, as shown in Fig. 8.21.

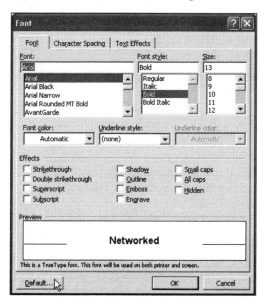

Fig. 8.21 Setting a New Default Font.

A warning box opens to make sure you really know what you are about to do. Pressing the **Yes** button, changes the default character settings for this and all subsequent new documents using the Normal template, but does not change already existing ones. Pressing **No** aborts the operation.

Special Characters and Symbols

Word 2002 has a redesigned Symbol dialogue box from which you can select characters and symbols and insert them into your document using the **Insert, Symbol** command. This is shown in Fig. 8.22 below.

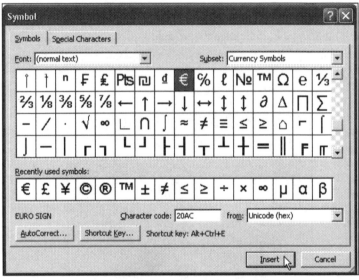

Fig. 8.22 The New Symbol Dialogue Box.

You should be able to find just about any symbol you require in the (normal text) font displayed. But if not, pressing the down-arrow button next to the **Font** box, will reveal the other available character sets. If you double-click the left mouse button on a character, it transfers it to your document at the insertion point.

Microsoft have made it easier to find symbols by grouping them into sets. Clicking the **Subset** button opens a drop-down menu for you to quickly move between them.

The **AutoCorrect** button opens the box shown in Fig. 7.1 (page 135) so that you can insert any of the symbols in the **Replace text as you type** section.

Inserting Other Special Characters

You can include other special characters in a document, such as optional hyphens, which remain invisible until they are needed to hyphenate a word at the end of a line; non-breaking hyphens, which prevent unwanted hyphenation; non-breaking spaces, which prevent two words from splitting at the end of a line; or opening and closing single quotes.

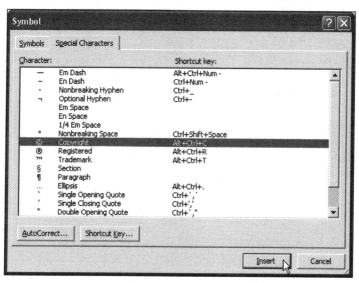

Fig. 8.23 The Special Characters Sheet.

There are two ways to insert these special characters in your document. One is to click the **Special Characters** tab of the Symbol dialogue box which reveals a long list of these special characters, as shown in Fig. 8.23 above. You then select one of them and click the **Insert** button.

The other way is to use the shortcut key combinations listed in Fig. 8.23, which does not require you to open the dialogue box. But you do have to remember them though!

* * *

Word has many more features, far too numerous to mention in the space allocated to this book, although we will be discussing later on how you can use Word to share information with other Microsoft applications and how to use mail merge techniques. What we have tried to do so far, is give you enough basic information so that you can have the confidence to forge ahead and explore the rest of Word's capabilities by yourself.

Perhaps, you might consider exploring page numbering, headers and footers, tables, frames, drawing, and outlining, in that order. We leave it to you. However, if you would prefer to be guided through these topics, then may we suggest you look up the later chapters of the book *Microsoft Word 2002 explained* (BP510), also published by BERNARD BABANI (publishing) Ltd.

* * *

9

The Works Spreadsheet

When you first enter the Works spreadsheet, the program sets up a huge electronic page, or worksheet, in your computer's memory, many times larger than the small part shown on the screen. Individual cells are identified by column and row location (in that order), with the present size extending to 256 columns by a massive 16,384 rows. The columns are labelled from A to Z, followed by AA to AZ, BA to BZ, and so on, to IV, while the rows are numbered from 1 to 16,384.

Clicking the **Programs** tab in the Task Launcher window, selecting **Works Spreadsheet**, and then clicking **Start a blank Spreadsheet** displays the following screen. The program can also be opened by selecting **Microsoft Works Spreadsheet** in the Windows **Start** menu system.

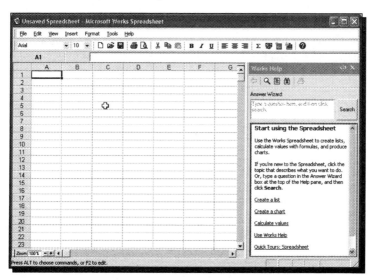

Fig. 9.1 The Works Blank Spreadsheet.

A spreadsheet can be thought of as a two-dimensional table made up of rows and columns. The point where a row and column intersect is called a cell, while the reference points of a cell are known as the cell address. The active cell (A1 when you first enter the program) is highlighted.

Worksheet Navigation

Navigation around the worksheet is achieved with the four arrow keys. Each time one of these keys is pressed, the active cell moves one position right, down, left or up, depending on which arrow key was pressed. The <PgDn> and <PgUp> keys can also be used to move vertically one full page at a time, while the <Ctrl+PgDn> and <Ctrl+PgUp> key combinations can be used to move horizontally one full page at a time. Pressing the arrow keys while holding down the <Ctrl> key causes the active cell to be moved to the extremities of the worksheet. For example, <Ctrl+⇨> moves the active cell to the IV column, while <Ctrl+⇩> moves the active cell to the 16,384th row.

You can move the active cell with a mouse by moving the mouse pointer to the cell you want to activate and clicking the left mouse button. If the cell is not visible, then move the window by clicking on the scroll bar arrowhead that points in the direction you want to move, until the cell you want to activate is visible. To move a page at a time, click in the scroll bar itself, or for larger moves, drag the scroll box in the scroll bar.

When you have finished navigating around the worksheet, press the <Ctrl+Home> keys which will move the active cell to the A1 position. This is known as the 'Home' position. If you press the <Home> key by itself, the active cell is moved to the 1st column of the particular row. Note that there are several areas on your screen; the displayed area within which you can move the active cell is referred to as the working area of the worksheet, while the letters and numbers in the border around the displayed portion of the worksheet form the reference points.

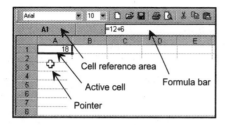

Fig. 9.2 The Spreadsheet Screen.

The location of the active cell is constantly monitored in the Cell Reference Area at the left end of the formula bar, below the toolbar. If you type text in the active cell, what you type appears both in the formula bar and in the cell itself. Typing a formula which is preceded by the equals sign (=) to, say, add the contents of two cells, causes the actual formula to appear in the 'formula bar', while the result of the actual calculation appears in the active cell when the <Enter> key is pressed.

The GoTo Command

To move to a distant address in the worksheet, use the **F5** function key which opens the Find and Replace dialogue box with a tab for the 'Go To' command. For example, to jump to cell HZ4000, type the address in the appropriate box (see Fig. 9.3) and press the **Go to** button.

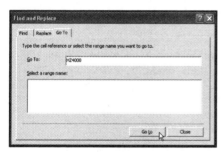

Fig. 9.3 The GoTo Sheet of the Find and Replace Dialogue Box.

To specify a cell address, you must always key one or two letters followed by a number. The letters can be in upper or lower case, and can range from A to IV (for columns), while the numbers can range from 1 to 16,384 (for rows). Specifying a column or row outside this range will cause an error message to be displayed which you have to clear by clicking on the **OK** button, before you can continue.

The other tabs on this dialogue box help you find and replace text (or numbers) in rows or columns.

The Spreadsheet Toolbar

As with the word processor tool, mouse lovers have an advantage when using the spreadsheet, in that they can make use of the toolbar. This occupies the third line down of the screen. If you prefer, you can turn it off by activating the **View**, **Toolbar** command. This is a toggle switch, when the '√' shows the toolbar will display, otherwise it will not. The only advantage to be gained by not showing the toolbar, is that you gain one line on your screen display. To use the toolbar you simply click the mouse on one of the icon buttons shown below, and the command selected will be effected on worksheet cells that are highlighted.

The meanings of the toolbar options are as follows:

Option	*Result*
Arial	Choose a font from the available list. Clicking the down arrow (▼) will open the list of fonts.
10 ▼	Choose from the available point sizes. Clicking the down arrow (▼) will open the list of sizes.
	Open new spreadsheet
	Open an existing file
	Save current document
	Print current document
	Print preview
	Cut to clipboard
	Copy to clipboard
	Paste from clipboard

B	Embolden selected text
I	Make selected text italic
U	Underline selected text
	Left align a paragraph
	Centre align a paragraph
	Right align a paragraph
Σ	Autosum a column, or row
$	Format selected cells as currency, with 2 decimal places
	Use Easy Calc to enter functions
	Create a chart using the selected entry data

Entering Information

We will now investigate how information can be entered into the worksheet. But first, return to the Home (A1) position by pressing <Ctrl+Home>, then type in the words:

```
PROJECT ANALYSIS
```

As you type, the characters appear in both the 'formula bar' and the active cell window.

If you make a mistake, press the <BkSp> key to erase the previous letter or the <Esc> key to start again. When you have finished, press <Enter>. Note that what you have just typed in has been entered in cell A1, even though part of the word ANALYSIS appears to be in cell B1. If you use the right arrow key to move the active cell to B1 you will see that the cell is indeed empty.

Note that the text displayed in the 'formula bar' is prefixed by double quotation marks (") which were added automatically by the program to indicate that the entry is a 'label' and not a number, or a date. Thus, typing a letter at the beginning of an entry into a cell results in a 'label' being formed. If the length of a label is longer than the width of a cell, it will continue into the next cell to the right of the current active cell, provided that cell is empty, otherwise the displayed label will be truncated.

To edit information already in a cell, move the pointer to the appropriate cell and either press the **F2** function key, or click in the 'formula bar'. The cursor keys, the <Home> and <End> keys, as well as the <Ins> and <Del> keys can be used to move the cursor and/or edit the information displayed in the formula bar, as required. After such editing of information in the formula bar, you must either press the <Enter> key, or click the '√' button on the formula bar, to enter it in the active cell.

Now use the arrow keys to move the active cell to B3 and type

        "Jan

Then press the right arrow key, which will automatically enter the abbreviation 'Jan' into the cell, as a label, and will also move the active cell to position C3. Had we only typed Jan (without the double quotes prefix) on pressing either <Enter> or the right-arrow key, the word 'January' would have appeared automatically in the cell, as a date. In cell C3, type

        "Feb

and again press the right arrow key.

The looks of a worksheet can be enhanced considerably by placing lines, or cell borders, to separate information in different rows. Select the cells A4 to C4 (from the keyboard use the <Shift+⇨> keystroke; with the mouse drag the active cell) and choose the **Format**, **Border** menu command. This opens the Border tabbed section of the Format Cells dialogue box (shown in Fig. 9.4), from which you can place any combination of lines along the borders of selected cells.

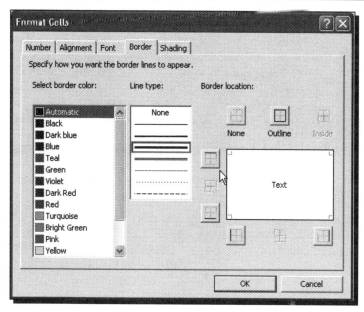

Fig. 9.4 The Format Cells Dialogue Box.

In our case, select the heavy line under the **Line type** option, click the button pointed to under the **Border location** option, as shown in Fig. 9.4, and press **OK** to accept the settings.

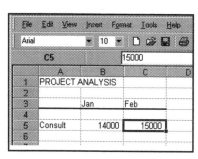

Fig. 9.5 Entering Data into a Sheet.

Finally, type in the label and amounts earned in columns A, B and C of row 5, as shown in the screen dump in Fig. 9.5.

Note how the labels 'Jan' and 'Feb' do not appear above the numbers 14000 and 15000. This is because by default, labels are left justified, while numbers are right justified.

Changing Text Alignment and Fonts

One way of improving the looks of this worksheet is to also right justify the labels 'Jan' and 'Feb' within their respective cells. To do this, move the active cell to B3 and mark the range B3 to C3 (from the keyboard use the <Shift+→> keystroke; with the mouse drag the active cell), choose the **Format, Alignment** command, then select the **Right** option listed in the Alignment tabbed section of the Format Cells dialogue box and click **OK**. The labels should now appear right justified within their cells. An easier way to carry out this operation is to select the cells and click the **Right Align** toolbar icon, shown here.

We could further improve the looks of the worksheet by choosing a different font for the heading 'Project Analysis'. To achieve this, move the active cell to A1, choose the **Format, Font and Style** command, then select Courier New, **Size** 8 and **Italic**, from the options listed in the displayed dialogue box, and press **OK**. The heading will now appear in Courier New 8, Italic font.

Once again the toolbar gives a much quicker way of carrying out these operations. Simply click the down arrow alongside the Font Name or Font Size icons, shown above, and make your selection from the menus that drop down.

Finally, since the entered numbers in cells B5 to C5 represent money, it would be better if these were displayed with two digits after the decimal point and prefixed with the £ sign. To do this, move the active cell to B5 and select the cell block B5 to C5, then choose the **Format, Number, Currency** command and accept the default number of decimals, which is 2. This formatting operation can also be done by clicking the **Currency** toolbar icon, shown here. The numbers within the marked worksheet range should now be displayed in the new format. If the width of the relevant cells had not been large enough to accommodate all the digits of the new format, they would have been filled with the hash character (#) to indicate insufficient space. The columns would then need to be widened.

Changing Column Widths

To change the width of a given column or a number of columns, activate a cell in the relevant column, or block the number of required column cells, then use the **Format Column Width** command. This causes a dialogue box in Fig. 9.6 to be displayed with the 'standard' column width offered as 10 characters, or a 'best fit' option which ensures all entries in the column fit. Typing 12 and clicking **OK**, changes the width of the selected columns to 12 characters.

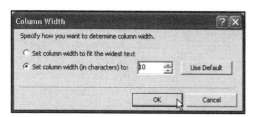

Fig. 9.6 The Column Width Dialogue Box.

Fig. 9.7 Changing the Width of a Column.

A quicker method of doing this, if you prefer, is to position the mouse pointer in the column headings at the top of the working area. It will change shape as you move it over the border of two columns. Dragging this new pointer right or left, will widen, or narrow, the column to the left.

If the currency symbol displays as a '$' don't panic, it just means your version of Windows is not set up for the UK. To remedy this open the Control Panel by clicking the **Start** button on the Windows TaskBar, followed by **Settings**, **Control Panel**. Double-click on the **Regional Settings** icon, shown here, and make sure that English (United Kingdom) is selected on the opening tabbed page. If the Currency page settings are not correct, simply change them. You can, of course, customise these Regional settings for wherever on the globe you happen to be.

Now change the contents of cell A5 from 'Consult' to 'Consultancy'.

Saving a Worksheet

At this point, you might like to stop entering information in your worksheet, and save the work so far carried out, before leaving the program. You can do this by choosing the **File, Save** command which, when used for the first time with a file, opens the Save As dialogue box shown in Fig. 9.8.

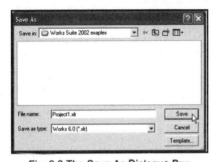

For our exercise, type the **File name** as **Project1** and press <Enter>, or click the **Save** button (the extension **.xlr** will be added by Works). If you prefer to save your work in a different folder, instead of in the default My Documents folder, you could make your

Fig. 9.8 The Save As Dialogue Box.

selection in the **Save in** box.

What you should see displayed on your screen after the above commands have been issued, is shown in Fig. 9.9 below, at a zoom factor of 150% for clarity.

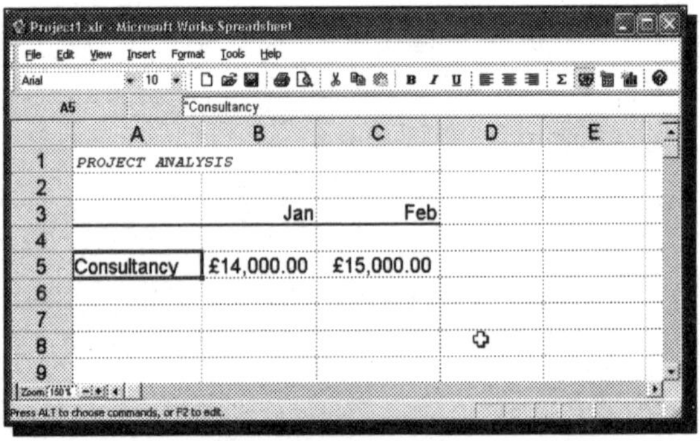

Fig. 9.9 The Formatted Works Worksheet.

At this point you could exit Works and Windows and then switch off your computer, safe in the knowledge that your work is saved on disc and can be retrieved at any time.

Exiting a Spreadsheet

To exit Works, either click the Application 'X' **Close** button, use the **File, Exit** command, or the <Alt+**F4**> keys. If you have made any changes to your work since the last time you saved it, an alert box will be displayed on your screen to ask you if you would like to save the file before leaving the program.

Filling in a Worksheet

We will use, as an example of how a spreadsheet can be built up, the few entries on 'Project Analysis' which we used previously. If you haven't saved the **Project1** example, don't worry as you could just as easily start afresh.

Retrieving a Worksheet

There are two main ways of retrieving, or opening, existing files. Which you use depends on whether you have the Task Launcher or the Spreadsheet itself open.

From the Spreadsheet Itself

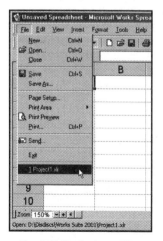

Fig. 9.10 Retrieving a File.

Use the **Open** toolbar button, or the **File**, **Open** command and select a spreadsheet file from the displayed list in the Open dialogue box.

A quick way to retrieve one of the last files used by Works is to open the **File** menu in a Spreadsheet window and click on the file's name at the bottom of the menu options, as shown here. As you highlight the files in this list their full path locations are shown on the status bar, as shown in Fig. 9.10.

From the Task Launcher
Clicking the **Hi̱story** tab in the Task Launcher opens a list of recently used files and documents, as shown below. Clicking one of these will open the file in the relevant application. In our case, this will be **Project1**, as shown in Fig. 9.11.

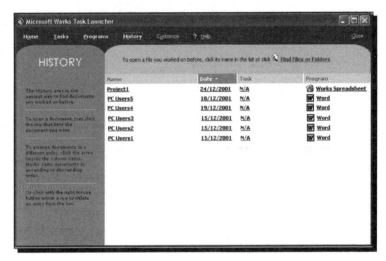

Fig. 9.11 Recently Used Files in Task Launcher's History Tab.

This list can get very untidy, often showing several references that are of no real use. To delete these from the history list, right-click a name, and select **Delete** on the shortcut menu. The entry in the history list is only a shortcut to a file, so when you delete an entry the file itself is not deleted from your computer's hard drive, only the shortcut.

If you don't know the document's actual location on your system, try using the **Find Files or Folders** link to search your whole hard disc system. When you have selected the file you want, in our case, **Project1**, just click to open it.

When the file is open, use the **F2** function key to 'Edit' the existing entries, or simply retype the contents of cells (see the next section for the formatting of the example) so that your worksheet looks like the one in Fig. 9.12 on the next page.

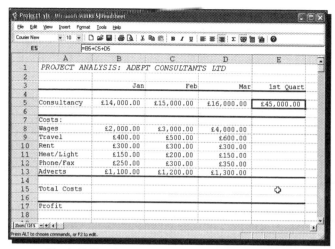

Fig. 9.12 First Quarter Figures of Adept Consultants.

Formatting Entries

Because of the length of some of the labels used and the formatting of the numbers, the default widths of cells in our worksheet were changed from the existing 10, to 12. If you haven't done this already, mark the cell block A1:E1, and choose the **Format, Column Width** command, and type 12 for the new width of the cells. The information in cell A1

```
PROJECT ANALYSIS: ADEPT CONSULTANTS LTD
```

was entered left justified and formatted by choosing the Courier New, size 12, **Italic** toolbar icon. The labels in the cell block B3-E3 were formatted with the **Right Align** icon, so they are displayed right justified.

The numbers within the cell block B5-E17 were formatted by clicking the **Currency** button. All the labels appearing in column A (apart from that in cell A1) were just typed in (left justified), as shown.

The lines in cells A4 to E4 and A14 to E14 were entered using the **Format, Border** command and selecting **Top**. Those in cells A6 to E6 and A16 to E16 were entered using **Format, Border** and selecting **Bottom**.

Entering Text, Numbers and Formulae

When text, numbers or formulae are entered into a cell, or reference is made to the contents of a cell by the cell address, or a Works function is entered into a cell, then the content of the message line changes from 'Press ALT to choose commands, or F2 to edit' to 'Press ENTER, or ESC to cancel'. This message can be changed back to the former one either by completing an entry and pressing <Enter> or one of the arrow keys, or by pressing the <Esc> key.

In our example, we can find the 1st quarter total income from consultancy, by activating cell E5 and typing the formula

    =B5+C5+D5

followed by <Enter>. The total first quarter consultancy income is added, using this formula, and the result is placed in cell E5. Note, however, that when cell E5 is activated, the 'formula bar' displays the actual formula used to calculate the contents of the cell.

Complete the insertion into the spreadsheet of the various amounts under 'costs' and then choose the **File, Save As** command to save the resultant worksheet under the filename **Project2**, before going on any further. Remember that saving your work on disc often is a good policy to get used to, as even the shortest power cut can cause the loss of hours of hard work!

Using Functions

In our example, writing a formula that adds the contents of three columns is not too difficult or lengthy a task. But imagine having to add 20 columns the same way! For this reason Works, like all spreadsheets, has an inbuilt summation function (for the many others see the Appendix) in the form of =SUM( ) which can be used to add any number of columns (or rows).

To illustrate how this function can be used, activate cell E5 and type

```
=SUM (
```

then use the mouse pointer to highlight the cells in the summation range (B5 to D5 in this case). What appears against the cell indicator is the entry

```
SUM(B5:D5
```

which has to be completed by typing the closing parenthesis (round bracket) and pressing <Enter>.

The Autosum Function

Another clever feature in Works is the facility to automatically enter the above =SUM() function into the worksheet. To automatically sum a series of numbers in either a column, or a row, place the active cell below the column, or to the right of the row, and click the **Autosum** toolbar button, shown here, or press the <Ctrl+M> quick key combination. Works enters the formula for you; all you have to do is press <Enter>, or click the **Enter** button (√) on the Formula bar, to accept it.

Easy Calc

The Easy Calc feature helps you add functions to your spreadsheets. To use it, place the active cell where you want to add a function (cell E8 in our example) and click the **Easy Calc** toolbar button shown here. If you prefer, use the **Tools**, **Easy Calc** menu command. Both open the dialogue box shown in Fig. 9.13, which should help to enter the correct function for your needs. Selecting **Add** opens the second box in which you are asked for the range to be added (B8:D8 in our example). Finally, in the third dialogue box you are asked to specify the cell in which the result should be placed.

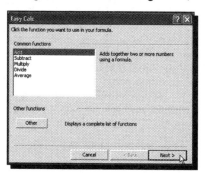

Fig. 9.13 The Easy Calc Function Box.

Copying Cell Contents

To copy information into other cells we could repeat the above procedure (in this particular case entering the SUM() function in each cell within the cell range E8 through E13), or we could choose the **Edit**, **Copy** command, point to the cell we would like to copy information into and **Edit**, **Paste** it.

To illustrate the copy command, activate cell E5 and click the **Copy** icon, or choose the **Edit**, **Copy** command, or press <Ctrl+C>, which copies the cell contents to the Windows clipboard. Move the highlighted cell to E8 and click the **Paste** icon, or press **Edit**, **Paste**, or the <Ctrl+V> quick key. Then, block the cell range E8:E13 (by either using the <Shift+↓> keystroke or dragging the mouse) and choose the **Edit, Fill Down** command, or press <Ctrl+D>. This is a good shortcut to remember!

Immediately this command is chosen the actual sums of the 'relative' columns appear in the target area. Notice that when you activate cell E5, the function target range is B5:D5, while when you activate cell E8 the function target range changes to B8:D8 which indicates that copying formulae with this method causes the 'relative' target range to be copied. Had the 'absolute' target range been copied instead, the result of the various summations would have been wrong.

Now complete the insertion of functions and formulae in the rest of the worksheet, noting that 'Total Costs' is the summation of rows 8 through 13, 'Profit' is the subtraction of 'Total Costs' from 'Consultancy', and that 'Cumulative' in row 19 refers to cumulative profit.

Then add another column to your worksheet to calculate (and place in column F) the average monthly values of earnings, costs, and profit, using the =AVG( ) function.

The worksheet, up to this point, should look like the one in Fig. 9.14 on the next page. To make room on the screen for all 6 columns, we changed the Font to Courier 10 points, but we could have used the **View**, **Zoom** feature instead. We also emboldened all the column and row titles.

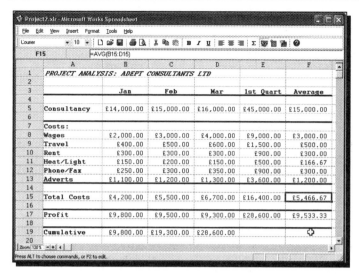

Fig. 9.14 The Completed First Quarter Worksheet of Adept Consultants.

Erasing Cell Contents

If you make any mistakes and copy information into cells you did not mean to, then choose the **Edit, Clear** command. To blank the contents within a range of adjacent cells, first select the cell block, then use the command.

There is also an **Edit**, **Undo...** menu option in the Works Spreadsheet, but unfortunately it is nowhere near as useful as that in the word processor.

Once you are satisfied that what appears on your screen is the same as our example, use the **File**, **Save As** command to save your worksheet under the filename **Project3**, as we shall be using this example in the next chapter.

Quick Key Combinations

We have already discussed how you can move around a worksheet, edit information in a cell, or mark a range of cells using the pull-down sub-menus, or the toolbar.

Another method of achieving these and other operations (some of which will be discussed in the next chapter) is using quick key combinations, which do not require the menu bar to be activated. As you get used to the Works package, you might find it easier to use some of the quick key combinations which can save you a lot of time.

The following key combinations are some of those for use with the Works spreadsheet.

File Handling
Open new file	Ctrl+N
Open an existing file	Ctrl+O
Close the current file	Ctrl+W
Save the current file	Ctrl+S
Print File	Ctrl+P

Moving and Selecting
Go To	F5 or Ctrl+G
Move right one window	Ctrl+PgDn
Move left one window	Ctrl+PgUp
Move to next named range	Shift+F5
Move to next unlocked cell	Tab
Move to previous unlocked cell	Shift+Tab
Select worksheet row	Ctrl+F8
Select worksheet column	Shift+F8
Select whole worksheet	Ctrl+Shift+F8
Activate Autosum	Ctrl+M

Editing
Undo / Redo last action	Ctrl+Z
Cut selection to the clipboard	Ctrl+X
Copy selection to the clipboard	Ctrl+C
Paste from the clipboard	Ctrl+V
Copy contents of cell above	Ctrl+' (apostrophe)
Re-calculate now	F9
Open object menu	Shift+F10
Activate menu bar	F10
Select all	Ctrl+A
Find	Ctrl+F
Replace	Ctrl+H

Fill cells to the right	Ctrl+R
Fill cells down	Ctrl+D
Check spelling	F7
Help	F1

Working in the Formula Bar

Activate/clear the formula bar	Backspace, or Del
Confirm information in a cell	Enter
Confirm a range of cells	Ctrl+Enter
Edit cell in formula bar	F2

Printing a Worksheet

When Windows was installed on your computer your printers should have been installed as well. Once a printer has been installed and selected, as described on Page 48, Works will happily print to that printer from all the tools.

To print a worksheet, choose the **File**, **Print** command, or use the <Ctrl+P> quick key combination, both of which open the Print dialogue box shown in Fig. 9.15.

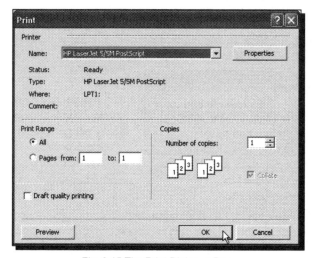

Fig. 9.15 The Print Dialogue Box.

Note that the default print settings are 1 copy, **All** pages, and all text styles, etc. You can change any of the options by choosing to print a different **Number of copies**, selecting which pages to print, and setting **Draft quality printing** output, if you wish. You can also change which printer to use, as well as setting its **Properties**.

 Note that clicking on the **Print** toolbar icon will send your work straight to the printer without giving you a chance to check, or change, your settings.

Before printing to paper, select the **File**, **Print Preview** command, or click the **Print Preview** toolbar icon, shown here, to see how much of your worksheet will fit on your selected paper size. This depends very much on the chosen font. If the **Print Preview** option displays only part of your worksheet, and you then direct output to the printer, what does not fit on one page will be printed out on subsequent pages. To fit more of your worksheet on one page, you should reduce the selected font. Thus, the **Print Preview** option allows you to see the layout of the final printed page, which can save a few trees and, equally important to you, a lot of frustration and wear and tear on your printer.

Setting a Print Area

To select a smaller print area than the current worksheet, first select the required area, then choose the **File**, **Print Area**, **Set Print Area** command and press **OK** on the displayed warning box shown here. You can then either preview the selected area, or print it on paper.

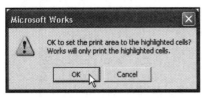

Fig. 9.16 The Set Print Area Warning Box.

To reset the print area to the entire worksheet, choose the **Edit**, **Select All** command, then **File**, **Print Area**, **Set Print Area** once more, before attempting to either preview your worksheet or send it to the printer.

Adding Headers and Footers

Headers and footers can be used in both the Works Spreadsheet and Database tools. These cannot be viewed in the actual spreadsheets, but appear on both the print preview and the print output. To add headers and footers, choose **View**, **Header and Footer**, then type the required information in the appropriate boxes, or select one of the standard codes listed in the drop-down menus, as shown in Fig. 9.17. The Preview area displays what the printout wil look like.

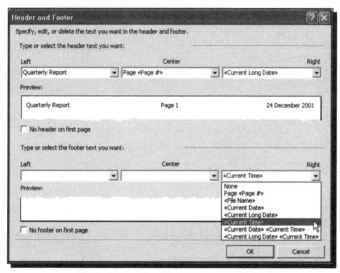

Fig. 9.17 Inserting Headers and Footers.

It can sometimes be useful to date and time stamp a spreadsheet so that you can tell exactly when it was produced. In our example above we selected the standard code for <<Current Long Date>> to appear at the top right of the printout and the standard code for <<Current Time>> to appear at the bottom right. Finally, you can prevent a header or footer from appearing on the first page of your printout by selecting either **No header on first page** or **No footer on first page**. You might want to use this when adding page numbers to a printout, which you don't want to show on the first page.

To see the results of any header and footer entries you have
added to your document, you only have to click the Print
Preview button. It is then very easy to make changes
until you get exactly the result you want without wasting
yet more paper!

```
Quarterly Report            Page 1           24 December 2001

PROJECT ANALYSIS: ADEPT CONSULTANTS LTD

                      Jan        Feb        Mar      1st Quart

Consultancy       £14,000.00 £15,000.00 £16,000.00 £45,000.00

Costs:
Wages              £2,000.00  £3,000.00  £4,000.00  £9,000.00
Travel               £400.00    £500.00    £600.00  £1,500.00
Rent                 £300.00    £300.00    £300.00    £900.00
Heat/Light           £150.00    £200.00    £150.00    £500.00
Phone/Fax            £250.00    £300.00    £350.00    £900.00
Adverts            £1,100.00  £1,200.00  £1,300.00  £3,600.00

Total Costs        £4,200.00  £5,500.00  £6,700.00 £16,400.00

Profit             £9,800.00  £9,500.00  £9,300.00 £28,600.00

Cumulative         £9,800.00 £19,300.00 £28,600.00


                                                       11.45
```

Fig. 9.18 Print Preview of a Worksheet Displaying Headers and Footers.

10

Spreadsheet Skills and Graphs

We will now use the worksheet saved under **Project3** in the previous chapter to show how we can add to it, rearrange information in it and freeze titles in order to make entries easier, before going on to discuss some more advanced topics. If you haven't saved **Project3** on disc, it will be necessary for you to enter the information into the Works spreadsheet so that you can benefit from what is to be introduced in this chapter.

Having done this, save your work before going on with the suggested alterations. If you have saved **Project3**, then click the **Open File** button on the toolbar and select the file from the displayed list. The worksheet should look like ours in Fig. 10.1.

	A	B	C	D	E	F
1	*PROJECT ANALYSIS: ADEPT CONSULTANTS LTD*					
2						
3		Jan	Feb	Mar	1st Quart	Average
4						
5	Consultancy	£14,000.00	£15,000.00	£16,000.00	£45,000.00	£15,000.00
6						
7	Costs:					
8	Wages	£2,000.00	£3,000.00	£4,000.00	£9,000.00	£3,000.00
9	Travel	£400.00	£500.00	£600.00	£1,500.00	£500.00
10	Rent	£300.00	£300.00	£300.00	£900.00	£300.00
11	Heat/Light	£150.00	£200.00	£150.00	£500.00	£166.67
12	Phone/Fax	£250.00	£300.00	£350.00	£900.00	£300.00
13	Adverts	£1,100.00	£1,200.00	£1,300.00	£3,600.00	£1,200.00
14						
15	Total Costs	£4,200.00	£5,500.00	£6,700.00	£16,400.00	£5,466.67
16						
17	Profit	£9,800.00	£9,500.00	£9,300.00	£28,600.00	£9,533.33
18						
19	Cumulative	£9,800.00	£19,300.00	£28,600.00		
20						

Cell reference F15: =AVG(B15:D15)

Fig. 10.1 The First Quarter Worksheet of Adept Consultants.

Controlling Cell Contents

We will now add some more information to the worksheet with the insertion of another quarter's figures between columns E and F. In fact, we need to insert four columns altogether.

In general, you can insert or delete columns and rows in a worksheet, copy cell contents (including formulae) from one part of the worksheet to another and freeze titles in order to make entries into cells easier.

Inserting Rows and Columns

To insert columns into a worksheet, point to the column heading where a column is to be inserted, in our case F, and press the left mouse button, which highlights the whole column. Then choose the **I**nsert, **Insert C**olumn command, or right-click with the mouse and select **Insert Column** from the opened object menu. Had you highlighted a specific cell, say F1, the **I**nsert menu command would give you the options of inserting either columns, or rows.

Repeat the insertion command three more times so that the column headed 'Average' appears in column J. To insert three columns in one operation, select the three columns to the right of where you want the insertion before you use the **Insert Column** command. We could now start entering information into the empty columns, but if we did this we would then have to re-enter all the formulae used to calculate the various results for the first quarter.

An alternative, and much easier, way is to copy every-thing from the first quarter to the second and then only edit the actual numeric information within the various columns. We will choose this second method to achieve our goal. First, highlight the cell block B3:E19, move the highlighter to the top border of the block where it will change to a DRAG pointer. Hold down the <Ctrl> key and Drag copy the block four columns to the right, as shown in Fig. 10.2 on the next page.

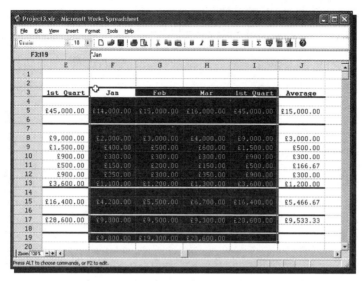

Fig. 10.2 Copying Blocks of Cells in a Worksheet.

If necessary, use the **Format, Column Width** command, to change the width of any cells from 10 characters to 12. Now the widths of the highlighted columns are suitably adjusted, edit the copied headings 'Jan', 'Feb', 'Mar', and '1st Quart' to 'Apr', 'May', 'Jun', and '2nd Quart'. Save the resultant work under the filename **Project4** (don't forget to use the **Save As** command)!

Freezing Titles

Note that by the time the highlighted bar is moved to column J, the 'titles' in column A have scrolled to the left and are outside the viewing area of the screen. This will make editing of numeric information very difficult if we can't see what refers to what. Therefore, before we attempt any further editing, it would be a good idea to use the 'Titles' command to freeze the titles in column A and rows 1 to 3.

To freeze row (or column) headings on a worksheet, move the highlighted bar to the cell below the row (or to the right of the column) you wish to freeze on the screen (in our case B4), and select the **Format, Freeze Titles** toggle command.

On execution, the headings on the chosen column (and row) are frozen but the highlighter can still be moved into the frozen area. Moving around the worksheet, leaves the headings in these rows (and/or columns) frozen on the screen. Carry this out and change the numbers in the worksheet cells F5 to H13 to those in Fig. 10.3.

A1		PROJECT ANALYSIS: ADEPT CONSULTANTS LTD				
	A	**F**	**G**	**H**	**I**	**J**
1	PROJECT ANALYS:					
2						
3		Apr	May	Jun	2nd Quart	Average
4						
5	Consultancy	£15,500.00	£16,000.00	£16,500.00	£48,000.00	£15,000.00
6						
7	Costs:					
8	Wages	£3,500.00	£4,000.00	£4,500.00	£12,000.00	£3,000.00
9	Travel	£500.00	£550.00	£580.00	£1,630.00	£500.00
10	Rent	£300.00	£300.00	£300.00	£900.00	£300.00
11	Heat/Light	£150.00	£120.00	£100.00	£370.00	£166.67
12	Phone/Fax	£300.00	£350.00	£400.00	£1,050.00	£300.00
13	Adverts	£1,250.00	£1,300.00	£1,350.00	£3,900.00	£1,200.00
14						
15	Total Costs	£6,000.00	£6,620.00	£7,230.00	£19,850.00	£5,466.67
16						
17	Profit	£9,500.00	£9,380.00	£9,270.00	£28,150.00	£9,533.33
18						
19	Cumulative	£9,500.00	£18,880.00	£28,150.00		
20						

Zoom 116%

Press ALT to choose commands, or F2 to edit.

Fig. 10.3 Worksheet Displaying Information on Second Quarter.

Save the file again, but this time use the **Save** toolbar icon, to keep the name **Project4**.

Note: If you examine this worksheet carefully, you will notice that two errors have occurred; one of these has to do with the average calculations in column J, while the other has to do with the accumulated values in the second quarter.

Non-contiguous Address Range

The calculations of average values in column J of the above worksheet are wrong because the range values in the formula are still those entered for the first quarter only.

To correct these, highlight cell J5 and press **F2** to edit the formula displayed in the formula bar from =AVG(B5:D5) to

    =AVG(B5:D5,F5:H5)

which on pressing <Enter> changes the value shown in cell J5.

Note the way the argument of the function is written when non-contiguous address ranges are involved. Here we have two such address ranges, B5:D5 and F5:H5, which we separate with a comma.

Now replicate the formula to the J8:J13 cell range by highlighting cell J5, choosing the **Edit, Copy** command, or <Ctrl+C>, move the highlight to cell J8 and use **Edit, Paste**. Then drag the highlight from J8 to J13 (to select the range) and choose the **Edit, Fill Down** command. Finally, repeat the **Paste** operation for the target cells J15 and J17 - You could also do all these actions with the Copy and Paste icons. The choice is yours!

Relative and Absolute Cell Addresses

Entering a mathematical expression into Works, such as the formula in cell C19 which was

```
=B19+C17
```

causes Works to interpret it as 'add the contents of cell one column to the left of the current position, to the contents of cell two rows above the current position'. In this way, when the formula was later replicated into cell address D19, the contents of the cell relative to the left position of D19 (i.e. C19) and the contents of the cell two rows above it (i.e. D17) were used, instead of the original cell addresses entered in C19. This is relative addressing.

To see the effect of relative versus absolute addressing, type in cell E19 the formula

```
=E5−E15
```

which will be interpreted as relative addressing. Now, add another row to your worksheet, namely 'Profit/Quart' in row 21, and copy the formula in cell E19 to cell E21, using the **Edit Copy** command. The displayed calculated value in E21 is, of course, wrong (negative) because the cell references in the copied formula are now given as

```
=E7−E17
```

as the references were copied relatively.

Now change the formula in E19 by editing it to

```
=$E$5-$E$15
```

which is interpreted as absolute addressing. Copying this formula into cell E21 calculates the correct result. Highlight cell E21 and observe the cell references in its formula; they have not changed from those of cell E19.

The $ sign must prefix both the column reference and the row reference. Mixed cell addressing is permitted; as for example when a column address reference is needed to be taken as absolute, while a row address reference is needed to be taken as relative. In such a case, only the column letter is prefixed by the $ sign.

Finally, correct the formulae in cells I19 and I21 (they should both contain '=$E$19+$I$17') in order to obtain the results shown in Fig. 10.4.

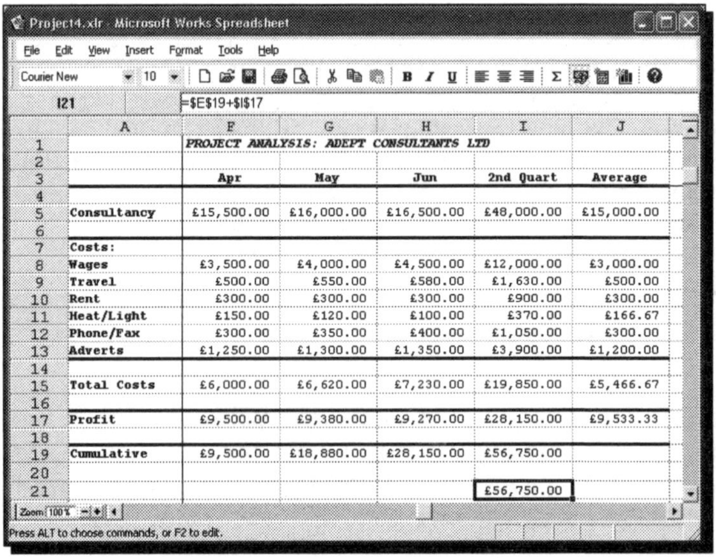

	A	F	G	H	I	J
1		PROJECT ANALYSIS: ADEPT CONSULTANTS LTD				
2						
3		Apr	May	Jun	2nd Quart	Average
4						
5	Consultancy	£15,500.00	£16,000.00	£16,500.00	£48,000.00	£15,000.00
6						
7	Costs:					
8	Wages	£3,500.00	£4,000.00	£4,500.00	£12,000.00	£3,000.00
9	Travel	£500.00	£550.00	£580.00	£1,630.00	£500.00
10	Rent	£300.00	£300.00	£300.00	£900.00	£300.00
11	Heat/Light	£150.00	£120.00	£100.00	£370.00	£166.67
12	Phone/Fax	£300.00	£350.00	£400.00	£1,050.00	£300.00
13	Adverts	£1,250.00	£1,300.00	£1,350.00	£3,900.00	£1,200.00
14						
15	Total Costs	£6,000.00	£6,620.00	£7,230.00	£19,850.00	£5,466.67
16						
17	Profit	£9,500.00	£9,380.00	£9,270.00	£28,150.00	£9,533.33
18						
19	Cumulative	£9,500.00	£18,880.00	£28,150.00	£56,750.00	
20						
21					£56,750.00	

Fig. 10.4 Demonstrating Relative and Absolute Cell Addressing.

Moving Cell Contents

To improve the printed output of **Project4**, we could move the caption to somewhere in the middle of the worksheet. Since the cell whose contents we propose to move is frozen, the move command could be preceded by additional keystrokes. From the keyboard, first unfreeze the title with the **Format**, **Freeze Titles** command. Now, highlight cell A1 and choose the **Edit, Cut** command (or <Ctrl+X>), which removes the cell contents from the worksheet and places them on the Windows clipboard, then highlight cell F1 and **Paste** the clipboard's contents. Save the resultant worksheet under the filename **Project5**.

Other Useful Features

Works includes several other spreadsheet features worth mentioning briefly.

Alignment

Another method of carrying out the title formatting in the last example would be to use the ability to centre a cell's contents within a selected range with the **Format**, **Alignment**, **Center across selection** command.

Some other features to note in this dialogue box are the vertical alignment options and the ability to **Wrap text within a cell** (but not numbers or formulae). You can now have several lines of text in the same cell.

Automatic Column Widths

Choosing the **Set column width to fit the widest text** radio button in the **Format**, **Column Width** dialogue box lets Works determine the best column width to accommodate all the entries in selected columns, or parts of columns. You could use this after selecting the whole sheet and not have to worry about cell widths again.

Inserting Functions

You can automatically choose a function with the **Insert**, **Function** command and Works inserts it, including its arguments, into the formula bar. This feature saves you having to remember all the available function names, and from looking up the argument details every time. In the **Select a category** list, functions are listed in suitable categories, under such headings as 'All', 'Financial', 'Date and Time', etc., as shown in Fig. 10.5.

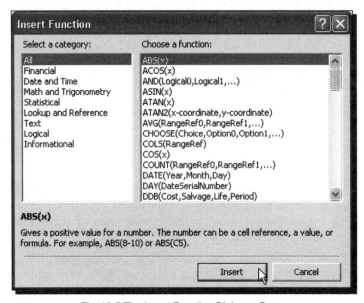

Fig. 10.5 The Insert Function Dialogue Box.

Nevertheless, and for your convenience, all functions with their required arguments are listed under appropriate headings in the Appendix at the back of this book.

The Undo Command

The **Edit**, **Undo..** command reverses certain commands, or deletes the last entry you typed, but only if it is used straight away. Immediately after you undo an action, this command changes to **Redo..**, which allows you to reverse the action.

Automatic Cell Fill

A useful feature which could save you much typing is the **Edit**, **Fill Series** command, which fills highlighted cells with a series of numbers or dates. You type the first entry, highlight the cells to fill and use this command to quickly enter the rest of a series of consecutive dates or numbers in the column or row.

Try typing 'Jan' in a heading cell and pressing <Enter>. Then highlight it and the next eleven cells to the right, use the **Edit**, **Fill Series** command, select **Month**, and see what happens. Computers do make things easier after all!

Cell Formatting Options

The **Format**, **Shading** command gives you control over the pattern and colour of the background of highlighted cells. To change the foreground colour of a cell's contents you must use the **Format**, **Font and Style**, **Color** option.

The **Format**, **AutoFormat** option gives a series of built-in formats you can apply to any highlighted range to give it a more professional appearance, as shown in Fig. 10.6.

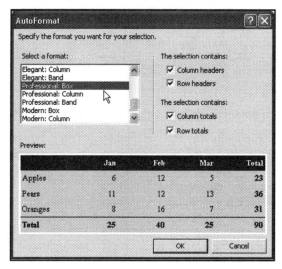

Fig. 10.6 The AutoFormat Dialogue Box.

Adding Spreadsheet Charts

Works allows you to represent information in graphical form which makes data more accessible to non-expert users who might not be familiar with the spreadsheet format. In any case, the well known saying 'a picture is worth a thousand words', applies equally well to charts and figures.

You use the charting facility of Works by first selecting a data range to be charted on your worksheet, such as A8:D13 on our file **Project5**, and then choosing the **Tools**, **Create** **New Chart** command, or pressing the **New Chart** toolbar icon. This opens the New Chart box, shown in Fig. 10.7.

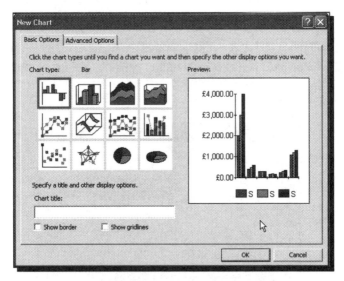

Fig. 10.7 The New Chart Dialogue Box.

As you click the icons in the **Chart type** section, an example of each, based on the selected spreadsheet data, is shown in the box. Although Works has eight main two-dimensional, and four three-dimensional, chart and graph types, there are many optional ways to view each type, and they can be grouped and overlapped, which allows you to add considerably to the list.

To enhance your charts you can add titles, legends, labels, and can select grids, fill types, scaling, fonts, etc. These charts (you can have several per spreadsheet) can be displayed on the screen and can be sent to an appropriate output device, such as a plotter or printer.

The main graph types available are listed next, with their **Charting** toolbar icons, where available. These chart types are normally used for the following relationships between data:

Bar

For comparing differences in data over a period of time. Displays the values of dependent variables as vertical columns. The stacked and 100% options, show relationships to the whole; with 2-D or 3-D options.

Area

For comparing value changes to the total over a period of time; 2-D or 3-D options available.

Line

For representing data values with points joined by lines and appearing at equal intervals along the x-axis. For such charts, the x-axis could be intervals in time, such as labels representing months; 2-D and 3-D options.

Stacked Line

For representing the total in each category. A line chart in which the lines are stacked.

Combination

For displaying related data measured in different units; used for comparing two different kinds of data or to show a correlation that might be difficult to recognise.

XY (Scatter)

For showing the relationship, or degree of relationship, between numeric values in different groups of data; used for finding patterns or trends in data.

Radar

For showing changes in data relative to a centre point and to other data; useful for relative comparisons.

Pie

For comparing parts with the whole. Displays data blocks as slices of a pie. Can contain only one series; 2-D or 3-D options available.

Charts can be displayed on the screen at the same time as the worksheet, but in a separate window. As charts are dynamic, any changes made to the data are automatically reflected on the defined charts.

Preparing for a Bar Chart

In order to illustrate some of the graphing capabilities of Works we will now plot an income from consultancies graph of the **Project5** file.

First we need to define what we want to chart. The specified range of data to be charted should be contiguous for each chart. But, in our example, the range of data is split into two areas; Jan-Mar (occupying cell positions B3:D3), and Apr-Jun (occupying cell positions F3:H3), with the corresponding income values in cells B5:D5 and F5:H5.

Thus, to create an appropriate contiguous data range, we must first replicate the labels and values of these two range areas in another area of the spreadsheet (say, beginning in cell B23 for the actual month labels and B24 for the values of the corresponding income), as shown on the next page.

To do this, use the **Edit, Copy** and **Paste** commands, or buttons, to copy the labels in the above two cell-ranges into the target area. However, before you replicate the cells containing numeric values, consider what might happen if these cells contain formulae, and you used the **Edit, Paste** command to replicate them. Using this command would cause the relative cell addresses to adjust to the new locations and each formula will then recalculate a new value for each cell which will give wrong results.

The Paste Special Command

The **Edit, Paste Special** command allows you to copy only cell references without adjusting to the new location. To do this, mark the cell range to be copied (in this case B5:D5) and choose the **Edit, Copy** command, move the highlighter to cell B24 and press **Edit, Paste Special**, select the **Insert the value in the cell** option from the displayed dialogue box and click **OK**. Now repeat the same procedure for the values under Apr-Jun, but copy them into E24 to form a contiguous data range.

Finally, add labels for 'Months' and 'Income' in cells A23 and A24, respectively, as shown in Fig. 10.8, and save the resulting spreadsheet as **Project6**.

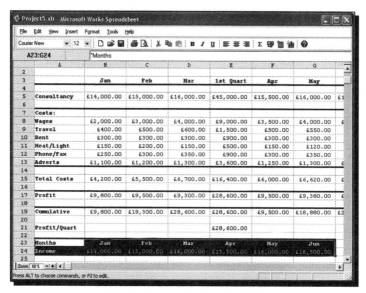

Fig. 10.8 Pasting Data by Value Only.

Note - The above way of copying cells is fine for our example where the data will not change. If you have data that changes, however, you would want your graphs to reflect these changes. This is easy to do; you set the graphing cells to 'mirror' the main sheet cells holding the variable data, by entering a formula consisting of a '+' sign followed by the cell address to be 'mirrored'. In our case, for example, cell B24 would contain the formula

    +B5

It would then always show the contents of that cell.

The Chart Editor

To obtain a chart of 'Income' versus 'Months', block cell range A23:G24 and choose the **Tools**, **Create New Chart** command, or the **New Chart** toolbar icon and type a **Chart title**, such as 'ADEPT MONTHLY INCOME'.

Select **OK** to accept the default Bar chart type and Works clears the screen and draws a bar chart of the information contained in the blocked range of cells. This places you in Charting mode with a new set of menu commands and a new toolbar, as shown in Fig. 10.9.

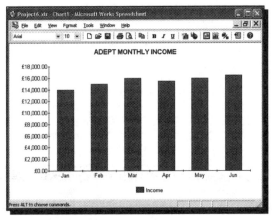

Fig. 10.9 The Adept Monthly Income Bar Chart.

The chart is displayed in its own window, so to return to the worksheet you click the **Go To 1st Series** toolbar button shown here, or you can press the <Ctrl+F6> keys, or use the **Window**, or **View** menu options. Choosing **View**, **Chart**, reveals that the chart just displayed on screen has been given the name **Chart1** in the list box.

To select a different type chart, you must return to Chart mode by selecting a Chart window. You can then choose the **Format**, **Chart Type** menu command to open the Chart Type box again, but with some extra options. You could select another type from the displayed list, but if you do your Bar chart will not be saved.

To select another type of chart, but still retain the first one, activate the **Tools**, **Create New Chart** command, which opens a new chart as **Chart2**. Choosing the Line option and selecting **OK** will produce a line chart similar to the one below.

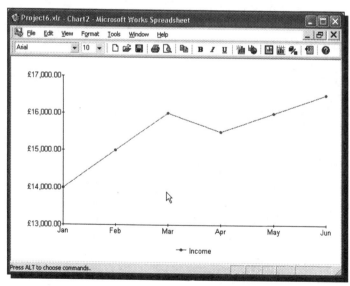

Fig. 10.10 Displaying Data in a Line Chart.

The shape of this line chart was improved by choosing the **Format**, **Vertical (Y) Axis** command and typing

```
13000
```

in the **Minimum value** box.

There are a lot of other options that you can specify when creating a chart. Some of these are self evident, like titles, legends, data labels, and the inclusion of axis labels and grid lines. These will be discussed only if needed in the examples that follow.

Saving Charts

Charts are saved with a spreadsheet when you save the spreadsheet to disc. Thus, saving the spreadsheet under the filename **Project7**, will ensure that your charts are also saved under the same name. Since each chart is linked to the spreadsheet from which it was derived, if information on the spreadsheet changes, the charts associated with it will also change automatically.

Naming Charts

You can give your charts more meaningful names than the default ones 'Chart1, Chart2, etc.,' that are given by Works. The **Tools**, **Rename Chart** command opens a dialogue box from which you can select any of your charts and give them new names.

Customising a Chart

In order to customise a chart, you need to know how to add extra titles and labels, how to change text fonts, the colour and pattern of the chart, and how to incorporate grid lines.

Drawing a Multiple Bar Chart

As an exercise, open **Project7**, if it is not already in memory, so we can build a new bar-type chart which deals with the monthly 'Costs' of Adept Consultants. As there are six different non-contiguous sets of costs, first copy them (including the cost description labels) using the **Edit, Paste Special** command, into a contiguous range below the 'Income' range (starting, say, at cell A27), as shown in Fig. 10.11.

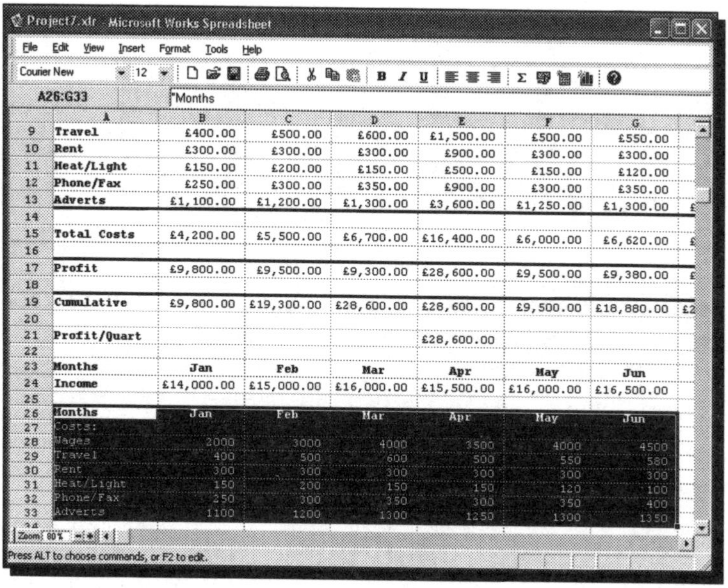

Fig. 10.11 Preparing for a Multiple Bar Chart.

Having done this, copy the 'Months' labels from row 23 to row 26 and save the resultant worksheet under the filename **Project8**. Next block the cell range A26:G33, as in Fig. 10.11 above, click the **New Chart** toolbar icon, type 'ADEPT CONSULTANTS' in the **Chart title** field and press **OK**.

Immediately this is done, the bar chart of the 6 different monthly costs is drawn automatically with each month in a different colour. The diagram in Fig. 10.12 on the next page shows the result, after using the **View**, **Display as Printed** command. As you can see, the colours have been replaced by shading patterns, as our default printer did not handle colours.

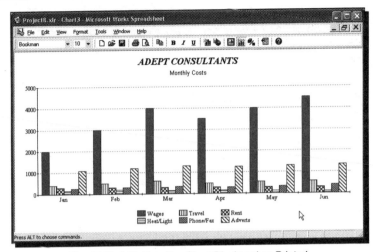

Fig. 10.12 A Multiple Bar Chart Displayed as Printed.

Chart Titles, Fonts and Sizes

To edit a chart title, choose the **Edit**, **Titles** command which causes this dialogue box to be displayed on your screen.

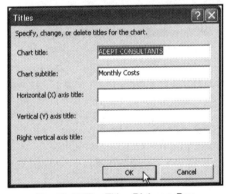

Fig. 10.13 The Titles Dialogue Box.

Type 'Monthly Costs' in the **Chart subtitle** field of the dialogue box and select **OK**, to complete the addition.

You can change the font and size of any contained text on a chart. For example, click the title, to select it, and then choose **Format**, **Font** to display the

Font dialogue box shown in Fig. 10.14. To change the font of **all** the other text and numbers in a chart, choose **Format**, **Font** without first selecting an item.

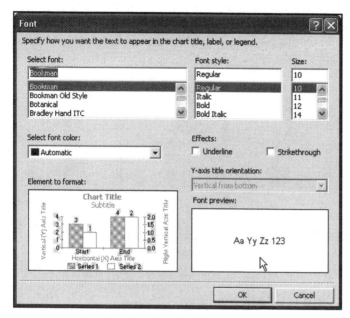

Fig. 10.14 The Chart Font Dialogue Box.

From this you can choose any of the fonts available to Windows, or set a new size by selecting from the list of sizes (given in points), or change the colour and set other attributes.

The fonts and sizes of the text in the chart of Fig. 10.15 were set as follows:

Chart title: Bookman, bold and italic, size 16

Other text & numbers: Bookman, Regular, size 10

Grid lines were added by selecting the **F<u>o</u>rmat**, **<u>V</u>ertical (Y) Axis** command and activating the **Show gridlines** option. We then saved the file as **Project9**.

Note that you can, to a certain extent, control the vertical scaling of the final chart, by dragging the bottom edge of the Works window up or down. This works for the screen display, but not when the chart is printed.

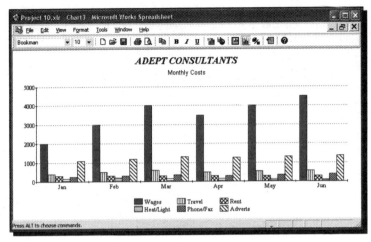

Fig. 10.15 A Formatted Multiple Bar Chart.

Printing a Chart

Before printing, or previewing a chart, you should check your page settings with the **File**, **Page Setup** command. This opens the dialogue box shown in Fig. 10.16 with the Source, Size & Orientation tab sheet displaying.

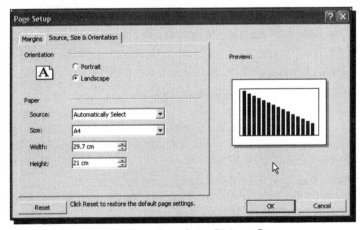

Fig. 10.16 The Page Setup Dialogue Box.

You use the options on this sheet to control how a chart will be orientated on the page. The Margins tab on the Page Setup dialogue is used to set the size of the margins and the depth of the headers and footers.

Before printing a chart it is wise to always preview it, using the toolbar icon. You may find that you have to adjust your text font settings to get all the chart text to display. When you are satisfied, press **Print** to record your chart on paper, or **Close**, to return to the chart window.

Drawing a Pie Chart

As a second example in chart drawing, use the 'Average' values of the costs from the worksheet of **Project9** to plot a pie chart. Select the range J8:J13 and again, click the **New Chart** toolbar icon, choose Pie as the chart type, then click the Variations tab of the Chart Type dialogue box. Next, select the last of the six pie chart type options (the one at the bottom right-hand corner) and press **OK**. Your range should now be displayed in a colourful pie chart.

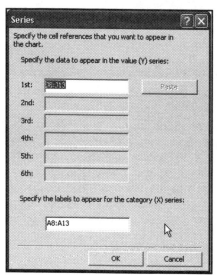

However, the labels on each segment of the pie chart are not very self explanatory. To remedy this, use the **Edit**, **Series** command, type A8:A13 in the **Specify the labels to appear for the category (X) series** text box, as shown in Fig. 10.17, and click **OK** to leave the box and return to your chart.

Fig. 10.17 The Series Box.

Next, use the **Edit, Titles** command to open the Titles dialogue box in which you can add an appropriate **Chart title** and **Chart subtitle**. Finally, allocate a font and size to it as described previously. Your chart should now look something like that shown in Fig. 10.18.

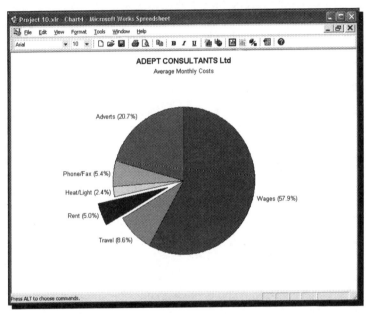

Fig. 10.18 A Pie Chart of Costs Displaying an Exploded Segment.

To explode one of the segments of the pie chart, choose the **Format, Shading and Color** command and select the number of the slice you would like to appear detached, from the displayed dialogue box. Slices, in this case, are numbered from 1 to 6 and are allocated to the pie chart in a clockwise direction. Thus, to explode the 'Rent' slice, select **3** in the **Slices** box, then activate the **Explode slice** option and press the **Format** and **Close** buttons. In this way, you can emphasise one or more portions of the chart.

To cancel an exploded selection, use the **Format**, **Shading and Colors** command (when the chart is in view), and press the **Format All** and **Close** buttons. Selecting other slices for exploding, without first cancelling previous selections, adds to the selection.

Finally, save the file as **Project 10**. Yes, with Windows 95/98/Me, Windows NT/2000, and Windows XP, you can give all your files long names (up to 255 characters), which can include spaces and capitals.

Mixing Chart Types

To illustrate a combination of a bar and line chart, we will consider the variable monthly costs of Adept Consultants with the introduction of average monthly costs in column 33 of the worksheet. We will leave it to you to work out and place the cell formulae for this operation. If you have worked your way to here, this should not be too much of a problem.

However, Works can only deal with a maximum of six categories and the addition of the average monthly costs to the list makes the costs categories for each month to seven. We, therefore, will have to reduce the costs categories to six by deleting one of them, say the 'Rent'.

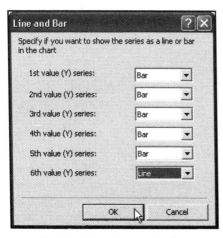

Fig. 10.19 The Line and Bar Box.

To create a mixed chart, first select the A26:G32 cell range, use the **New Chart** icon, choose the Combination chart and press **OK**. The chart may be a little mixed up, so use the **Format**, **Line and Bar** command, select **Bar** for the first five series and **Line** for the sixth, as shown in Fig. 10.19, then press **OK**.

The final Combination chart should look like the one in Fig. 10.20 below.

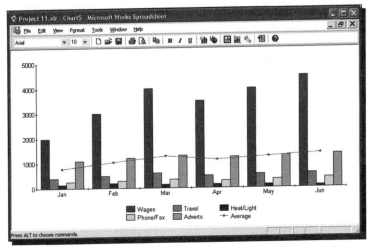

Fig. 10.20 A Combination Chart of Monthly Costs and their Average Value.

As you can see, Works provides a very powerful charting facility which deserves exploring. We hope you spend a few hours looking seriously at this facility. Good luck.

11

The Works Database

A Works database is a file which contains related information, such as 'Customers' Names', 'Consultancy Details', 'Invoice No.', etc. A phone book is a simple database, stored on paper. In Works, each record is entered as a worksheet row, with the fields of each record occupying corresponding columns.

The next section deals with the basic concepts of using a simple database, along with the database 'jargon' that is used in this book. If you are not familiar with database terminology then you should read this section first.

A database is a collection of data that exists, and is organised around a specific theme, or requirement. A database is used for storing information, so that it is quickly accessible. In the case of Works, data is stored in **data-files** which are specially structured files kept on disc like other disc-files. To make accessing the data easier, each row or **record** of data within a database is structured in the same fashion, i.e., each record will have the same number of columns, or **fields**.

We define a database and its various elements as follows:

Database	A collection of data organised for a specific theme.
Data-file	Disc-file in which data is stored.
Record	A row of information relating to a single entry and comprising one or more fields.
Field	A single column of information of the same type, such as people's names.
Form	A screen in which one record of data can be entered, displayed, or edited.
List	The whole database displayed in a spreadsheet-like format. Multiple records can be entered and edited.
Filter	A set of instructions to search the database for records with specific properties.

A good example of a database is a telephone directory. To cover the whole country many directories are needed, just as a database can comprise a number of data-files. The following shows how data is presented in such a directory.

```
Prowse H.B., 91 Cabot Close ....................... Truro 76455
Pruce T.A., 15 Woodburn Road ................ Plymouth 223248
Pryce C.W., 42 North Gate Road  .............. St Austell 851662
Pryor A., 38 Western Approach  ................ Plymouth 238742
Pryor B.E., 79 Trevithick Road ..................... Truro 742310
Queen S.R., 4 Ruskin Crescent .............. Camborne 712212
Regan R.B., 1 Woodland Avenue  ................ Bodmin 78236
```

Information is structured in fields which are identified below, for a single record, as follows:

Name	Address	Town	Tel No.
Pryor B.E.	79 Trevithick Road	Truro	742310

Creating a Database

A database file in Works, is created either using a Template, or manually. Several useful templates to help you rapidly design specific databases are provided with the package and are briefly described in a later Chapter.

Here, we are going to step you through the process of manually designing and building a simple database, suitable for keeping track of the invoices issued by a small engineering consulting company.

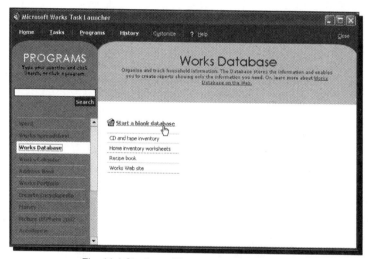

Fig. 11.1 Starting a Blank Works Database.

Clicking the **Programs** tab in the Task Launcher window, selecting **Works Database**, and then clicking **Start a blank Database** as shown above, displays the screen shown on the next page in Fig. 11.2.

The program can also be opened by selecting **Microsoft Works Database** in the Windows **Start** menu system and selecting **Blank Database**, as shown here.

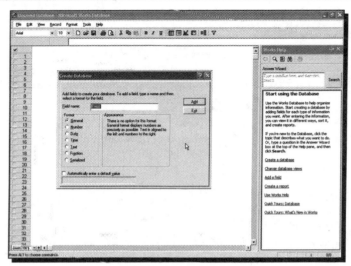

Fig. 11.2 The Works Blank Database.

As shown, the Database window has its own menu and toolbar, and the Create Database dialogue box is opened automatically waiting for you to enter your database fields.

Entering Fields

Type 'Customer Name' as Field 1 in the highlighted **Field name** text box and click the **Add** button to accept **General** as the format for the field data. The format determines how your data will be stored and displayed in your database. Clicking each format type in the list will show its description.

Enter the remaining fields as shown in the table below.

Field Name	Width	Format	
Details	20	**General**	
Inv.No	7	**Number**	(01234 - but 4 digits)
Issued	12	**Date**	(20/01/02)
Paid	10	**Number**	(True/False)
O/D	5	**Number**	(01234 - but 1 digit)
Total	10	**Number**	(£1,234.56 - 2 dec's)

The format examples shown above are those to select from the list of options given to you.

There are no more fields to enter so press **Done**. You should now have a basic, but empty, database in List View form (see below) which looks like the one shown in Fig. 11.3.

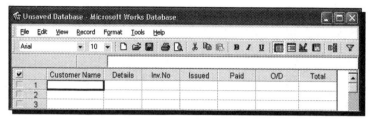

Fig. 11.3 An Empty Database in List View.

This List screen now has a row of field titles along the top, above an empty 'spreadsheet' working area. The default

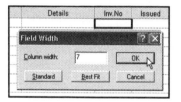

column width for a List screen is 10, and we want some of our fields to be different from that, so click the cursor in the title of the 'Inv.No' field, to select the column and choose the **Format, Field Width** command. Type **7** as the **Column width**, as shown here, and press **OK**.

Database Screens

As we have seen, the opening screen of a Works database is a 'List View' window, which gives a spreadsheet type view of the database, with the numbers down the left-hand side referring to individual records, and the column headings referring to the database fields. The status line shows which record the cursor is in, how many records are currently displayed, and how many are in the database.

The other way of looking at, and accessing, a Works database is through a 'Form' window, as shown in Fig. 11.4 when inserting a new record in the database, which is a 'front end' to easily enter, and access, data. You use the **F9** key, or the **Form View** toolbar icon shown here, or the **View, Form** menu command, to change to the Form window.

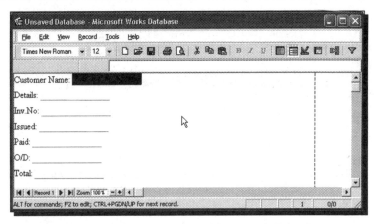

Fig. 11.4 Inserting a New Record in a Database in Form View.

Pressing <Ctrl+F9>, or the **Form Design** toolbar icon, or choosing **View, Form Design** will open a window in which you can customise the 'basic' form produced by Works, as shown in our example in Fig. 11.5.

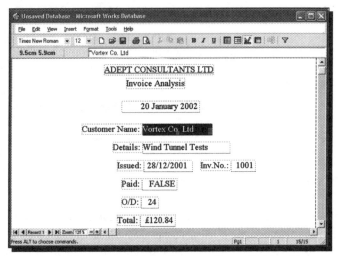

Fig. 11.5 Viewing an Existing Database Record in Form View.

 Pressing <Shift+F9>, or the **List View** toolbar icon, or choosing **View, List,** will return you to the List screen.

Form Editing

We suggest you click the **Form Design** toolbar icon, shown here, and use the Form Design window to alter the entry form for your database to something a little nearer ours in Fig. 11.5 shown on the previous page.

As it is a multi-page window, the co-ordinate information on the line below the toolbar could be needed to keep track of the current cursor position. This gives X and Y co-ordinates in the current system dimension units, (measured from the top left-hand corner of each printed page). The page number of the current cursor position is shown on the Status Bar, as shown in Fig. 11.6. The overall maximum form dimensions can be 3 pages long by 3 screens wide. A form can contain up to 256 database fields, as well as titles, labels and other text. Each field can hold up to 256 characters, and a database can contain up to 32,000 records, which should be enough for most people!

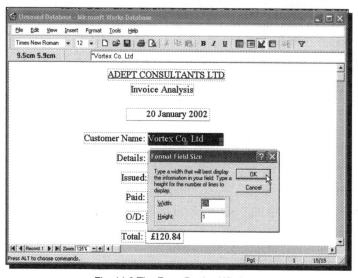

Fig. 11.6 The Form Design Window.

Before entering any records, the entry form would benefit from some cosmetic attention. The List screen field widths are in fact independent of those of the Form screen. In our example, we want them to be the same, so place the cursor in the 'Details' field, click to select it and choose the **Format, Field Size** command. This opens the box shown above, in which you can set the **Width** or **Height** of form fields. Type **20** as the width and press **OK**. Then alter the other form widths to those given in our table on page 230.

When a field is selected in the Design window the mouse pointer changes and lets you drag an outline of the field around the screen, as shown here. You could move the fields so that all the colons are in one vertical line, or until you have a layout you prefer. With the Drag and Drop function you simply select a field with your mouse pointer and drag it to a new position.

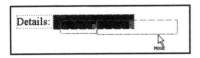

To place a label on your form, click the cursor where you want it to start and type the label text. In our example, type the database title 'ADEPT CONSULTANTS LTD' and drag it until you are happy with its position. Labels can be placed in any unused space on the form screen. With the title still highlighted it is a good time to carry out any enhancements. Click on the **Underline** toolbar icon and then enter the other labels shown in our example (on page 232).

Hiding a Field Name

The 'date' cell, shown in our example as '20 January 2002', is not a label. It actually has a dotted line below it and is, in fact, a database field (called Date:), containing a formula to generate the current date, but with its field name switched off.

To do this, place the cursor in position, and create a 'Date' field with the **Insert, Field** command. For the moment we will leave this cell empty. To hide it, highlight its field name, and choose the **Format, Show Field Name** command. The field name 'Date:' should now be turned off. If you wanted, you could now place a different label on top of it. This technique is useful if you want to keep actual field names short, but need longer descriptive ones on the database form, as could have been used with the 'O/D:' field (Overdue), shown in our example.

Entering Data in a Form

Now change to the Form view and enter the first record into the database. If your form is the same as ours, your cursor should be in the date cell. Press <Tab> to move to the 'Customer Name:' field, and type the following:

Vortex Co. Ltd	press <Tab> and type,
Wind Tunnel Tests	press <Tab> and type,
28/12/2001	press <Tab> and type,
1001	press <Tab> and type,
0	press <Tab> twice, and type,
120.84	press <Tab>

Nothing should have been entered in the 'O/D' field. The last <Tab> should have completed the entry of record 1, and brought up an empty form for the next record. Press <Ctrl+PgUp>, to move back one record, to the date cell of record 1.

When moving about a form, <Tab> and <Shift+Tab>, move the cursor between fields, whereas <Ctrl+PgUp> and <Ctrl+PgDn>, move between adjacent records.

The arrow buttons at the bottom of a form window can also be used to step through the records of a database, as shown in Fig. 11.7.

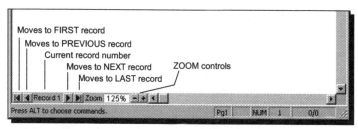

Fig. 11.7 Function of Arrow Buttons at Bottom of a Form Window.

Using Formulae in a Field

Database formulae have two main applications; to automatically force the same entry in each similar field of every record in the database, or to calculate the contents of one field based on those of another. Each database field can only contain one formula. Once it is entered in the field of one record, it is automatically entered into all the other records. As in the spreadsheet, a formula is preceded by an equal sign (=).

In our database example we will enter formulae in two fields, the date formula next, and one that calculates the contents of a field, a little later on. Change to List view and with the cursor in the date cell, type:

```
=NOW()
```

This formula is shown on the screen, both in the cell and in the formula bar at the top of the screen.

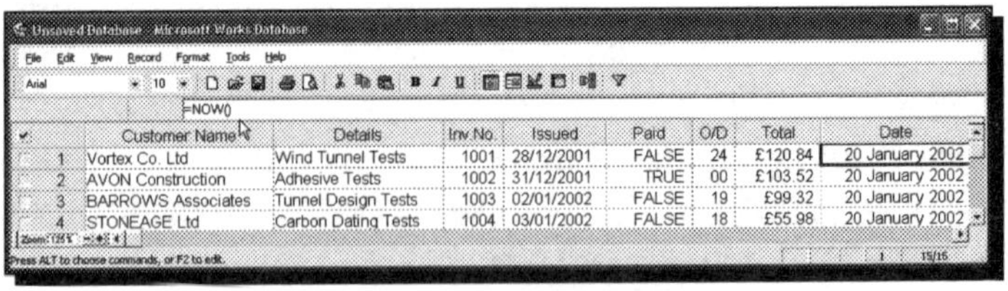

Fig. 11.8 Entering a Formula in a Date Field of a Database.

When you press <Enter>, the cell may fill with the hash character (#). Do not panic, it only means the date is too long for the cell width. Simply re-size it with the pointer.

Protecting Fields

You can 'lock' fields in your database to prevent their contents being accidentally changed, or to force the <Tab> key to ignore the cell when you are moving around the form, or entering data. To demonstrate this, highlight the Date field in List View and use the **Format**, **Protection** command, click the **Protect field** box and press the **OK** button. The date field should now be fully protected. In fact, it is now inaccessible until the field's protection is toggled off again.

Now complete the data entry by typing in the remaining records shown in the screen dump below. You can do this in either Form or List view, but you may find it easier in Form view. In the 'Paid' field, enter 1 (TRUE) if the invoice has been paid, or 0 (FALSE) if not. When you have saved the database as **Invoice1**, a List view should then be similar to our printout. In future to access a saved database use the **Start** menu system and select **Open an existing Database** (see page 229).

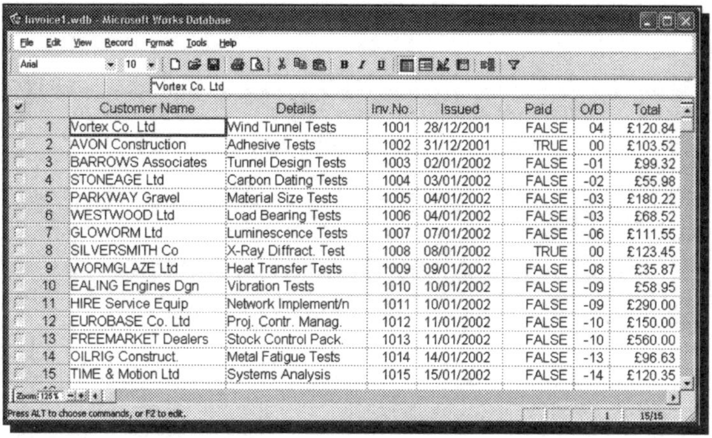

		Customer Name	Details	Inv.No	Issued	Paid	O/D	Total
	1	Vortex Co. Ltd	Wind Tunnel Tests	1001	28/12/2001	FALSE	04	£120.84
	2	AVON Construction	Adhesive Tests	1002	31/12/2001	TRUE	00	£103.52
	3	BARROWS Associates	Tunnel Design Tests	1003	02/01/2002	FALSE	-01	£99.32
	4	STONEAGE Ltd	Carbon Dating Tests	1004	03/01/2002	FALSE	-02	£55.98
	5	PARKWAY Gravel	Material Size Tests	1005	04/01/2002	FALSE	-03	£180.22
	6	WESTWOOD Ltd	Load Bearing Tests	1006	04/01/2002	FALSE	-03	£111.55
	7	GLOWORM Ltd	Luminescence Tests	1007	07/01/2002	FALSE	-06	£68.52
	8	SILVERSMITH Co	X-Ray Diffract. Test	1008	08/01/2002	TRUE	00	£123.45
	9	WORMGLAZE Ltd	Heat Transfer Tests	1009	09/01/2002	FALSE	-08	£35.87
	10	EALING Engines Dgn	Vibration Tests	1010	10/01/2002	FALSE	-09	£58.95
	11	HIRE Service Equip	Network Implement/n	1011	10/01/2002	FALSE	-09	£290.00
	12	EUROBASE Co. Ltd	Proj. Contr. Manag.	1012	11/01/2002	FALSE	-10	£150.00
	13	FREEMARKET Dealers	Stock Control Pack.	1013	11/01/2002	FALSE	-10	£560.00
	14	OILRIG Construct.	Metal Fatigue Tests	1014	14/01/2002	FALSE	-13	£96.63
	15	TIME & Motion Ltd	Systems Analysis	1015	15/01/2002	FALSE	-14	£120.35

Fig. 11.9 Records to be Entered in Invoice1 Database.

Sorting a Database

The records in our database are in the order in which they were entered, with the invoice numbers, in the 'Inv.No' field, shown in ascending order. However, once records have been entered, you might find it easier to browse through the database if it were sorted in a different way, say, in alphabetical order of 'Customer Name'. This might also make it easier to use the database for other operations, such as a mail merge. The Works database has an easy to use sort function, which can be accessed from either the Form or List screen.

With the cursor in any location, choose the **Record**, **Sort Records** command. Click the arrow in the **Sort by** drop-down list, select 'Customer Name', make sure **Ascending** is selected, and press **OK** to sort the database.

This sorts the field in an ascending order, from A - Z, and from 0 - 9. A descending sort order is the reverse. If you decide to have a secondary sort field (say you want invoices for the same company to appear in ascending order of invoice number), it is a simple matter to define a secondary sort range in the **Then by** box, before sorting. The three sort ranges available should be enough for most purposes.

Issuing these commands should produce the display shown in Fig. 11.10.

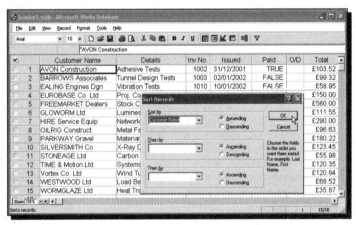

Fig. 11.10 Sorting Records in Ascending Order of Customer Names.

Now resort the database, in ascending order on the 'Inv.No' field, to return it to the original format.

Date Arithmetic

There are several date functions which can be used in Works to carry out date calculations. For example, typing the function =DATE(2002,01,20) - that is 20/01/2002 backwards - works out the number of days between 31 December 1899 and that date. These functions are included to make Works more compatible with older versions, but Works 2002 has an easier, and quicker, way of dealing with date arithmetic. Just typing a date into a cell, in one of the accepted date formats, allows Works to use the date number in any calculations.

When a date is typed in a field, or a spreadsheet cell, what actually shows in that cell depends on the cell format. If '20/1/02', (a date in short date format), is typed into a cell, it will be shown as 20/01/2002 in date or general format, or as "20/1/02, in any of the other formats.

The function

```
=NOW()-1/01/02
```

gives the difference in days (if the appropriate cell is formatted for integer numbers) between now and the mentioned date.

We will use this function to work out the number of overdue days for the unpaid invoices in our example, by typing the following formula into an O/D field cell in List View:

```
=NOW()-Issued
```

However, before we go any further, we should take into consideration the fact that, normally, such information would not be necessary if an invoice has already been paid. Therefore, we need to edit the formula to make the result conditional on non-payment of the issued invoice.

The IF Function

The =IF function allows comparison between two values with the use of special 'logical' operators. The logical operators we can use are listed below.

Logical operators

=	Equal to
<	Less than
>	Greater than
<=	Less than or Equal to
>=	Greater than or Equal to
<>	Not Equal to

The general format of the IF function is as follows:

=IF(Comparison, Outcome-if-true, Outcome-if-false)

which contains three arguments separated by commas. The first argument is the logical comparison, the second is what should happen if the outcome of the logical comparison is 'true', while the third is what should happen if the outcome of the logical comparison is 'false'.

Thus, we can incorporate an =IF function in the formula we entered in the O/D cell, to calculate the days overdue, only if the invoice has not been paid, otherwise '0' should be written into that cell. The test will be on the contents of the corresponding 'Paid' field of a record, and will look for anything else but '0', or FALSE.

To edit the formula in the O/D cell, highlight any cell in that field and press the Edit key <F2>. Then press the <Home> cursor key, followed by →, to place the cursor after the '=' of the existing formula in the formula line at the top of the screen and change the formula to:

```
=IF(Paid=0,NOW()-Issued,0)
```

The edited formula should now correspond to that shown in the screen printout in Fig. 11.11.

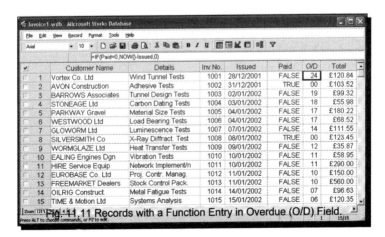

Fig. 11.11 Records with a Function Entry in Overdue (O/D) Field.

Note that once a formula is entered into any one field cell it is automatically copied to all the other cells in that field of the database. Save the file under the name **Invoice2**, but make sure you use the **Save As** command. Your results will almost certainly differ from those above. The reason for this is, of course, that the NOW() function returns different numerical values when used on different dates. To get the same results as those shown in Fig. 11.11, you will have to reset your computer's clock to the date used in our example, as follows:

> Save your work and Exit Works. Open the Control Panel, double-click the **Date/Time** icon, reset the **Date** to '20/01/02' and press **OK**. Close the Control Panel and the new date will be operational when you re-enter Works.

WARNING - Make sure you have saved your work before doing this, and when you have finished this section remember to reset the date in the Control Panel.

Searching a Database

 A database can be searched for specific records, that meet several complex criteria, with the **Tools, Filters** command, once a filter has been set as described below. Or, more simply, by clicking the toolbar **Filters** icon, shown here. For a simple search, on one field only, the **Edit, Find** command is, however, both quicker and easier.

We will use the previously saved database **Invoice2** to illustrate both these methods.

Let us assume we needed to find a record, from our database, containing the text 'x-ray'. In the List View window, choose **Edit, Find**, type **x-ray** in the **Find what** box, and select the option, **All records**. The record for 'SILVERSMITH Co' is brought to the screen, and the status line (1/15) indicates that this is the only record that meets the search criterion. Only the one record is shown, and all the others are hidden. The command, **Record, Show, 1 All Records** will display the complete database again.

Database Filtering

Sometimes it is necessary to find records in a database that satisfy a variety of conditions. For example, in a warehouse stock database, you may need to find all the items that were purchased between May and July of last year, that were ordered by a specific person, cost between £5.00 and £100.00, and that remained in stock for more than 60 days. In Works this kind of search is called a filter.

When a filter operation is carried out in Works, all the records that match the filter criteria are extracted. In List View these are all displayed, whereas in Form view you see one matching record at a time. Every time a filter is applied the program searches the complete database for matches. A database can have up to 8 filters saved with it.

If necessary, retrieve the file **Invoice2**, and select the List View. Clicking the **Filters** icon presents the Filter box, as shown in Fig. 11.12, after you have entered a Filter Name.

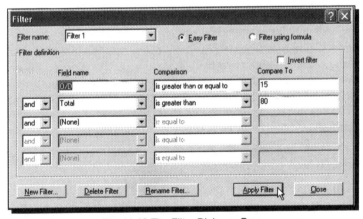

Fig. 11.12 The Filter Dialogue Box.

The above box is completed assuming that we would like to search the database for all the details of our customers whose invoices are overdue by 15 or more days, and who owe more than £80.

This intuitive approach to filters is very much easier than having to develop long logical expressions yourself. In fact what is actually created, in the above case, is the expression

```
='O/D'>=VALUE("15")#AND#Total>VALUE("80")
```

which is placed in the 'O/D' field cell of the filter.

When all the required criteria have been entered, select the **Apply Filter** button to action the filter. Unless you have renamed it, this first filter in your database will be **Filter 1**.

You are then returned to List view, where only the records which meet the search requirements will be listed. In our case this should be three only. The screen should now look similar to that shown here.

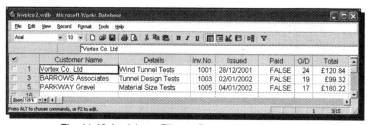

Fig. 11.13 Applying a Filter to Records in a Database.

To view all the records again, choose **Record**, **Show**, **1 All Records**. The filter criteria will remain intact until next edited.

Save the file with the name **Invoice3**, but again make sure you use the **Save As** command.

Marking Records

You can also manually mark records that do not easily filter, by clicking in the box to the left of their row number, as can be seen above.

Using the **Record**, **Show**, **2 Marked Records** will separate them for processing, or inclusion in a report.

The Database Toolbar

Most of the database toolbar icons are common to the other Toolbars already described, but there are six icons on this bar specific to the database tool, whose meanings are as follows:

Option	*Result*
▤	Change to List view
▤	Change to Form view
▨	Change to Form Design view
▣	Change to Report view
▤	Insert new record
▽	Carry out a filter

Once you get used to all of these buttons, you will find that designing and manipulating databases becomes very much easier!

12

Database Applications

Once a database has been created, the data sorted in the required order, and specific records have been searched for, the retrieved data can be browsed on the screen, either one record at a time, or in the list format, one full screen at a time. Some form of hard copy will almost certainly be required at some stage, by printing part, or all, of the database to paper.

Printing from a Database

There are three main ways of printing information from a database. In the 'Form' view, selected records are printed out in the same format as the screen form. Printing from a 'List' view will produce rows and columns just as they appear on the screen; little manipulation of the printed result is possible. To obtain a customised print-out, possibly containing selected fields only, but with report and page titles, totals and sub-totals, a 'Report' must first be defined. Data can then be printed from the Report screen. To see what will actually print use the **Print Preview** toolbar icon.

What is printed from the List and Form windows is controlled by the settings in the **File**, **Page Setup**, **Other Options** dialogue box shown in Fig. 12.1. Printing from List view, will produce a spreadsheet-like layout, which will only be of use if your database has only a few fields per record.

Printing from the Form view could probably be best used with a diary type appointment database, or with a simple database designed to hold, say, personnel lists or parts inventories. Space could maybe be built into each form to hold a scanned photograph, for example.

To demonstrate the process, load the database **Invoice3**, which was created in the last chapter. From the Form view choose **File**, **Page Setup** command, and click the **Other Options** tab to display the dialogue box shown in Fig. 12.1.

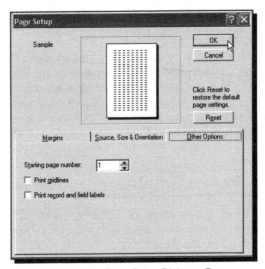

Fig. 12.1 The Page Setup Dialogue Box.

When you accept these settings a print preview should show neatly spaced fields on one or two pages. For our example, if you want to see all the fields on one page, select the **Source, Size & Orientation** tab and select **Landscape**.

Creating a Report

A report can present records sorted and grouped, with summaries, totals, and with explanatory text. Once a report format has been set up, producing a report is a quick, almost automatic process. The current records 'displayed' in a database are those used to make the body of a report. The initial process is to create a report definition, which indicates what information will be in a report, and where it will be placed. Works has a 'semiautomatic front end' to make the production of simple report formats much easier.

Using the database we built up in the last chapter, we will step through the process of setting up a report definition. If necessary, retrieve the file saved as **Invoice3**, which was a database to store details of the invoices sent out by a small company. It would be very useful, for both the accountant and the company management of Adept, if a report like that of Fig. 12.2 could be 'instantly' produced, and printed out.

ADEPT CONSULTANTS LTD
Invoice Alalysis Report

Summary of Overdue Invoices

Customer Name	Invoice Number	Days Overdue	Total Amount
TIME & Motion Ltd	1015	6	£120.35
0 - 1 Weeks Overdue	1	6	£120.35
OILRIG Construct.	1014	7	£96.63
EUROBASE Co. Ltd	1012	10	£150.00
FREEMARKET Dealers	1013	10	£560.00
EALING Engines Dgn	1010	11	£58.95
HIRE Service Equip	1011	11	£290.00
WORMGLAZE Ltd	1009	12	£35.87
1 - 2 Weeks Overdue	6	11	£1,191.45
GLOWORM Ltd	1007	14	£111.55
PARKWAY Gravel	1005	17	£180.22
WESTWOOD Ltd	1006	17	£88.52
STONEAGE Ltd	1004	18	£55.98
BARROWS Associates	1003	19	£99.32
2 - 3 Weeks Overdue	5	17	£515.59
Vortex Co. Ltd	1001	24	£120.84
3 - 4 Weeks Overdue	1	24	£120.84
Overall Totals and Averages	13	14	£1,948.23

Fig. 12.2 Report on Overdue Invoices of Adept Consultants.

This summarises all the unpaid invoices and ranks them in groups depending on the number of weeks they have been overdue. Once we have defined the format of this report, it will only take a few keystrokes, at any time in the future, to produce a similar but updated report.

To start the process, change to the Form Design screen of **Invoice3**, as we must first add an extra field to the form. This will show the number of weeks an invoice is overdue. We will need it, to provide the basis for sorting the database records, and breaking them up into groups.

Create a new field called 'Weeks' with the **Insert**, **Field** command, placed wherever you like on the form, but give it the integer **Number** format (01234) with **1** digit. Next, change to Form View, and type the formula

```
=Int(O/D/7)
```

in the highlighted empty cell and press <Enter>. Note that Works places single inverted commas around the field name O/D, to show it as a label; this is because it contains the slash character '/'. The formula produces the integer part of the number of days overdue, divided by seven; approximately the whole number of weeks.

We are now ready to create the report definition. Choose the **Tools**, **ReportCreator** command, or click the toolbar **Report View** button. Ignore the initial Report Name box, but type ADEPT CONSULTANTS LTD into the **Report title** box of the main ReportCreator dialogue box, which is shown in Fig. 12.3.

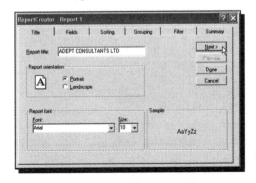

Fig. 12.3 The Report Creator's Title Tab Sheet.

Click the **Next** button to move to the **Fields** tabbed section, select the field 'Customer Name' in the **Fields available** list box and press **Add>**, or <Alt+A>, to add the field to the **Field order** list. In the same way add the fields 'Inv.No', 'O/D' and 'Total' as shown in Fig. 12.4.

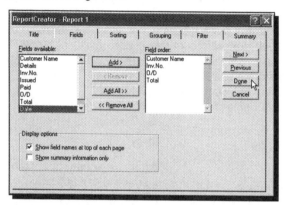

Fig. 12.4 The Report Creator's Fields Tab Sheet.

The other tabbed sheets provide a quick way of entering instructions and formulae into the report definition, to carry out calculations and produce totals or averages, for example. In the future you may find this an easier way to generate rapid reports, but at this stage we will not use this method, so press **Done** to move to the report definition screen shown in Fig.12.5.

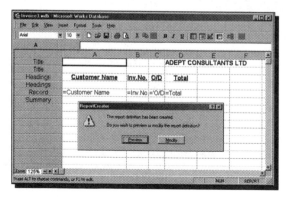

Fig. 12.5 The Report Definition Screen.

The message in the pop-up box suggests you use the Print Preview to see what your report will look like when printed, at this stage there is not much point, so select **Modify** which places you in Modify Report mode.

The working area of the screen contains columns and rows which intersect, as in the spreadsheet, to form cells. The row types, shown on the left part of the screen, determine the order the rows will be printed in the report, and what action will be taken in that row. The row type and what it prints are listed below, although at this stage the 'Intr' and 'Summ' line types do not appear on our screen in Fig. 12.5, as there are no breakpoints defined for this report (more on this shortly).

Row type	*Prints*
Title	At the beginning of a report.
Headings	At the top of each page.
Intr *1st breakfield*	At the beginning of each group created by the 1st breakfield.
Intr *2nd breakfield*	At the beginning of each group created by the 2nd breakfield.
Intr *3rd breakfield*	At the beginning of each group created by the 3rd breakfield.
Record	Each displayed record.
Summ *3rd breakfield*	At the end of each group created by the 3rd breakfield.
Summ *2nd breakfield*	At the end of each group created by the 2nd breakfield.
Summ *1st breakfield*	At the end of each group created by the 1st breakfield.
Summary	At the end of a report.

If you printed the report generated from our initial procedure which resulted in the Report definition in Fig. 12.5, we don't think you would be overly impressed with the results. As long as you can persevere, though, and follow us to the end of the chapter, we are sure you will be impressed with the power of the report generating facility.

Naming a Report

If you open the **View** sub-menu you will see that the **Report** option button is depressed, which when selected opens a box showing the option **Report 1**. Works gives any reports generated a series of names, numbered 1, 2, 3, etc. To change this report name, choose **Tools**, **Rename Report**, type 'Overdue' in the text box and click **Rename** followed by **OK**. The **View**, **Report** box should now contain the option Overdue. When a database is saved, any report definitions generated are saved with it, including sorting instructions. Obtaining a similar report in the future is simply a matter of selecting it from the **View**, **Report** box.

Defining a Report

The definition to automatically produce the report in Fig. 12.2 is shown in the screen dump of Fig. 12.6. This was designed to print on an A4 sheet of paper.

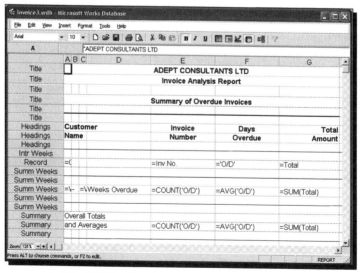

Fig. 12.6 The Overdue Invoices Report Definition.

As an example we will step through the procedure of producing this report. Most of the reporting features should become apparent during the operation. You may also find it useful to spend a few minutes with the Works Help sections.

This report definition will be easier to prepare from an empty work area, so choose **Edit**, **Select All** and then **Edit, Clear** to clear the working area cells.

The first operation is to reset the column widths. Set columns A, B and C to a width of 2, by selecting these columns, choosing **Format, Column Width** and typing 2, followed by <Enter>. In the same way, alter the other columns as follows: D, E and F to 17 and G to 16.

Adding a Report Title

The 'Title' rows hold any text that is to appear at the top of the first printed page of the report. In our example we will need six rows of this type, so we must insert four more. Press <Ctrl+Home> to move the cursor to the Home cell, highlight the top four rows by selecting their headers and choose **Insert**, **Insert Row**. The next box asks what type of rows are to be inserted; we want 'Title', which is highlighted, so press <Enter> to complete the operation.

To position the main report title in the centre of the printed page, move the cursor to column A of the top row, type

```
ADEPT CONSULTANTS LTD
```

and press <Enter>. We will leave it to you to add the other two title lines in column A of rows 2 and 4. Now highlight the first four rows of columns A to G and use the **Format**, **Alignment**, **Center across selection** command, then embolden the selected titles.

To place the horizontal line across the page, select the cells A5 to G5 and place a **Bottom** line with the **Format**, **Border** command. There are several line options to choose from.

Adding Page Titles

Page titles are placed in 'Headings' type rows, and appear below the report title on the first page of a report, and at the top of all subsequent pages. We will need three of this type of row, so insert one more, as described earlier. The top two of these rows will hold the four report column titles, as shown on page 227. To enter these, place:

Customer and **Name**	-	left aligned	-	in column A
Invoice and **Number**	-	centre aligned	-	in column E
Days and **Overdue**	-	centre aligned	-	in column F
Total and **Amount**	-	right aligned	-	in column G

The way to select the above alignments is from the **F**o**rmat**, **A**lignment box. Produce any lines with the **F**o**rmat**, **B**order command, as described previously.

Using Formulae in a Cell

The body of the report will be produced by the contents of the 'Record' row. If we type a field name, preceded by an equal sign, in a 'Record' cell, Works places the contents of that field for each record into the report.

There are also a series of statistical operators that can be included in cell formulae. These are mainly used in 'Summ' type rows, to produce totals, averages, etc. When placed in a 'Summ fieldname' row they give field statistics for the previous group printed. In a 'Summary' row the statistics refer to that field for the whole report.

Statistic	*Calculates*
SUM	Total of the group.
AVG	Average of the group.
COUNT	Number of items in the group.
MAX	Largest number in the group.
MIN	Smallest number in the group.
STD	Standard deviation of the group.
VAR	Variance of the group.

There are several ways to enter formulae in a cell. If you can remember all your database fields, you could simply type the formulae in.

If not, the **Insert**, **Field Name** command places the selected field name in a cell, **Insert**, **Field Entry** places an '=' followed by the name; both dialogue boxes list all the fields of the database. The **Insert**, **Field Summary** box lists not only the database fields, but all the above functions, which you can select to place formulae in a 'Summ', or 'Summary', type row.

In our example, to complete the 'Record' row, enter the following formulae into the cells shown below and format the cells, in the **Format**, **Number** box as follows:

Cell	Contents	Alignment	Format
A	=Customer Name	Left justified	
E	=Inv.No.	Centre justified	Fixed (0)
F	=O/D	Centre justified	Fixed (0)
G	=Total	Right justified	Currency (2)

Sorting a Report

A report is sorted to arrange the database entries in a certain order, such as alphabetical (order) or by date. A sort order specified in a report stays with that report, until it is physically changed. The main sort field, in our case, is on the Weeks field. We must specify the sort parameters now, as 'Summ' type rows cannot be used without a breakpoint having been entered.

The **Tools**, **Report Sorting** command opens the Report Settings dialogue box. The selections shown in Fig. 12.7 are those required for our example. To obtain them, select 'Months' in the **Sort by** box and an **Ascending** sort. In our case, for neatness, we have also specified a **Then by** ascending sort on the 'O/D' field. If our database contained many hundreds of records, with several for each customer, we could also sort, and break, on the 'Customer Name' field. A summary for each customer would then be produced.

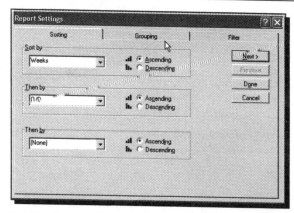

Fig. 12.7 The Sorting Tab Sheet of the Report Settings Dialogue Box.

Next, click the **Grouping** tab and select the **When contents change** option, which will cause the report to split its output every time the value of the sorted field 'Weeks' changes.

Filtering a Report

For a report to show the correct records, the database must first be searched using the required retrieval criteria, as was described in the previous chapter.

In our case, the report should include all the invoices which have not been settled. Click the **Filter** tab and choose **Create New Filter**, giving it the name 'Overdue'. Select the field 'Paid' in the **Field name** box, the statement 'is equal to' in **Comparison** and type '0' in the **Compare to** section, as shown in Fig. 12.8, and press **OK** followed by **Finish**.

When the above settings are accepted, two extra rows, 'Intr Months' and 'Summ Months', are placed in the report definition. An 'Intr' row is placed before a report break section and can contain headings to identify the following data. In our case we will leave this line blank (you could delete it, but in this case we will not). It is only by 'playing around' like this and checking the printed results with Print Preview that you can fully master the Report Generator.

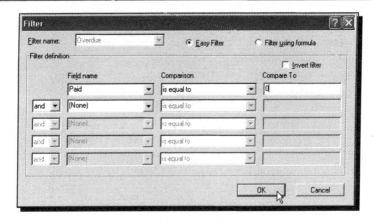

Fig. 12.8 The Filtering Tab Sheet of the Report Settings Dialogue Box.

Completing the Report Definition

Insert four more 'Summ Weeks' rows, and enter the following formulae in the middle row cells, with the formats and styles shown, as before.

Cell	Contents	Alignment	Format
A	=Weeks	Left justified	Fixed (0)
B	"–	Left justified	
C	=Weeks+1	Right justified	Fixed (0)
D	" Weeks Overdue	Left justified	
E	=COUNT('O/D')	Centre justified	Fixed (0)
F	=AVG('O/D')	Centre justified	Fixed (0)
G	=SUM(Total)	Left justified	Currency (2)

When you have completed this row, place horizontal lines, as described previously, above and below it.

Our report definition is almost complete now, only the 'Summary' rows remain to be done. If you have worked your way to this stage, entering these rows on your own should present no problems.

Insert two more 'Summary' type rows. Place a line in the bottom one, and type the following in the remaining two rows:

Cell	Contents	Alignment	Format
Row 17			
A	"Overall Totals	Left justified	
Row 18			
A	"and Averages	Left justified	
E	=COUNT('O/D')	Centre justified	Fixed (0)
F	=AVG('O/D')	Centre justified	Fixed (0)
G	=SUM(Total)	Right justified	Currency (2)

Printing a Report

Printing a report is similar to printing a word processor document, except that the facility to force column page breaks is included, as is the case with spreadsheets. From the Report screen choose **File**, **Page Setup** and make sure your page is set up with a 3.2 cm left margin, and select Print Preview to see what your report will look like on paper. It should be similar to the screen dump shown in Fig. 12.9 on the next page. Press **Print** to start printing, or **Cancel** to return to the Report definition screen.

Our report definition is now complete. It probably took several hours to build, but an instant report can now be generated from it, no matter how big the database gets. Also you should by now be able to tackle any reports of your own design.

Save the file with the name **Invoice4**, but yet again make sure you use the **Save As** command.

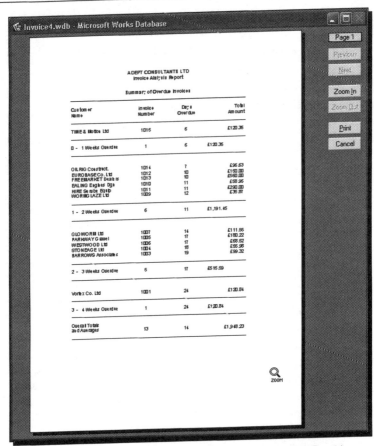

Fig. 12.9 The Print Preview Screen of the Overdue Invoices Report.

Form Letters

We are now in a position to use the mail merge capability of Works to create customised 'form letters', which make use of information stored in a database. As an example of this, you could create the simple database shown in Fig. 12.10, which contains the personal details of our potential customers. Save this database as **Business address**.

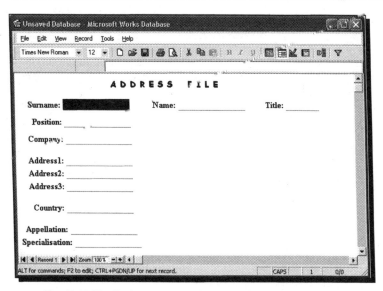

Fig. 12.10 The Business Address Database Design in Form View.

Next, type in your word processor the letter shown in Fig. 12.11, but before doing so read the next paragraph.

Note the way the various field names are enclosed by angled brackets. These 'field name markers' cannot be just typed in place. Move the cursor to where you want a field name marker and choose the **Insert**, **Database Field** command. Click the **Merge information from another type of file** option and select the file name of the database to use, in our case **Business address**. In the **Insert Fields** box choose the field name you want, press **Insert** and Works will place the field name in the document.

You can use the **View Results** button to get the word processor to substitute the database field information in your letter. This way you can make sure you have selected the correct field!

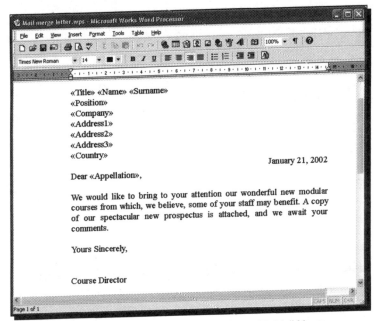

Fig. 12.11 The Design of a Letter to be Used in Mail Merge.

When the letter is completed, close the **Insert Fields** box and save the document with the name of **Mail merge letter**.

Note the field 'Appellation' which could be 'Sir', if you didn't know the name of the recipient, 'Mr Brown', if you did or 'John', if he was a friend of yours.

The field 'Specialisation' is included so that your form letters are only sent to relevant people. You would use information in this field in a Filter to select records.

Printing Form Letters

Works will print one copy of the letter for each record displayed in the database, assuming of course that you have entered some records.

Open the word processor file holding the form letter, in our case **Mail merge letter**. Before continuing make sure the database has been searched and sorted to display the records you need. You now do this from the word processor, with the **Tools**, **Mail Merge**, **Filter and Sort** command.

Next, complete the various options in the Print dialogue box (Fig. 12.12) for, say, **Number of copies**, etc., and finally press **OK** to start the print run. Obviously if you don't want to actually print the letters you would press **Cancel**.

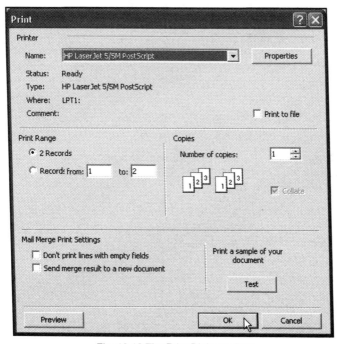

Fig. 12.12 The Print Dialogue Box.

When your printer is set up correctly, choose **File**, **Print**, select what options you want from **Mail Merge Print Settings** and click the **Preview** button to see what will be printed.

That is all there is to it. As long as your printer does not run out of paper, Works will print as many letters as there are records selected.

This procedure is not, of course, restricted to producing letters. It can be used for any word processed document which extracts information from a database.

Note: If you have all your important names and addresses stored in the Works Address Book, as described at the beginning of Chapter 14, you could use the Address Book in this procedure instead of the database.

13

E-mail with Outlook Express

To be able to communicate electronically with the rest of the world, many users will need to connect their PC through a modem to an active phone line. This is a device that converts data so that it can be transmitted over the telephone system. Installing such a modem is quite easy with Windows XP.

Modem Properties

Before using your modem, check to ensure it is correctly configured. To do this, double-click the **Phone and Modem Options** icon in the Control Panel. Windows will open the relevant dialogue box which we show on the left in Fig. 13.1 with its Modems tab selected. Click the **Properties** button, then select the Diagnostics tab and click the **Query Modem** button. If it displays the word 'success' your modem is working fine.

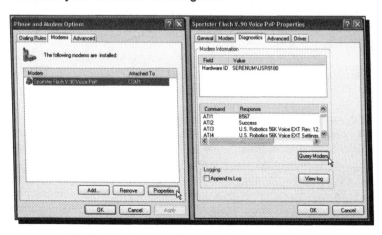

Fig. 13.1 Performing a Diagnostic Test on your Modem.

Microsoft Outlook Express

Works Suite 2002 comes with the very powerful mail and news facility, Outlook Express 6 (Works 6.0 with version 5.5), built into it, which makes it very easy for you to send and receive e-mail messages. What follows is applicable to both versions of the program which should already have been added to your PC by **Setup** (an entry being placed on the **Start** menu left column. To start the program, left-click the menu option, shown here which displays the screen shown in Fig. 13.2 below.

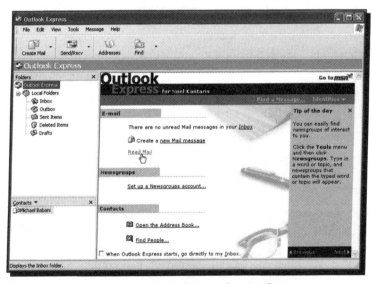

Fig. 13.2 The Outlook Express Opening Screen.

Obviously, to send and receive electronic mail over a modem, you must make an arrangement with a commercial server. There are quite a few around now, and most have Internet options. Try and find one that is free or can provide you with a reduced rate for local telephone calls, to minimise your phone bills. Once you have registered with such a service, you will be provided with all the necessary information to enter in the Internet Connection Wizard, so that you can fully exploit all the available facilities.

Connecting to your Server

To tell Outlook Express how to connect to your server's facilities, you must complete your personal e-mail connection details in the Internet Connection Wizard shown in Fig. 13.3, which opens when you first attempt to use the Read Mail facility pointed to in Fig. 13.2.

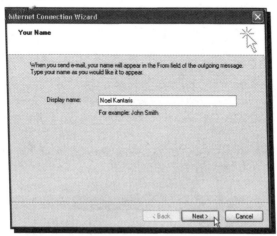

Fig. 13.3 The First Internet Connection Wizard Screen.

If the Wizard does not open, or if you want to change your connection details, use the **Tools**, **Accounts** menu command, select the mail tab and click the **Add** button and select **Mail**.

In the first screen of the Wizard, type your name in the text box, shown above, and click the **Next** button to display the second screen, shown in Fig. 13.4 on the next page. Enter your e-mail address in the text box, if you have not organised one yet you could always sign up for free e-mail with Hotmail. Hotmail is a free browser-based e-mail service owned by Microsoft.

In the third Wizard screen enter your e-mail server details, as shown for us in Fig. 13.5. To complete some of the details here you may need to ask your Internet Service Provider (ISP), or system administrator, for help.

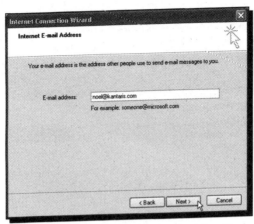

Fig. 13.4 The Second Internet Connection Wizard Screen.

The details shown below will obviously only work for the writer, so please don't try them!

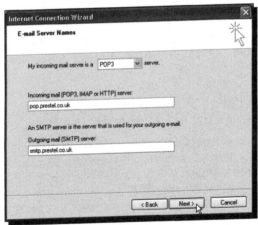

Fig. 13.5 The Third Internet Connection Wizard Screen.

The next Wizard screen asks for your user name and password. Both these would have been given to you by your ISP. Type these in, as shown for us in Fig. 13.6, and click the **Next** button.

If you select the **Remember password** option in this box, you will not have to enter these details every time you log on. **BUT** it may not be wise to do this if your PC is in a busy office - for security reasons.

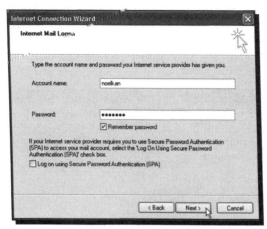

Fig. 13.6 The Fourth Internet Connection Wizard Screen.

This leads to the final Wizard screen informing you of your success, which completes the procedure, so press **Finish** to return you to the Internet Accounts dialogue box, with your new account set up as shown below for us.

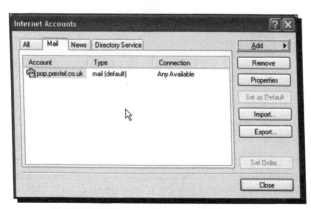

Fig. 13.7 The Internet Accounts Dialogue Box.

In the future, selecting the account in this box and clicking the **Properties** button will give you access to the settings sheets (to check, or change, your details).

Once your connection is established, you can click the Read Mail coloured link, or the **Inbox** entry in the Folder List on the left side of the Outlook Express opening window. Both of these actions open the Inbox, which when opened for the first time, will probably contain a message from Microsoft, like that shown in Fig. 13.8 below.

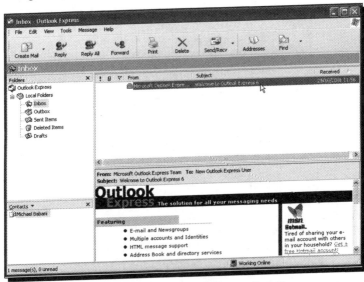

Fig. 13.8 The Inbox Outlook Express Screen.

This shows the default Outlook Express Main window layout, which consists of a Folders List to the left with a Contacts list (from the Address Book) below it, a Message List to the right and a Preview Pane below that. The list under Folders contains all the active mail folders, news servers and newsgroups.

Clicking on one of these displays its contents in the Message List, and clicking on a message opens a Preview of it below for you to see. Double-clicking on a message opens the message in its own window.

A Trial Run

To check your mail, click the Send/Recv Toolbar icon which will connect you to the Internet and download any new messages from your mailbox to your hard disc. You can then read and process your mail at your leisure without necessarily still being connected to the Internet.

Before explaining in more detail the main features of Outlook Express we will step through the procedure of sending a very simple e-mail message. The best way to test out any unfamiliar e-mail features is to send a test message to your own e-mail address. This saves wasting somebody else's time, and the message can be very quickly checked to see the results. To start, click the New Mail icon to open the New Message window, shown in Fig. 13.9 below.

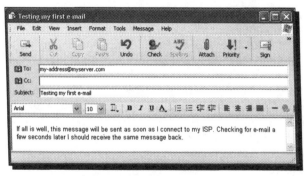

Fig. 13.9 Creating a New E-mail.

Type your own e-mail address in the **To:** field, and a title for the message in the **Subject:** field. The text in this subject field will form a header for the message when it is received, so it helps to show in a few words what the message is about. Type your message and when you are happy with it, click the Send Toolbar icon shown here.

By default, your message is stored in an Outbox folder, and pressing the Send/Recv Toolbar icon will connect to the Internet and then send it, hopefully straight into your mailbox. When Outlook Express next checks for mail, it will find the message and download it into the Inbox folder, for you to read and enjoy!

The Main Outlook Express Window

After the initial opening window, Outlook Express uses three other main windows, which we will refer to as: the Main window which opens next; the Read Message window for reading your mail; and the New Message window, to compose your outgoing mail messages.

The Main window consists of a Toolbar, a menu, and five panes with the default display shown in our example in Fig. 13.8. You can choose different pane layouts, and customise the Toolbar, with the **View**, **Layout** menu command, but we will let you try these for yourself.

The Folders List

The folders pane contains a list of your mail folders, your news servers and any newsgroups you have subscribed to. There are always at least five mail folders, as shown in Fig. 13.10. You can add your own with the **File**, **Folder**, **New** menu command from the Main window. You can delete added folders with the **File**, **Folder**, **Delete** command. These operations can also be carried out after right-clicking a folder in the list. You can drag messages from the Message list and drop them into any of the folders, to 'store' them there.

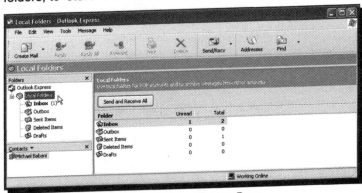

Fig. 13.10 The Local Folders Pane.

Note the icons shown above, any new folders you add will have the same icon as that of the first added folder.

The Contacts Pane

This pane simply lists the contacts held in your Address Book. Double-clicking on an entry in this list opens a New Message window with the message already addressed to that person.

The Message List

When you select a folder, by clicking it in the Folders list, the Message list shows the contents of that folder. Brief details of each message are displayed on one line, as shown in Fig. 13.11.

Fig. 13.11 Received Messages in Ascending Date Order.

The first column shows the message priority, if any, the second shows whether the message has an attachment, and the third shows whether the message has been 'flagged'. All of these are indicated by icons on the message line. The 'From' column shows the message status icon (listed on the next page) and the name of the sender, 'Subject' shows the title of each mail message, and 'Received' shows the date it reached you. You can control what columns display in this pane with the **View**, **Columns** menu command.

To sort a list of messages, you can click the mouse pointer in the title of the column you want the list sorted on, clicking it again will sort it in reverse order. The sorted column is shown with a triangle mark, as shown in Fig. 13.12 below.

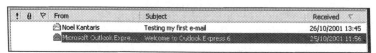

Fig. 13.12 Received Messages in Descending Date Order.

As seen on the screen dump above, the received messages have been sorted by date, with the most recently received message appearing at the top. This is our preferred method of display.

Message Status Icons

This icon	Indicates this
0	The message has one or more files attached.
!	The message has been marked high priority by the sender.
↓	The message has been marked low priority by the sender.
📖	The message has been read. The message heading appears in light type.
✉	The message has not been read. The message heading appears in bold type.
🔄	The message has been replied to.
📨	The message has been forwarded.
📝	The message is in progress in the Drafts folder.
🔏	The message is digitally signed and unopened.
🔐	The message is encrypted and unopened.
🔏	The message is digitally signed, encrypted and unopened.
🔓	The message is digitally signed and has been opened.
🔓	The message is encrypted and has been opened.
🔓	The message is digitally signed and encrypted, and has been opened.
⊞	The message has responses that are collapsed. Click the icon to show all the responses (expand the conversation).
⊟	The message and all of its responses are expanded. Click the icon to hide all the responses (collapse the conversation).
✉	The unread message header is on an IMAP server.
✗	The opened message is marked for deletion on an IMAP server.
⚑	The message is flagged.
⚡	The IMAP message is marked to be downloaded.
⊞⚡	The IMAP message and all conversations are marked to be downloaded.
⊟⚡	The individual IMAP message (without conversations) is marked to be downloaded.

Fig. 13.13. Table of Message Status Icons.

The Preview Pane

When you select a message in the Message list, by clicking it once, it is displayed in the Preview pane, which takes up the rest of the window. This lets you read the first few lines to see if the message is worth bothering with. If so, double clicking the header, in the Message list, will open the message in the Read Message window, as shown later in the chapter.

You could use the Preview pane to read all your mail, especially if your messages are all on the short side, but it is easier to process them from the Read Message window.

The Main Window Toolbar

Selecting any one of the local folders displays the following buttons on Outlook's Toolbar.

 Opens the New Message window for creating a new mail message, with the To: field blank.

 Opens the New Message window for replying to the current mail message, with the To: field pre-addressed to the original sender. The original Subject field is prefixed with Re:.

 Opens the New Message window for replying to the current mail message, with the To: field pre-addressed to all that received copies of the original message. The original Subject field is prefixed with Re:.

 Opens the New Message window for forwarding the current mail message. The To: field is blank. The original Subject field is prefixed with Fw:.

 Prints the selected message.

 Deletes the currently selected message and places it in the Deleted Items folder.

 Connects to the mailbox server and downloads waiting messages, which it places in the Inbox folder. Sends any messages waiting in the Outbox folder.

 Opens the Address Book.

 Finds a message or an e-mail address using Find People facilities of the Address Book.

The Read Message Window

If you double-click a message in the Message list of the Main window the Read Message window is opened, as shown below.

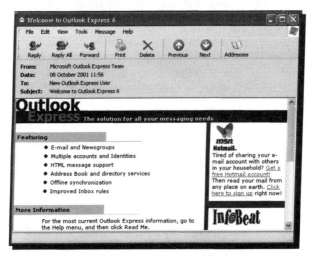

Fig. 13.14 The Read Message Window.

This is the best window to read your .mail in. It has its own menu system and Toolbar, which lets you rapidly process and move between the messages in a folder.

The Read Message Toolbar

This window has its own Toolbar, but only two icons are different from those in the Main window.

Previous - Displays the previous mail message in the Read Message window. The button appears depressed if there are no previous messages.

Next - Displays the next mail message in the Read Message window. The button appears depressed if there are no more messages.

Creating New Messages

We briefly looked into the creation of a new message and the New Message window earlier in the chapter (Fig. 13.9). However, before we activate this window again and discuss it in detail, let us first create a signature to be appended to all outgoing messages.

Your Own Signature

You create a signature from the Main window using the **Tools**, **Options** command which opens the Options dialogue box shown below when its Signature tab is selected and the **New** button is clicked.

Fig. 13.15 The Options Dialogue Box.

You could also create a more fancy signature file in a text editor like Notepad, or WordPad, including the text and characters you want added to all your messages, and point to it in the **File** section of this box. You could choose to **Add signatures to all outgoing messages** which is preferable, or you could leave this option blank and use the **Insert**, *Signature* command from the New Message window menu system.

The New Message Window

This is the window, shown below, that you will use to create any messages you want to send electronically from Outlook Express. It is important to understand its features, so that you can get the most out of it.

Fig. 13.16 The New Message Window.

As we saw, this window can be opened by using the **Create Mail** Toolbar icon from the Main window, as well as the **Message**, **New Message** menu command. From other windows you can also use the **Message**, **New Message** command, or the <Ctrl+N> keyboard shortcut. The newly opened window has its own menu system and Toolbar, which let you rapidly prepare and send your new e-mail messages.

Message Stationery

Another Outlook Express feature is that it lets you send your messages on pre-formatted stationery for added effect.

To access these, click the down arrow next to the **Create Mail** button in the Main window and either select from the **1** to **7** list, as shown here, or use the **Select Stationery** command to open a box with many more stationery types on offer.

Fig. 13.17 Stationery.

The New Message Toolbar

The icons on the New Message Toolbar window have the following functions:

 Send Message - Sends message, either to the recipient, or to the Outbox folder.

 Cut - Cuts selected text to the Windows clipboard.

 Copy - Copies selected text to the Windows clipboard.

 Paste - Pastes the contents of the Windows clipboard into the current message.

 Undo - Undoes the last editing action.

 Check Names - Checks that names match your entries in the address book, or are in correct e-mail address format.

 Spelling - Checks the spelling of the current message before it is sent, but is only available if you have Word, Excel, or PowerPoint.

 Attach File - Opens the Insert Attachment window for you to select a file to be attached to the current message.

 Set Priority - Sets the message priority as high or low, to indicate its importance to the recipient.

 Digitally sign message - Adds a digital signature to the message to confirm to the recipient that it is from you.

 Encrypt message - Encodes the message so that only the recipient can read it.

 Work Offline - Closes connection to the Internet so that you can process your mail offline. The button then changes to **Work Online.**

Message Formatting

Outlook Express provides quite sophisticated formatting options for an e-mail editor from both the **Format** menu and Toolbar. These only work if you prepare the message in HTML format, as used in Web documents. You can set this to be your default mail sending format using the Send tab in the **Tools**, **Options** box.

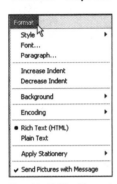

Fig. 13.18 The Format Sub-menu.

To use the format for the current message only, select **Rich Text (HTML)** from the **Format** menu, as we have done here. If **Plain Text** is selected, the black dot will be placed against this option on the menu, and the formatting features will not then be available.

The Format Toolbar shown below is added to the New Message window when you are in HTML mode and all the **Format** menu options are then made active.

Fig. 13.19 The Format Toolbar.

All of the formatting features are well covered elsewhere in the book so we will not repeat them now. Most of them are quite well demonstrated in Microsoft's opening message to you. You should be able to prepare some very easily readable e-mail messages with these features, but remember that not everyone will be able to read the work in the way that you spent hours creating. Only e-mail programs that support MIME (Multi-purpose Internet Mail Extensions) can read HTML formatting. When your recipient's e-mail program does not read HTML, and many people choose not to, the message appears as plain text with an HTML file attached.

Note: At the risk of being called boring we think it is usually better to stick to plain text without the selection of any message stationery; not only can everyone read it, but it is much quicker to transmit and deal with.

Using E-mail Attachments

If you want to include an attachment to your main e-mail message, you simply click the **Attach** Toolbar button in the New Message window, as shown in Fig. 13.20 below.

Fig. 13.20 Adding an Attachment to an E-mail.

This opens the Insert Attachment dialogue box (Fig. 13.21), for you to select the file, or files, you want to go with your message.

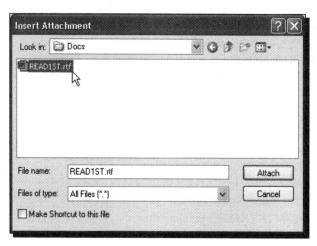

Fig. 13.21 The Insert Attachment Dialogue Box.

In Outlook Express the attached files are placed below the **Subject** text box. In Fig. 13.22 we show two attachments, each with a distinctive icon that tells the recipient what each file is; the first a graphics .jpg file, the second a text .rtf document. It is only polite to include in your e-mail a short description of what the attachments are, and which applications were used to create them; it will help the recipient to decipher them.

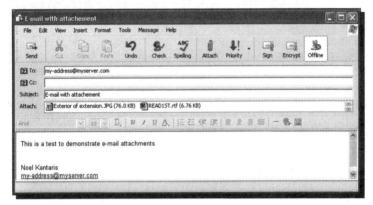

Fig. 13.22 Adding an Attachment to an E-mail.

Clicking the **Send** icon on the Toolbar, puts each e-mail (with its attachments, if any) in Outlook's **Outbox** folder. Next time you click the **Send/Recv** Toolbar icon, Outlook Express connects to your ISP and sends all the e-mails stored in it.

Receiving Attachments with an E-mail

To demonstrate what happens when you receive an e-mail with attachments, we have sent the above e-mail to our ISP, then a minute or so later we received it back, as shown in Fig. 13.23 on the next page.

Note that the received e-mail shows the graphics (.jpg) file open at the bottom of the Preview pane, but there is no indication of any other attachments. To find out how many attachments were included with the received e-mail, double-click the e-mail to open it in its own window and reveal all of them in the **Attach** box shown in Fig. 13.24 on the next page.

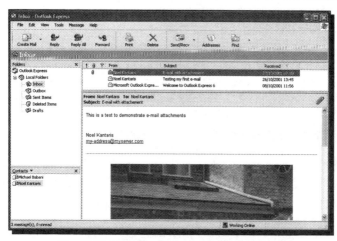

Fig. 13.23 A Received E-mail with Attachments.

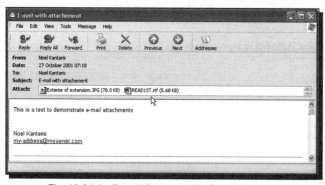

Fig. 13.24 An E-mail Opened in its Own Window.

To view or save an attachment file, left-click its entry on the list. This opens the Warning box shown in Fig. 13.25.

Each attached file can be opened in situ or saved to disc by selecting **Open it** or **Save it to disk**.

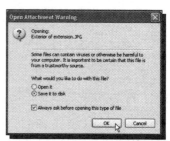

Fig. 13.25 The Open Attachment Warning Window.

Replying to a Message

When you receive an e-mail message that you want to reply to, Outlook Express makes it very easy to do. The reply address and the new message subject fields are both added automatically for you. Also, by default, the original message is quoted in the reply window for you to edit as required.

With the message you want to reply to still open, click the Reply to Sender Toolbar icon to open the New Message window and the message you are replying to will, by default, be placed under the insertion point.

With long messages, you should not leave all of the original text in your reply. This can be bad practice, which rapidly makes new messages very large and time consuming to download. You should usually edit the quoted text, so that it is obvious what you are referring to. A few lines may be enough.

Removing Deleted Messages

Whenever you delete a message it is actually moved to the Deleted Items folder. If ignored, this folder gets bigger and bigger over time, so you need to check it frequently and manually re-delete messages you are sure you will not need again.

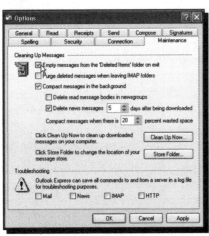

If you are confident that you will not need this safety net, you can opt to **Empty messages from the 'Deleted Items' folder on exit** in Maintenance tab settings of the **Tools**, **Options** box, opened from the Main window, as shown in Fig. 13.26.

Fig. 13.26 Cleaning up Messages.

Organising your Messages

Perhaps most of the e-mail messages you get will have no 'long term' value and will be simply deleted once you have dealt with them. Some however you may well need to keep for future reference. After a few weeks it can be surprising how many of these messages can accumulate. If you don't do something with them they seem to take over and slow the whole process down. That is the reason for the Folders List.

As we saw earlier you can open and close new folders in this area, and can move and copy messages from one folder into another.

Fig. 13.27 Moving a Message.

To move a message, you just select its header line in the Message List and with the left mouse button depressed 'drag' it to the folder in the Folders List, as shown in Fig. 13.27. When you release the mouse button, the message will be moved to that folder.

The copy procedure is very much the same, except you must also have the <Ctrl> key depressed when you release the mouse button. You can tell which operation is taking place by looking at the mouse pointer. It will show a '+' when copying, as on the right.

The System Folders

Outlook Express has five folders which it always keeps intact and will not let you delete. Some of these we have met already.

The *Inbox* holds all incoming messages; you should delete or move them from this folder as soon as you have read them.

The *Outbox* holds messages that have been prepared but not yet transmitted. As soon as the messages are sent they are automatically removed to the *Sent Items* folder. You can then decide whether to 'file' your copies of these messages, or whether to delete them. As we saw earlier, deleted messages are placed in the *Deleted Items* folder as a safety feature.

The **Drafts** folder is used to hold a message you closed down without sending it - the program will ask you whether to save such a message in this folder. We also use the Drafts folder to store our message pro-formas and unfinished messages that will need more work before they can be sent.

Spell Checking

Many of the e-mail messages we receive seem to be full of errors and spelling mistakes. Some people do not seem to read their work before clicking the 'Send' button. With Outlook Express this should be a thing of the past, as the program is linked to the spell checker that comes with other Microsoft programs. If you do not have any of these, the option will be greyed out, meaning that it is not available.

To try it out, prepare a message in the New Message window, but make an obvious spelling mistake, maybe like ours below. Pressing the Spelling Toolbar button, the **F7** function key, or using the **Tools, Spelling** menu command, reveals the drop-down sub-menu shown below in Fig. 13.28.

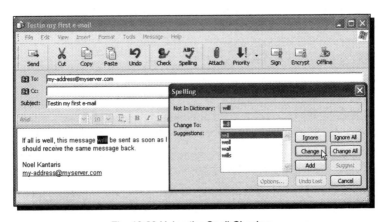

Fig. 13.28 Using the Spell Checker.

Any words not recognised by the checker will be flagged up as shown. If you are happy with the word just click one of the **Ignore** buttons, if not, you can type a correction in the **Change To:** field, or accept one of the **Suggestions:**, and then click the **Change** button. With us the **Options** button always seemed 'greyed out', but you can get some control over the spell checker on the settings sheet opened from the main Outlook Express menu with the **Tools**, **Options** command, and then clicking the Spelling tab.

The available options, as shown in Fig. 13.29, are self-explanatory so we will not dwell on them. If you want every message to be checked before it is sent, make sure you select the **Always check spelling before sending** option.

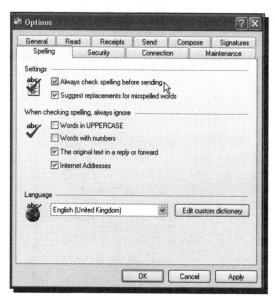

Fig. 13.29 The Options Spelling Dialogue Box.

In the above dialogue box, you could also choose to have the Spell Checker ignore **Words with numbers**, if you so wished, before clicking the **Apply** button.

Connection at Start-up

While you are looking at the program settings, open the **Tools**, **Options**, Connection tabbed sheet, shown in Fig. 13.30.

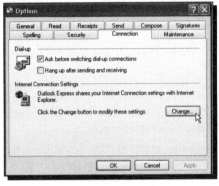

This gives you some control of what happens when you open Outlook Express, depending on your connection settings for Internet Explorer. If you have a modem connection to the Internet, it can be annoying when a program goes into dial-up mode un-expectedly. To look at these settings, click

Fig. 13.30 The Options Connection Dialogue Box.

the **Change** button which displays the dialogue box in Fig. 13.31.

Fig. 13.31 The Internet Properties Dialogue Box.

Next, select the **Never dial a connection** option so that you only 'go on line' (as long as you have not chosen to **Work Offline** from the **File** menu option), when you click the Send/Recv toolbar icon shown here. If you have more than one Internet connection, the down arrow to the right of the icon lets you select which one to use.

If, on the other hand, you have a permanent Internet connection, you might like to deselect the **Never dial a connection** option.

Printing your Messages

It was originally thought by some, that computers would lead to the paperless office. That has certainly not proved to be correct. It seems that however good our electronic communication media becomes, most people want to see the results printed on paper. As far as books are concerned, long may that last!

Outlook Express 5 lets you print e-mail messages to paper, but it does not give you any control over the page settings it uses. You can, however, alter the font size of your printed output as it depends on the font size you set for viewing your messages. As shown here, you have five 'relative' size options available from the **View**, **Text Size** menu command.

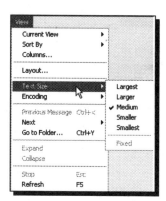

Fig. 13.32 The View Menu.

When you are ready to print a message in the Read Message window, use the <Ctrl+P> key combination, or the **File**, **Print** menu command, to open the Print dialogue box shown in Fig. 13.33 on the next page with its General tab selected.

Fig. 13.33 The Print Dialogue Box.

Make sure the correct printer, **Page Range**, and **Number of copies** you want are selected, then click **Print**. You can also start the printing procedure by clicking the Print Toolbar icon shown here.

If the message has Web page links on it, there are two useful features in the Options tab of the Print dialogue box shown above. These are:

* The **Print all linked documents** option, which when checked not only prints the message, but also all the Web pages linked to it.

* The **Print table of links** option, which when checked, gives a hard copy listing of the URL addresses of all the links present in the page.

Outlook Express Help

Outlook Express has a built-in Help system, which is accessed with the **Help**, **Contents and Index** menu command, or the **F1** function key. These open a Windows type Help window, as shown in Fig. 13.34 below.

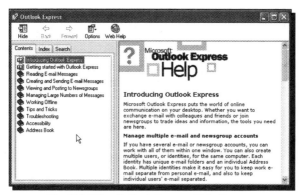

Fig. 13.34 The Outlook Express Help System.

We strongly recommend that you work your way through all the items listed in the **Contents** tabbed section. Clicking on a closed book icon will open it and display a listing of its contents. Double-clicking on a list item will then open a window with a few lines of Help information.

Another way of browsing the Help system is to click the **Index** tab and work your way through the alphabetic listing. The **Search** tab, on the other hand, opens a search facility you can use by typing your query in the **Type in the keyword to find** text field and clicking the **List Topics** button, then selecting one of the topics found and clicking **Display** to open Help information on it.

The Help provided by Microsoft with Outlook Express, is a big improvement over some earlier versions of the program, and it is well worth spending some time getting to grips with it. If you are connected to the Internet, the Web Help icon accesses the Support Online from Microsoft Technical Support, which can give more specific help with the program.

14

The Address Book & Calendar

In this chapter, we shall discuss two important features which are included in the Works package.

The Address Book

You open the Address Book from the **Programs** page of the Task Launcher, the same way as the other Works applications, by clicking **Start the Address Book**, as pointed to in Fig. 14.1.

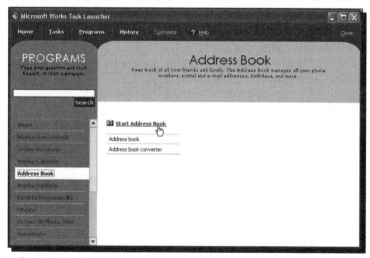

Fig. 14.1 The Works Address Book Link in the Task Launcher Screen.

The program can also be opened by selecting Address Book in the Works section of the Windows cascade **Start** menu.

E-mail addresses are often quite complicated and not at all easy to remember. With Outlook Express there is a very useful Address Book built in and accessed by clicking the menu icon with the same name. When open, it looks like our example in Fig. 14.2 which shows only a few entries.

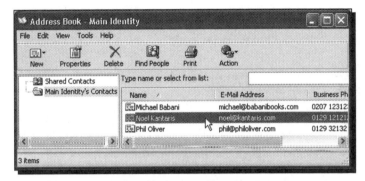

Fig. 14.2 The Address Book Screen.

Once in the Address Book, you can manually add a person's full details and e-mail address, in the Properties box that opens when you click the New Toolbar icon and select **New Contact**, as shown here. Selecting **New Group** from this drop-down menu lets you create a grouping of e-mail addresses, you can then send mail to everyone in the group with one operation.

To send a new message to anyone listed in your Address Book, open a New Message window and use the **Tools**, **Select Recipients** command, or click on any of the **To:** or **Cc:** icons shown here on the left.

In the Select Recipients box which is opened (Fig. 14.3), you can select a person's name and click either the **To:->** button to place it in the **To:** field of your message, the **Cc:->** button to place it in the **Cc:** field, or the **Bcc:->**button to place it in the **Bcc:** field.

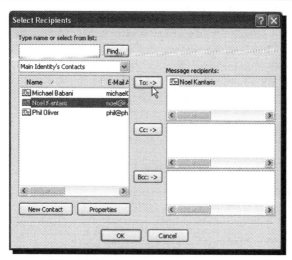

Fig. 14.3 The Select Recipients Screen.

The **New Contact** button lets you add details for a new person to the Address Book, and the **Properties** button lets you edit an existing entry, as shown in Fig. 14.4.

Fig. 14.4 A Recipient's Properties Screen.

To edit details of any of your Address Book entries, simply select one from the main list and click the **Properties** toolbar button. This opens the same dialogue box as before, but with a summary sheet on the front as shown in Fig. 14.5.

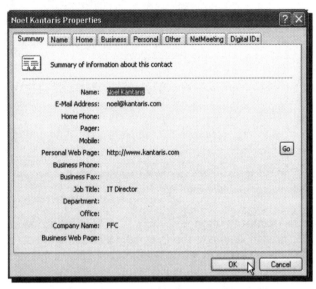

Fig. 14.5 The Properties Summary Screen.

It is easy to add an individual name to your address book when reading e-mails in Outlook Express itself. From a message you are viewing or replying to, just right-click the person's name, and then click **Add to Address Book**. From the message list of any mail folder or the Inbox, right-click a message, and then click **Add Sender to Address Book**.

Using E-mail Groups

This feature lets you create a grouping of e-mail addresses, you can then send mail to everyone in the group with one operation.

To create a group, click the **New** button on the toolbar, and then click **New Group**. The Properties dialogue box, shown in Fig. 14.6, opens.

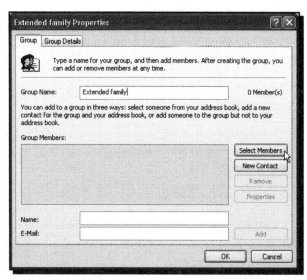

Fig. 14.6 The Group Properties Dialogue Box.

In the **Group Name** box, type the name of the group, which then forms part of the box title, as shown above. To add a person from your address book list, click **Select Members**, highlight their name in the address book list and then click the **Select** button, as shown in Fig. 14.7.

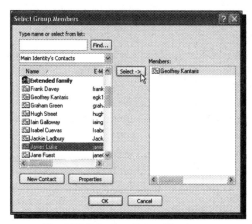

Fig. 14.7 Selecting Group Members.

To add a person directly to the group without adding them to your address book, type the person's **Name** and **E-Mail** address straight into the lower half of the Properties dialogue box, and then click the **Add** button.

Click **OK** to get back to the Address Book, then double-click the **Extended family** entry to find the new contact listed, as shown in Fig. 14.8.

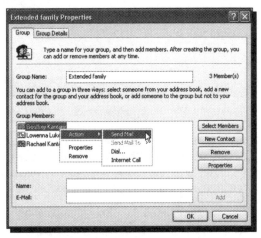

Fig. 14.8 A New Item in the Address Book.

To send a new message to a person in a group listed in your Address Book right-click the person's name and select **Action**, **Send Mail** from the drop-down menu, as shown in Fig. 14.8 above. As long as Outlook Express is set up properly its New Message window should be opened with the addressing details already completed.

To send a message to an individual person listed in your address book, or to all the members within a group, select the person or the group and left-click the **Action** toolbar button shown to the left, and select **Send Mail** from the drop-down menu.

Finding People

The Address Book gives you two main ways of finding people's

details, both from the **Find People** toolbar button shown here. If your Address Book has hundreds of entries you can use this feature to find a particular person. But how many faraway friends do you have that you would love to contact, but whose e-mail address you have lost or never even known? No problem with the Address Book, if they have an e-mail address you should be able to find it, as it supports LDAP (Lightweight Directory Access Protocol) for accessing directory services, and has built-in access to several popular directory services. Directory services are powerful search tools that you use to find people and businesses around the world.

If the Address Book is open, click the **Find People** toolbar button. If it is not, you can simply open the Windows **Start** menu and select **Search**, **Computers and People**. Both methods open the box shown in Fig. 14.9.

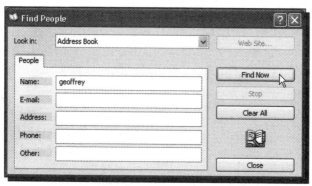

Fig. 14.9 The Find People Dialogue Box.

To search the Address Book itself, make sure it is selected in the **Look in** text box, type as many search details as you can remember in the **People** boxes, and click on **Find Now**.

To use a directory service, click the down arrow next to the **Look in** text box and select one of the listed options, as

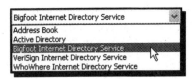

Fig. 14.10 Available Search
Directories for Finding People.

shown in Fig. 14.10. The Find People dialogue box then changes to that shown in Fig. 14.11 below, which also shows the result of the specific search. However, to get a result, you must connect to the Internet, then type the **Name** or **E-mail** address of the person you want to look for on the **People** tab, and then click **Find Now**.

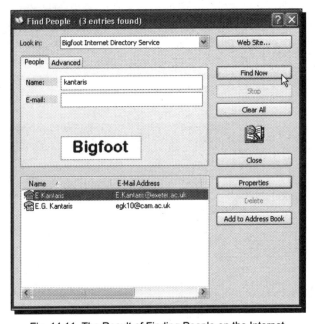

Fig. 14.11. The Result of Finding People on the Internet.

The **Advanced** tab lets you define extra search criteria to use. Clicking the **Web Site** button lets you access the directory Web site itself in which there is also a more sophisticated facility for searching for People.

Managing Identities

When Address Book is first installed, the default identity name, called Main Identity, is created and all your new contacts appear in that named folder (see Fig. 14.7). The name of this folder can be changed to your name, and additional identities can be created so that each member of your family can have their own separate contacts, by carrying out the following steps while the Address Book is open:

• Use the **File, Switch Identity** command and in the displayed dialogue box, shown in Fig. 14.12a, click the **Manage Identities** button to open the dialogue box shown in Fig. 14.12b.

(a)   (b)

Fig. 14.12 Changing the Main Identity's Name.

• Next, click the **Properties** button on the Manage Identities dialogue box to open the Identity Properties dialogue box shown in Fig. 14.13. It is in this box that you type your name to replace the default. You can also select a password, if so desired. Pressing the **OK** button, returns you to the Manage Identities dialogue box of Fig. 14.12b.

Fig. 14.13 Changing the Main Identity's Name.

299

- If you want to create another identity, click the **Properties** button on the Manage Identities dialogue box to open the dialogue box of Fig. 14.13 again, where you supply the new identity's name.

- To display all the available identities, and switch between identities, use the **File, Show All Contents** command.

Exporting and Importing an Address Book

Amongst the most valuable assets you might have on your old computer is your Address Book. After all, you have spent endless hours (over a period of time) compiling it and the last thing you want is to lose it, either because you are changing computer or because of some mishap.

Outlook Express has the facility to export your Address Book from your old computer, then import it into your new one. The same method can also be used to make a backup of your Address Book.

In your old computer, start Outlook Express, then in the Address Book:

- Use the **File, Export** command and click the **Address Book (WAB)** option.

- In the displayed Select Address Book File to Export to dialogue box, type a suitable name in the **File name** box and click the **Save** button.

In your new computer, start Outlook Express, then in the Address book:

- Use the **File, Import** command and click the **Address Book (WAB)** option.

- In the displayed **Select Address Book File to Import from** dialogue box, locate the drive and file holding your Address Book information and click the **Open** button.

It takes less time to do than to read how to do it, and you can save yourself hours of work and frustration!

Address Book Help

We will leave it to you to find your way round this very comprehensive facility. Don't forget that it has its own Help system that you can use with the **Help, Contents and Index** menu command. An example section is shown open in Fig. 14.14.

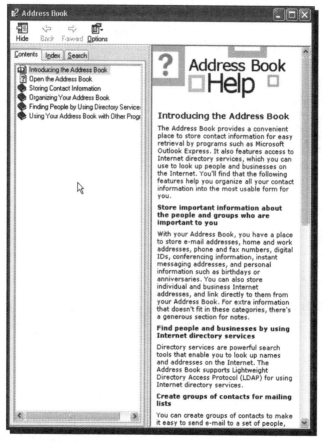

Fig. 14.14 The Address Book Help System.

We find the Address Book to be a very useful feature of the package, but like all such things it is only fully functional if you keep it up to date!

The Works Calendar

You use the Works Calendar to keep track of appointments, meetings and events such as holidays and birthdays, and to set reminders. As long as you keep it up to date, and check it every day, you need never miss appointments again!

Like the other Works applications you open the Calendar from the Task Launcher, by selecting **Works Calendar** in the **Programs** window list and then clicking on the **Start the Calendar** link, shown in Fig. 14.15.

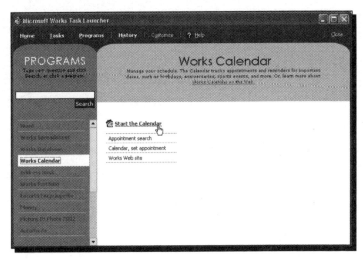

Fig. 14.15 The Works Calendar Link in the Task Launcher Screen.

The Calendar Screen

Before we get too involved with entering dates and appointments in the calendar perhaps we should look at the parts that make up the screen.

As shown in Fig. 14.16, it has its own menu and toolbar and shows either the current month, week or day, depending on the setting. Also shown open is the **Category Filter** bar on the left. This bar has its own toggle button on the toolbar and will be discussed a little later on.

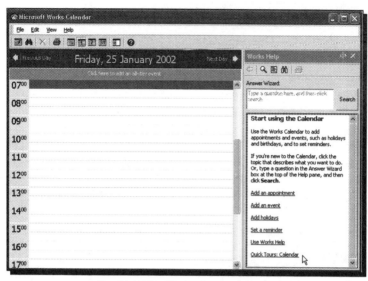

Fig. 14.16 The Works Calendar Screen.

The Toolbar

Most of the toolbar buttons are new to the Calendar so we will describe their operation before we go on.

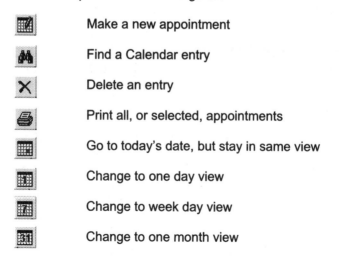

Make a new appointment

Find a Calendar entry

Delete an entry

Print all, or selected, appointments

Go to today's date, but stay in same view

Change to one day view

Change to week day view

Change to one month view

Toggle the Category Filter on and off

    Open the Calendar Help pane.

The toolbar can be switched on and off with the **View**, **Toolbar**, **Show Toolbar** menu command, and the same sub-menu gives you the option of using large icons on the bar.

Viewing Appointments

There are three main ways to view your calendar, one day, one week and one month at a time. In all these views you can see any diary entries that have been made, or you can click in a day's area to make a new appointment entry.

In any view, to look at the next day, week or month just left-click on the respective button on the right of the black Date bar, as shown here. The Previous day, week or month buttons on the left of the bar take you back one day, week or month.

To change between the views, simply click the appropriate button on the toolbar as shown above, or use the **View**, **Day** command (<Alt+1>), the **View**, **Week** command (<Alt+->), or the **View**, **Month** command (<Alt+=>). The choice is yours, whichever method you use the result is the same.

Entering Appointments

To start with, let us type in a recurring appointment to, say, meet Section Managers, that takes place on the first Thursday of every month starting at 10:00 a.m. on 31 January and lasts for 2 hours.

To do so, go to Month View, select January 2002 and double-click the 31 January on the calendar. This opens the New Appointment dialogue box shown in Fig. 14.17 in which you can type 'Managers' meeting' in the **Title** box, and 'My Office' in the **Location** box. In the **When Appointment starts** box enter 10.00 and in the **When Appointment ends** box enter 12.00, as shown.

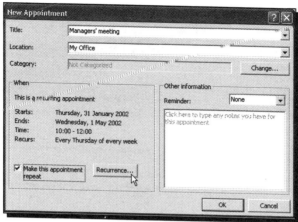

Fig. 14.17 The Edit Appointment Dialogue Box.

Next, select to **Make this appointment repeat** and click the **Recurrence** button. In the Recurrence Options dialogue box, click the **Monthly** radio button and select **The last Thursday of every 1 month(s)**, as shown in Fig. 14.18 and click **OK** to return to the previous dialogue box in which you could place notes about the meetings if you wanted to. Finally click **OK** to return to the Calendar.

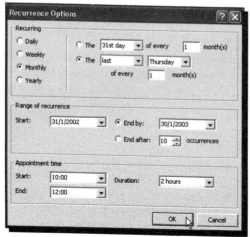

Fig. 14.18 The Recurrence Options Dialogue Box.

Your Calendar now shows the series of entries on the correct days. Fig. 14.19 shows the Day View of January 31, 2002.

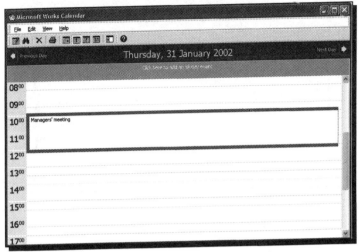

Fig. 14.19 The Day View of Works Calendar.

If you want to make any changes to the newly created appointment, double-click on it. Select **Open this occurrence**, from the menu box that opens, to make changes that only affect it on that date, or select **Open the Series** to open the Recurring Options dialogue box where you can make changes that will affect all future appointments.

To delete an appointment, select it and either click the **Delete** toolbar icon, or right-click and select **Delete Item**. Both methods will open a warning box to give you a chance to 'change your mind'.

Category Filters

A category is an assigned name that can help you define and organize the appointments in your calendar. You associate appointments with categories to help you remember, and view them, based on the categories assigned to them. For example, you can view only those appointments that have the Entertainment category assigned.

To add a category, click and select an appointment in the calendar and action the **File**, **Open Appointment** menu command. Click the **Change** button followed by the category you want to assign to the appointment, as shown below.

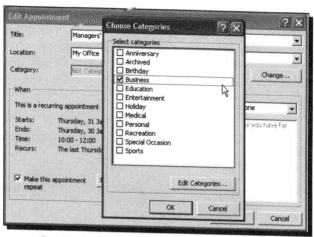

Fig. 14.20 Assigning Categories to Appointments.

Clicking on **OK** will complete the operation. The Choose Categories box in Fig. 14.20 shows all the default categories built into the calendar. You can change any of these by clicking the **Edit Categories** button, maybe by adding new ones and deleting those that you will never use.

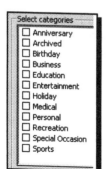

Once you have added categories to your appointments, you can use the **Category Filter** button to open the filter, shown to the left. This lets you control which appointments are displayed at any one time.

If **Not Categorized** is selected in the filter, only appointments with no categories will show on the calendar. If you select another category from the filter list and deselect **Not Categorized**, then only entries with that category will be displayed. In our example here only **Business** appointments will be visible.

Adding Holidays

When you first open the Works calendar it is empty and has no appointments or other entries. You can soon change this by adding what holidays you want to show, such as the national holidays of your country (and others if you like), or religious holidays, such as Christian, Jewish or Islamic.

To do this, use the **Edit**, **Add Holidays** menu command, or <Ctrl+H>, and select the holidays you want to add to your calendar. Fig. 14.21 below shows us adding the United Kingdom holidays to the Calendar and what it looks like after this addition takes place.

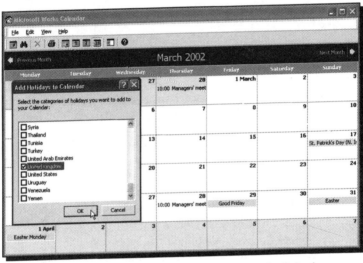

Fig. 14.21 The Effect of Adding Public Holidays to the Calendar.

We suggest you don't go too mad here, the calendar screen can get very easily cluttered with duplicate holiday entries which are not always easy to get rid of. Be warned. If you need to, you can delete holiday entries the same as other appointments, as described earlier.

Adding Birthdays

If you have already entered birthdays and anniversaries in the Address Book, you can add them to your calendar automatically with the **Edit**, **Birthdays** menu command which displays the dialogue box in Fig. 14.22.

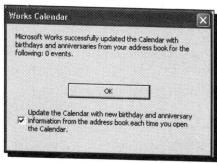

Fig. 14.22 The Birthdays Update Dialogue Box.

To add birthdays manually is a little more time consuming. You add them in the Month View the same as any other appointments, but give them the Birthday category, as shown in Fig. 14.23 below. Remember to make them recur yearly in the New Appointment dialogue box, or they will only show for the day you enter them, not every year from then on.

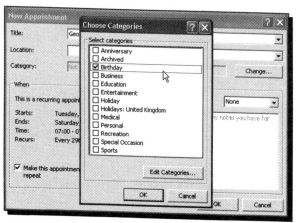

Fig. 14.23 The Birthdays Update Dialogue Box.

Managing Appointments

You can use the **Find** toolbar button not only to find specific appointments, but also to manage your Calendar entries. For example, clicking the **Find** toolbar button displays the dialogue box in Fig. 14.24 below.

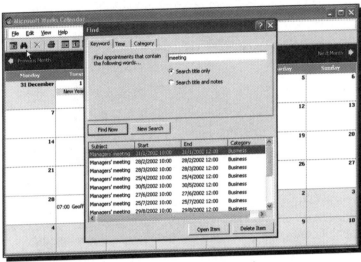

Fig. 14.24 The Birthdays Update Dialogue Box.

In the Find dialogue box you can use as a search criteria either a Keyword (as shown above), a Time, or a Category. Furthermore, you can make your search applicable to either the 'title' only, or the 'title and notes'.

Once an entry or a series of entries has been found, you

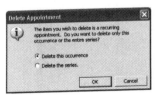

have the option to open or delete the particular item by clicking the appropriate buttons at the bottom of the Find dialogue box. Clicking the **Delete Item** button displays the Delete Appointment warning box shown here to the left.

Calendar Printing

Your calendar information can be printed on paper. Simply use the **File, Print** command to open the dialogue box in Fig. 14.25 below.

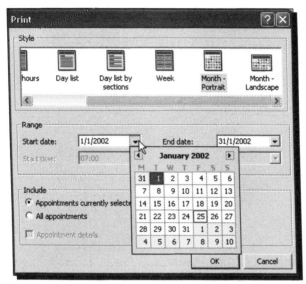

Fig. 14.25 The Print Calendar Dialogue Box.

As you can see, this gives you plenty of control on what parts of the calendar to print and what style to use. Note the drop-down 'calendar views' to help you select the start and end dates of your printout. You will need to experiment a little here to find the settings that suit you best.

When you click on **OK** to accept the settings selected, the 'normal' Print box is opened so that you can control your printer and paper settings, etc. It's a pity there is no Preview option to save a few trees!

15

Works Tasks & Templates

There are two more features included in the Works package that need some coverage. These are Tasks and Templates, both of which are designed to make the package more useful and easier to use.

Works Tasks

With Tasks, you get step-by-step assistance in creating particular types of documents. There are eleven groups of Tasks, as shown in Fig. 15.1, which can be displayed by clicking the tab sheet of the Works Task Launcher.

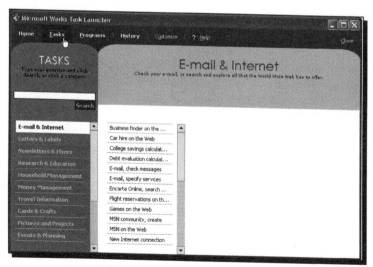

Fig. 15.1 The Tasks Sheet of the Works Task Launcher.

Letters and Labels

If you are new to Works, or to computing in general for that matter, you can use the Works Tasks to quickly get started on a particular job, or task. Most people write letters at some time so we will see what is on offer here.

Fig. 15.2 Starting a Specific Task.

Selecting one of these opens a relevant picture and a few lines of descriptive text, with a **Start this task** link. Clicking this link will start the task procedure, which usually involves one of the inbuilt Wizards.

Whether the Works 6.0 word processor or Word 2002 is opened depends on which version of Microsoft Works is installed on your computer. In our case, Word 2002 was opened with a very elegant letter template visible in the background and with the Letter Wizard screen, shown in Fig. 15.3 on the next page, activated.

In this first Wizard screen, you select from one of the five pre-formatted letter styles. To see what each one looks like you can select it and then click the **Minimize Wizard** button to see the resulting letter in the word processor window behind and then click **Maximize Wizard** to continue.

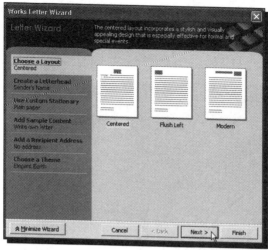

Fig. 15.3 Selecting Position of Sender's Address.

When you have chosen your letter style (mainly the position of your address), leave it selected and click the **Next** button to display the second Wizard screen (Fig. 15.4) in which you enter your own name and address details. If you don't want your own name to appear at the top of the letter, then delete this entry.

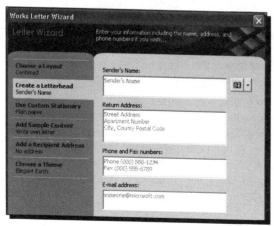

Fig. 15.4 Inserting Sender's Name and Address.

Press **Next**, and the third Wizard screen is displayed in which you give the details of any pre-printed stationery you plan to use. Otherwise just press **Next** again and go straight to the screen shown in Fig. 15.5 below.

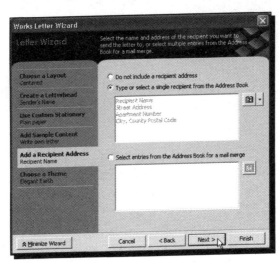

Fig. 15.5 Adding the Recipient's Address.

This lets you add details of the Recipient's name and address. This information can also be inserted from the Address Book, if you already have it there. Alternatively, you can select more than one entry from the Address Book for a mail merge. When you have entered the required information, click the **Next** button to open the fourth Wizard screen, shown in Fig. 15.6 on the next page.

In this penultimate Wizard screen, you can select a theme and colour for your letter, and when this is done clicking **Finish** opens the final product as shown in Fig. 15.7. We did not bother to fill in our personal details but you obviously would need to! You must agree that this is a fine way to generate well formatted letters.

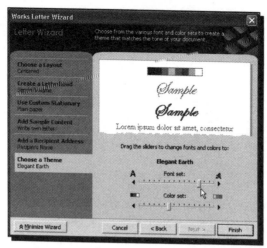

Fig. 15.6 Selecting a Theme and Colouring.

Fig. 15.7 The Final Document.

We suggest you work your way through the available Tasks, each one of which opens the Works application necessary to complete the task. Remember that pressing the **Next** button moves you to the next screen, and pressing **Cancel** will close the Task Wizard you are using.

Templates

A Template is a document 'blank' which can contain titles, text, formatting and other features, which do not change between documents of the same type. Once it has been created, you can open a Template, and adapt the resulting open file in any way you want, without affecting the original template file.

With Works many of the Tasks actually open templates for you, but you can also create your own. These can be either from scratch, or based on a document created from one of the Tasks.

Creating a Template in Word 2002

A useful Template for almost everyone, would be a blank letter heading with your address, date, etc., all laid out and ready to enter the letter contents. You could use one of the Tasks to set up such a letter for the first time. Then to save time in the future, save the letter format as a Template before adding its text.

We suggest you prepare a letter blank that you would be proud to send to anybody. It could be fairly simple, or be more sophisticated and include 'fancy fonts' and a graphic logo, etc. When you are happy with its layout and contents, choose the **File**, **Save As** menu command, click the down arrow against the **Save as type** command, select **Document Template (*.dot)**, type a suitable name, maybe 'My Letterhead', in the **File name** box shown in Fig. 15.8, and press **OK**.

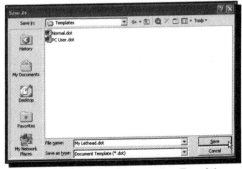

Fig. 15.8 Saving a Document as Template.

In the future, whenever you want to send a letter, use your new Template instead of starting from scratch. To do this, go to the Tasks section of the Task Launcher, click on **Word** and you will find the new option 'My Letterhead' has been added to the list of available tasks, as shown in Fig. 15.9 below.

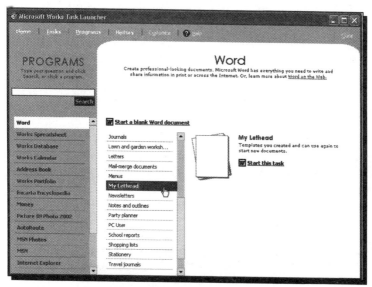

Fig. 15.9 Your Personal Letterhead Template.

Selecting this option and pressing **Start this task** will open a new document with all the text and formatting already included. All you have to do then is complete the body of your letter.

Creating a Template in Works 6.0 WP

The procedure for preparing a template in Works 6.0 word processor is similar to that described in Word. Having created your letterhead, save it using the **File**, **Save As** menu command. In the **Save as type** box of the displayed dialogue box, select **Works Template (*.wpt)**. Works selects automatically the **Template** folder to save your creation in. Next, type a suitable name, maybe 'My Letterhead', in the **File name** box as shown in Fig. 15.10 below, and click **OK**.

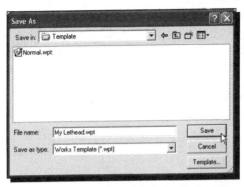

Fig. 15.10 Saving a Template in Works 6.0 WP.

In the future, whenever you want to send a letter, use your new Template instead of starting from scratch. To do this, go to the Tasks section of the Task Launcher, click on **Works Word Processor** and you will find the new option 'My Letterhead' has been added to the list of available tasks, as shown in Fig. 15.11 below.

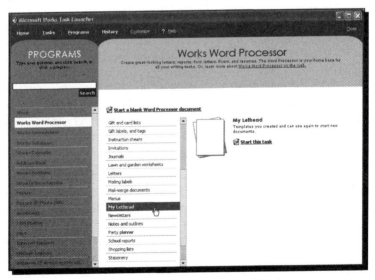

Fig. 15.11 Your Personal Letterhead Template.

Travel Information

Works Suite 2002 includes AutoRoute 2002 (with choices for Europe and World) which is an invaluable tool to finding places or organising your travel route. To look at what is offered, start the Works Launcher and select Travel Information, followed by Driving directions, as shown in Fig. 15.12.

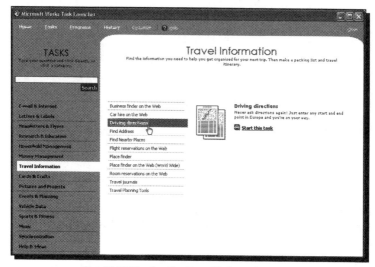

Fig. 15.12 Starting the Travel Information Task.

We tested the program on driving information between Redruth (Cornwall) and Cambridge, a route often used and familiar to us. Below we go through the various steps in selecting the best route and examining other available options.

To start the program click the **Start this task** link. Depending on your installation, you might be asked to insert the relevant Works disc in the CD-ROM drive before the first screen shown in Fig. 15.13 on the next page is displayed. Note the two choices under the **Find** button, **World** and **Europe**.

The next step is to specify the starting and finishing points of your journey. We typed 'Redruth' to replace the text **Type place or address** in the top box and clicked **Find**.

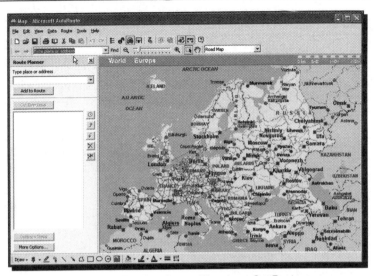

Fig. 15.13 The First Screen Planning a Car Route.

The reason for this is to make sure that the correct place is selected - there might be more than one Redruth on the map in which case they will be displayed in a drop-down list. Select the correct starting place and click the **Add to Route** button. The area of your starting place will now be displayed on the map. Next type your destination (Cambridge in our case), and add it

to the route. The map now displays the destination area. We now have all the required information and clicking the **Get Directions** button, shown here to the left, displays the colourful dialogue box in Fig. 15.14 below.

In a very short time a very detailed route of your journey is displayed with a summary at the end, as shown in Fig. 15.15 on the next page.

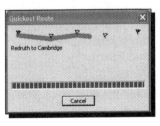

Fig. 15.14 Working out the Quickest Route.

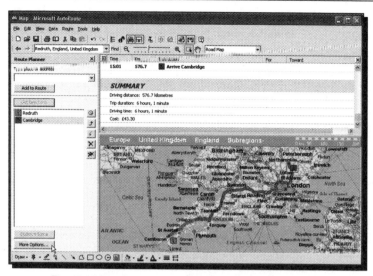

Fig. 15.15 The Quickest Route Between Specified Points.

If this route does not suit you, you can specify other options by clicking the **More Options** button pointed to above. This opens the More Route Options dialogue box shown in Fig. 15.16.

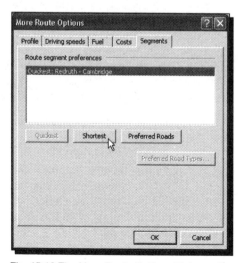

Fig. 15.16 The More Route Options Dialogue Box.

The available options are many and varied. We selected to have a look at the shortest route between the specified points. To get this, after you click the **Shortest** button on the More Route Options dialogue box, click **OK**, then click the area shown below, which appears at the top of the right panel of your screen.

The route is then recalculated and the results are shown in Fig. 15.17.

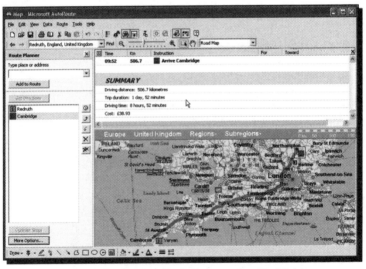

Fig. 15.17 The Shortest Route Between Specified Points.

Note that although this route is the shortest and costs less (rather a debatable point), it takes several hours more which we also found to be true. At the end the choice is yours - the quickest route is not very interesting, while the shortest route is, but you might get too tired to enjoy it!

Finally, we will not spent any more time covering other Task Wizards for two very good reasons:

1. They are very user friendly and almost anyone should be able to work through them without too many problems.

2. We feel strongly that you will become more proficient with the Works program, as a whole, if you build your own applications.

*   *   *

Works has more commands and functions which can be used to build and run your applications and to link with other applications in special ways. What this book has tried to do is to introduce you to the overall subject and give you a solid foundation on which to build your future knowledge.

*   *   *

16

Glossary of Terms

Access control	A security mechanism that determines which operations a user is authorised to perform on a PC, a file, a printer, etc.
Active	Describes the folder, window or icon that you are currently using or that is currently selected.
Active partition	A partition from which an x86-based computer starts up. The active partition must be a primary partition on a basic disc.
ActiveX	A set of technologies that enables software components to interact with one another in a networked environment, regardless of the language in which the components were created.
Add-in	A mini-program which runs in conjunction with another and enhances its functionality.
Address	A unique number or name that identifies a specific computer or user on a network.
Anonymous FTP	Anonymous FTP allows you to connect to a remote computer and transfer public files back to your local computer without the need to have a user ID and password.

Applet	A program that can be downloaded over a network and launched on the user's computer.
Application	Software (program) designed to carry out certain activity, such as word processing, or data management.
Archie	Archie is an Internet service that allows you to locate files that can be downloaded via FTP.
ASCII	A binary code representation of a character set. The name stands for 'American Standard Code for Information Interchange'.
ASP	Active Server Page. File format used for dynamic Web pages that get their data from a server based database.
Association	An identification of a filename extension to a program. This lets Windows open the program when its files are selected.
Attachment	A file that is added to an e-mail message for transmission.
Authoring	The process of creating web documents or software.
AVI	Audio Video Interleaved. A Windows multimedia file format for sound and moving pictures.
Backbone	The main transmission lines of the Internet, running at over 45Mbps (million bits per second).
Background	An image, colour or texture which forms the background of a Web page or document.
Backup	To make a back-up copy of a file or a disc for safekeeping.

Banner	An advertising graphic shown on a Web page.
BASIC	Beginner's All-purpose Symbolic Instruction Code - a high-level programming language.
Baud rate	The speed at which a modem communicates.
BBS	Bulletin Board System, a computer equipped with software and telecoms links that allow it to act as an information host for remote computer systems.
Binary	A base-2 number system in which values are expressed as combinations of two digits, 0 and 1.
Bit	The smallest unit of information handled by a computer.
Bitmap	A technique for managing the image displayed on a computer screen.
Bookmark	A marker inserted at a specific point in a document. Used as a target for a hypertext link, or to enable a user to return for later reference.
Boot partition	The partition on a hard disc that contains the operating system and its support files.
Boot up	To start your computer by switching it on, which initiates a self test of its Random Access Memory (RAM), then loads the necessary system files.
Browse	A button in some Windows dialogue boxes that lets you view a list of files and folders before you make a selection. Also to view a Web page.

Browser	A program, like the Internet Explorer, that lets you view Web pages.
Bug	An error in coding or logic that causes a program to malfunction.
Button	A graphic element or icon in a dialogue box or toolbar that performs a specified function.
Bytes	A unit of data that holds a single character, such as a letter, a digit.
Cable modem	A device that enables a broadband connection to the Internet by using cable television infrastructure.
Cache	An area of memory, or disc space, reserved for data, which speeds up downloading.
Card	A removable printed-circuit board that is plugged into a computer expansion slot.
CD-R	Recordable compact disc.
CD-ROM	Compact Disc - Read Only Memory; an optical disc which information may be read from but not written to.
CD-RW	Rewritable compact disc. Data can be copied to the CD on more than one occasion and can be erased.
Chart	A graphical view of data that is used to visually display trends, patterns, and comparisons.
Click	To press and release a mouse button once without moving the mouse.
Client	A computer that has access to services over a computer network. The computer providing the services is a server.

Client application	A Windows application that can accept linked, or embedded, objects.
Clipboard	A temporary storage area of memory, where text and graphics are stored with the cut and copy actions. The Office XP clipboard can store up to 24 items.
Command	An instruction given to a computer to carry out a particular action.
Configuration	A general purpose term referring to the way you have your computer set up.
Context menu	A menu that opens when you right-click the mouse button on a feature.
Controls	Objects on a form, report, or data access page that display data, perform actions, or are used for decoration.
Cookies	Files stored on your hard drive by your Web browser that hold information for it to use.
CPU	The Central Processing Unit; the main chip that executes all instructions entered into a computer.
Cyberspace	Originated by William Gibson in his novel 'Neuromancer', now used to describe the Internet and the other computer networks.
Data access page	A Web page, created by Access, that has a connection to a database; you can view, add, edit, and manipulate the data in this page.
Data packet	A unit of information transmitted as a whole from one device to another on a network.
Database	A collection of data related to a particular topic or purpose.

DBMS	Database management system - A software interface between the database and the user.
Default	The command, device or option automatically chosen.
Desktop	The Windows screen working background.
Device driver	A special file that must be loaded into memory for Windows to be able to address a specific procedure or hardware device.
Device name	A logical name used by an operating system to identify a device, such as LPT1 or COM1 for the parallel or serial printer.
Dial-up Connection	A popular form of Net connection for the home user, over standard telephone lines.
Dialogue box	A window displayed on the screen to allow the user to enter information.
Digital signature	A means for originators of a message, file, or other digitally encoded information to bind their identity to the information.
Direct Connection	A permanent connection between your computer system and the Internet.
Directory	An area on disc where information relating to a group of files is kept. Also known as a folder.
Disc	A device on which you can store programs and data.
Disconnect	To detach a drive, port or computer from a shared device, or to break an Internet connection.

Display adapter	An expansion board that plugs into a PC to give it display capabilities.
DLL	Dynamic Link Library; An OS feature that allows files with the .dll extensions to be loaded only when needed by the program.
Document	A file produced by an application program. When used in reference to the Web, a document is any file containing text, media or hyperlinks that can be transferred from an HTTP server to a browser.
Domain	A group of devices, servers and computers on a network.
Domain Name	The name of an Internet site, for example www.kantaris.com, which allows you to reference Internet sites without knowing their true numerical address.
DOS	Disc Operating System. A collection of small specialised programs that allow interaction between user and computer.
Double-click	To quickly press and release a mouse button twice.
Download	To transfer to your computer a file, or data, from another computer.
DPI	Dots Per Inch - a resolution standard for laser printers.
Drag	To move an object on the screen by pressing and holding down the left mouse button while moving the mouse.
Drive name	The letter followed by a colon which identifies a floppy or hard disc drive.

Drop-down list	A menu item that can be clicked to open extra items that can be selected.
DSL	Digital Subscriber Line - a broad-band connection to the Internet through existing copper telephone wires.
Dual boot	A PC configuration that can start two different operating systems.
DVD	Digital Video Disc; a type of optical disc technology. It looks like a CD but can store greater amounts of data.
E-mail	Electronic Mail - A system that allows computer users to send and receive messages electronically.
Embedded object	Information in a document that is 'copied' from its source application. Selecting the object opens the creating application from within the document.
Encrypted password	A password that is scrambled.
Engine	Software used by search services.
Ethernet	A very common method of networking computers in a LAN.
Expansion slot	A socket in a computer, designed to hold expansion boards and connect them to the system bus.
FAQ	Frequently Asked Questions - A common feature on the Internet, FAQs are files of answers to commonly asked questions.
FAT	The File Allocation Table. An area on disc where information is kept on which part of the disc a file is located.
File extension	The suffix following the period in a filename. Windows uses this to identify the source application program.

Filename	The name given to a file. In Windows 95 and above this can be up to 256 characters long.
Filter	A set of criteria that is applied to data to show a subset of the data.
Firewall	Security measures designed to protect a networked system from unauthorised access.
Floppy disc	A removable disc on which information can be stored magnetically.
Folder	An area used to store a group of files, usually with a common link.
Font	A graphic design representing a set of characters, numbers and symbols.
Format	The structure of a file that defines the way it is stored and laid out on the screen or in print.
Freeware	Software that is available for downloading and unlimited use without charge.
FTP	File Transfer Protocol. The procedure for connecting to a remote computer and transferring files.
Function key	One of the series of 10 or 12 keys marked with the letter F and a numeral, used for specific operations.
Gateway	A computer system that allows otherwise incompatible networks to communicate with each other.
GIF	Graphics Interchange Format, a common standard for images on the Web.
Gigabyte	(GB); 1,024 megabytes. Usually thought of as one billion bytes.

Graphic	A picture or illustration, also called an image. Formats include GIF, JPEG, BMP, PCX, and TIFF.
Graphics card	A device that controls the display on the monitor and other allied functions.
Group	A collection of users, computers, contacts, and other groups.
GUI	A Graphic User Interface, such as Windows 98, the software front-end meant to provide an attractive and easy to use interface.
Handshaking	A series of signals acknowledging that communication can take place between computers or other devices.
Hard copy	Output on paper.
Hard disc	A device built into the computer for holding programs and data.
Hardware	The equipment that makes up a computer system, excluding the programs or software.
Help	A Windows system that gives you instructions and additional information on using a program.
Hit	A single request from a web browser for a single item from a web server.
Home page	The document displayed when you first open your Web browser, or the first document you come to at a Web site.
Host	Computer connected directly to the Internet that provides services to other local and/or remote computers.
Hotlist	A list of frequently used Web locations and URL addresses.

HTML	HyperText Markup Language, the format used in documents on the Web.
HTML editor	Authoring tool which assists with the creation of HTML pages.
HTTP	HyperText Transport Protocol, the system used to link and transfer hypertext documents on the Web.
Hub	A common connection point for devices in a network.
Hyperlink	A segment of text, or an image, that refers to another document on the Web, an Intranet or your PC.
Hypermedia	Hypertext extended to include linked multimedia.
Hypertext	A system that allows documents to be cross-linked so that the reader can explore related links, or documents, by clicking on a highlighted symbol.
Icon	A small graphic image, or button, that represents a function or object. Clicking on an icon produces an action.
ICS	Internet Connection Sharing.
Image	See graphic.
Insertion point	A flashing bar that shows where typed text will be entered into a document.
Interface	A device that allows you to connect a computer to its peripherals.
Internet	The global system of computer networks.
Intranet	A private network inside an organisation using the same kind of software as the Internet.

IP	Internet Protocol - The rules that provide basic Internet functions.
IP Address	Internet Protocol Address - every computer on the Internet has a unique identifying number.
ISA	Industry Standard Architecture; a standard for internal connections in PCs.
ISDN	Integrated Services Digital Network, a telecom standard using digital transmission technology to support voice, video and data communications applications over regular telephone lines.
ISP	Internet Service Provider - A company that offers access to the Internet.
Java	An object-oriented programming language created by Sun Microsystems for developing applications and applets that are capable of running on any computer, regardless of the operating system.
JPEG/JPG	Joint Photographic Experts Group, a popular cross-platform format for image files. JPEG is best suited for true colour original images.
Kernel	The core of layered architecture that manages the most basic operations of the operating system and the computer's processor.
Kilobyte	(KB); 1024 bytes of information or storage space.
LAN	Local Area Network - High-speed, privately-owned network covering a limited geographical area, such as an office or a building.

Laptop	A portable computer small enough to sit on your lap.
LCD	Liquid Crystal Display.
Linked object	An object that is inserted into a document but still exists in the source file. Changing the original object automatically updates it within the linked document.
Links	The hypertext connections between Web pages.
Local	A resource that is located on your computer, not linked to it over a network.
Location	An Internet address.
Log on	To gain access to a network.
MCI	Media Control Interface - a standard for files and multimedia devices.
Megabyte	(MB); 1024 kilobytes of information or storage space.
Megahertz	(MHz); Speed of processor in millions of cycles per second.
Memory	Part of computer consisting of storage elements organised into addressable locations that can hold data and instructions.
Menu	A list of available options in an application.
Menu bar	The horizontal bar that lists the names of menus.
MIDI	Musical Instrument Digital Interface - enables devices to transmit and receive sound and music messages.

MIME	Multipurpose Internet Mail Extensions, a messaging standard that allows Internet users to exchange e-mail messages enhanced with graphics, video and voice.
MIPS	Million Instructions Per Second; measures speed of a system.
Modem	Short for Modulator-demodulator devices. An electronic device that lets computers communicate electronically.
Monitor	The display device connected to your PC, also called a screen.
Mouse	A device used to manipulate a pointer around your display and activate processes by pressing buttons.
MPEG	Motion Picture Experts Group - a video file format offering excellent quality in a relatively small file.
MS-DOS	Microsoft's implementation of the Disc Operating System for PCs.
Multimedia	The use of photographs, music and sound and movie images in a presentation.
Multitasking	Performing more than one operation at the same time.
My Documents	A folder that provides a convenient place to store documents, graphics, or other files you want to access quickly.
Network	Two or more computers connected together to share resources.
Network adapter	A device that connects your computer to a network.
Network server	Central computer which stores files for several linked computers.

Node	Any single computer connected to a network.
OLE	Object Linking and Embedding - A technology for transferring and sharing information among software applications.
Online	Having access to the Internet.
Online Service	Services such as America On-line and CompuServe that provide content to subscribers and usually connections to the Internet.
Operating system	Software that runs a computer.
Page	An HTML document, or Web site.
Parallel port	The input/output connector for a parallel interface device. Printers are generally plugged into a parallel port.
Partition	A portion of a physical disc that functions as though it were a physically separate disc.
Password	A unique character string used to gain access to a network, program, or mailbox.
PATH	The location of a file in the directory tree.
PCI	Peripheral Component Interconnect - a type of slot in your computer which accepts similar type peripheral cards.
Peripheral	Any device attached to a PC.
Pixel	A picture element on screen; the smallest element that can be independently assigned colour and intensity.

Plug-and-play	Hardware which can be plugged into a PC and be used immediately without configuration.
POP3	Post Office Protocol - a method of storing and returning e-mail.
Port	The place where information goes into or out of a computer, e.g. a modem might be connected to the serial port.
PostScript	A page-description language (PDL), developed by Adobe Systems for printing on laser printers.
Print queue	A list of print jobs waiting to be sent to a printer.
Program	A set of instructions which cause a computer to perform tasks.
Protocol	A set of rules or standards that define how computers communicate with each other.
Query	The set of keywords and operators sent by a user to a search engine, or a database search request.
Queue	A list of e-mail messages waiting to be sent over the Internet.
RAM	Random Access Memory. The computer's volatile memory. Data held in it is lost when power is switched off.
Refresh	To update displayed information with current data.
Registered file type	File types that are tracked by the system registry and are recognised by the programs you have installed on your computer.

Registry	A database where information about a computer's configuration is deposited. The registry contains information that Windows continually references during its operation.
Remote computer	A computer that you can access only by using a communications line or a communications device, such as a network card or a modem.
Resource	A directory, or printer, that can be shared over a network.
Right-click	To click the right mouse button once.
Robot	A Web agent that visits sites, by requesting documents from them, for the purposes of indexing for search engines. Also known as Wanderers, Crawlers, or Spiders.
ROM	Read Only Memory. A PC's non-volatile memory. Data is written into this memory at manufacture and is not affected by power loss.
RTF	Rich Text Format. An enhanced form of text that includes basic formatting and is used for transferring data between applications, or in e-mail messages.
Screen saver	A moving picture or pattern that appears on your screen when you have not used the mouse or keyboard for a specified period of time.
Script	A type of program consisting of a set of instructions to an application or tool program.
Scroll bar	A bar that appears at the right side or bottom edge of a window.
Search	Submit a query to a search engine.

Search engine	A program that helps users find information across the Internet.
Serial interface	An interface that transfers data as individual bits.
Server	A computer system that manages and delivers information for client computers.
Shared resource	Any device, program or file that is available to network users.
Shareware	Software that is available on public networks and bulletin boards. Users are expected to pay a nominal amount to the software developer.
Shortcut	A link to any item accessible on your computer or on a network, such as a program, file, folder, disc drive, Web page, printer, or another computer.
Signature file	An ASCII text file, maintained within e-mail programs, that contains text for your signature.
Site	A place on the Internet. Every Web page has a location where it resides which is called its site.
SMTP	Simple Mail Transfer Protocol - a protocol dictating how e-mail messages are exchanged over the Internet.
Software	The programs and instructions that control your PC.
Spamming	Sending the same message to a large number of mailing lists or newsgroups. Also to overload a Web page with excessive keywords in an attempt to get a better search ranking.
Spider	See robot.

Spooler	Software which handles transfer of information to a store to be used by a peripheral device.
SQL	Structured Query Language, used with relational databases.
SSL	Secure Sockets Layer, the standard transmission security protocol developed by Netscape, which has been put into the public domain.
Subscribe	To become a member of.
Surfing	The process of looking around the Internet.
SVGA	Super Video Graphics Array; it has all the VGA modes but with 256, or more, colours.
Swap file	An area of your hard disc used to store temporary operating files, also known as virtual memory.
Sysop	System Operator - A person responsible for the physical operations of a computer system or network resource.
Task bar	The bar that by default is located at the bottom of your screen whenever Windows is running. It contains the Start button, buttons for all the applications that are open, and icons for other applications.
Task Manager	A utility that provides information about programs and processes running on the computer. Using Task Manager, you can end or run programs and end processes, and display a dynamic overview of your computer's performance.

Task Pane	A pane or sub-window that gives a range of options pertaining to the task currently being performed. New to Office XP applications.
TCP/IP	Transmission Control Protocol/ Internet Protocol, combined protocols that perform the transfer of data between two computers. TCP monitors and ensures the correct transfer of data. IP receives the data, breaks it up into packets, and sends it to a network within the Internet.
Telnet	A program which allows people to remotely use computers across networks.
Text file	An unformatted file of text characters saved in ASCII format.
Thumbnail	A small graphic image.
TIFF	Tag Image File Format - a popular graphic image file format.
Toggle	To turn an action on and off with the same switch.
Tool	Software program used to support Web site creation and management.
Toolbar	A bar containing buttons or icons giving quick access to commands.
TrueType fonts	Fonts that can be scaled to any size and print as they show on the screen.
Uninstall	When referring to software, the act of removing program files and folders from your hard disc and removing related data from your registry so the software is no longer available.

Upload/Download	The process of transferring files between computers. Files are uploaded from your computor to another and downloaded from another computer to your own.
URL	Uniform Resource Locator, the addressing system used on the Web, containing information about the method of access, the server to be accessed and the path of the file to be accessed.
Usenet	Informal network of computers that allow the posting and reading of messages in newsgroups that focus on specific topics.
User ID	The unique identifier, usually used in conjunction with a password, which identifies you on a computer.
Virtual Reality	Simulations of real or imaginary worlds, rendered on a flat two-dimensional screen but appearing three-dimensional.
Virus	A malicious program, downloaded from a web site or disc, designed to wipe out information on your computer.
W3C	The World Wide Web Consortium that is steering standards development for the Web.
WAIS	Wide Area Information Server, a Net-wide system for looking up specific information in Internet databases.
Watermark	Toned down image or text that appears in the background of a printed page.

WAV	Waveform Audio (**.wav**) - a common audio file format for DOS/Windows computers.
Web	A network of hypertext-based multimedia information servers. Browsers are used to view any information on the Web.
Web Page	An HTML document that is accessible on the Web.
Webmaster	One whose job it is to manage a web site.
WINSOCK	A Microsoft Windows file that provides the interface to TCP/IP services.
Wizard	A Microsoft tool that shows how to perform certain operations, or asks you questions and then creates an object depending on your answers.

Appendix

Works Functions

Microsoft Works' functions are built-in formulae that perform specialised calculations in both the spreadsheet and database applications. Their general format is:

=name(arg1,arg2,...)

where 'name' is the function name, and 'arg1', 'arg2', etc., are the arguments required for the evaluation of the function. Arguments must appear in a parenthesised list as shown above and their exact number depends on the function being used. However, there are seven functions that do not require arguments and are used with empty parentheses. These are: =ERR( ), =FALSE( ), =NA( ), =NOW( ), =PI( ), =RAND( ) and =TRUE( ).

There are three types of arguments used with =functions: numeric values, range values and text strings, the type used being dependent on the type of function. Numeric value arguments can be entered either directly as numbers, as a cell address, a cell range name or as a formula. Range value arguments can be entered either as a range address or a range name.

Types of Functions

There are several types of functions, such as math and trigonometry, logical, financial, statistical, text, date and time, lookup and reference and informational. Each type requires its own number and type of arguments. These are listed in the following pages under the various function categories together with what they return.

Math and Trigonometry Functions

Mathematical functions evaluate a result using numeric arguments.

Function	*Returns*
=ABS(X)	The absolute value of X.
=ACOS(X)	The angle in radians, whose cosine is X (arc cos of X).
=ASIN(X)	The angle in radians, whose sine is X (arc sin of X).
=ATAN(X)	The angle (radians), between $\pi/2$ and $-\pi/2$, whose tangent is X (arc tan of X - 2 quadrant).
=ATAN2(X,Y)	The angle (radians), between π and $-\pi$ whose tangent is Y/X (arc tan of Y/X - 4 quadrant).
=COS(X)	The cosine of angle X, (X must be in radians).
=EXP(X)	The value of e raised to the power of X.
=INT(X)	The integer part of X.
=LN(X)	The natural logarithm (base e) of X.
=LOG(X)	The logarithm (base 10) of X.
=MOD(X,Y)	The remainder of X/Y.
=PI( )	The value of π (3.141593).
=RAND( )	A random number between 0 and 1, excluding 1.
=ROUND(X,N)	The value of X rounded to N places.
=SIN(X)	The sine of angle X (X must be in radians).
=SQRT(X)	The square root of X.
=TAN(X)	The tangent of angle X (X must be in radians).

Logical Functions

Logical functions produce a value based on the result of a conditional statement, using numeric arguments.

Function	*Returns*
=AND(Ag0,Ag1...)	The logical value 1 (TRUE) if all of the arguments are TRUE.
=FALSE( )	The logical value 0.
=IF(Cr,X,Y)	The value X if Cr is TRUE and Y if Cr is FALSE.
=NOT(Ag)	The opposite of logical value Ag.
=OR(Ag0,Ag1...)	The logical value 1 (TRUE) if any of the arguments are TRUE.
=TRUE( )	The logical value 1.

Financial Functions

Financial functions evaluate loans, annuities, and cash flows over a period of time, using numeric arguments.

Function	*Returns*
=CTERM(Rt,Fv,Pv)	The number of compounding periods for an investment of present value Pv, to grow to a future value Fv, at a fixed interest rate Rt.
=DDB(Ct,Sg,Lf,Pd)	The double-declining depreciation allowance of an asset, given the original cost Ct, predicted salvage value Sg, the life Lf of the asset, and the period Pd.
=FV(Pt,Rt,Tm)	The future value of a series of equal payments, each of equal amount Pt, earning a periodic interest rate Rt, over a number of payment periods in term Tm.
=IRR(Gs,Rg)	The internal rate of return of the series of cash flows in a range Rg, based on the approximate percentage guess Gs.

=NPV(Rt,Rg)	The present value of the series of future cash flows in range Rg, discounted at a periodic interest rate Rt.
=PMT(Pl,Rt,Tm)	The amount of the periodic payment needed to pay off the principal Pl, at a periodic interest rate Rt, over the number of payment periods in term Tm.
=PV(Pt,Rt,Tm)	The present value of a series of equal payments, each of equal amount Pt, discounted at a periodic interest rate Rt, over a number of payment periods in term Tm.
=RATE(Fv,Pv,Tm)	The periodic interest rate necessary for a present value Pv to grow to a future value Fv, over the number of compounding periods in term Tm.
=SLN(Ct,Sg,Lf)	The straight-line depreciation allowance of an asset for one period, given the original cost Ct, predicted salvage value Sg, and the life Lf of the asset.
=SYD(Ct,Sg,Lf,Pd)	The sum-of-the-years' digits depreciation allowance of an asset, given the original cost Ct, predicted salvage value Sg, the life Lf of the asset, and the period Pd.
=TERM(Pt,Rt,Fv)	The number of payment periods of an investment, given the amount of each payment Pt, the periodic interest rate Rt, and the future value of the investment Fv.

Statistical Functions

Statistical functions evaluate lists of values using numeric arguments or cell ranges.

Function	Returns
=AVG(Rg0,Rg1,...)	The average of values in range(s) Rg0, Rg1, ...
=COUNT(Rg0,Rg1,...)	The number of non-blank entries in range(s) Rg0, Rg1, ...
=MAX(Rg0,Rg1,...)	The maximum value in range(s) Rg0, Rg1, ...
=MIN(Rg0,Rg1,...)	The minimum value in range(s) Rg0, Rg1, ...
=STD(Rg0,Rg1,...)	The standard deviation of values in range(s) Rg0, Rg1, ...
=SUM(Rg0,Rg1,...)	The sum of values in range(s) Rg0, Rg1, ...
=VAR(Rg0,Rg1,...)	The variance of values in range(s) Rg0, Rg1, ...

Text Functions

Text functions operate on strings and produce numeric or string values dependent on the function.

Function	Returns
=EXACT(Sg1,Sg2)	The value 1 (TRUE) if strings Sg1 and Sg2 are exactly alike, otherwise 0 (FALSE).
=FIND(Ss,Sg,Sn)	The position at which the first occurrence of search string Ss begins in string Sg, starting the search from search number Sn.
=LEFT(Sg,N)	The first (leftmost) N characters in string Sg.
=LENGTH(Sg)	The number of characters in string Sg.
=LOWER(Sg)	A string Sg with all the letters converted to lowercase.

=MID(Sg,Sn,N)	The N characters from string Sg beginning with the character at Sn.
=N(Rg)	The numeric value in the upper left corner cell in range Rg.
=PROPER(Sg)	A string with all letters in Sg changed to first letter in uppercase and the rest in lowercase.
=REPEAT(Sg,N)	A repeated string Sg N times. Unlike the repeating character (\), the output is not limited by the column width.
=REPLACE(O,S,N,Ns)	A string with N characters removed from original string O, starting at character S and then inserts new string Ns in the vacated place.
=RIGHT(Sg,N)	The last (rightmost) N characters in string Sg.
=S(Rg)	The string value in the upper left corner cell in range Rg.
=STRING(X,N)	The numeric value X as a string, with N decimal places.
=TRIM(Sg)	A string Sg with no leading, trailing or consecutive spaces.
=UPPER(Sg)	All letters in string Sg converted to uppercase.
=VALUE(Sg)	The numeric value of string Sg.

Date and Time Functions

Date and time functions generate and use serial numbers to represent dates and times. Each date between 1 January, 1900 and 31 December 2079 has an integer serial number starting with 1 and ending with 65534. Each moment during a day has a decimal serial number starting with 0.000 at midnight and ending with 0.99999 just before the following midnight.

Function	*Returns*
=DATE(Yr,Mh,Dy)	The date number of Yr,Mh,Dy.
=DAY(Dn)	The day of the month number (1-31) of date number Dn.
=HOUR(Tn)	The hour number (0-23) of time number Tn.
=MINUTE(Tn)	The minute number (0-59) of time number Tn.
=MONTH(Dn)	The month number (1-12) of date number Dn.
=NOW( )	The serial number for the current date and time.
=SECOND(Tn)	The second number (0-59) of time number Tn.
=TIME(Hr,Ms,Ss)	The time number of Hr,Ms,Ss.
=YEAR(Dn)	The year number of date number Dn.

Lookup and Reference Functions

Special functions perform a variety of advanced tasks, such as looking up a value in a table.

Function	*Returns*
=CHOOSE(I,L0,...,Ln)	The Ith value in the list L0,...,Ln.
=COLS(Rg)	The number of columns in the range Rg.
=HLOOKUP(X,Rg,Rn)	The value of indicated cell by performing a horizontal table look-up by comparing the value X to each cell in the top index row in range Rg, then moves down the column in which a match is found by the specified row number Rn.
=INDEX(Rg,Cn,Rw)	The value of the cell in range Rg at the intersection of column Cn and row Rw.
=ROWS(Rg)	The number of rows in a range.

=VLOOKUP(X,Rg,Cn)   The value of indicated cell by performing a vertical table look-up by comparing the value X to each cell in the first column, or index column, in range Rg, then moves across the row in which a match is found by the specified column number Cn.

Informational Functions

Tests cells of a range of cells for specific conditions or errors.

Function	*Returns*
=ERR( )	The value of ERR.
=ISERR(X)	The value 1 (TRUE) if X contains ERR, else 0 (FALSE).
=ISNA(X)	The value 1 (TRUE) if X contains N/A, else 0 (FALSE).
=NA( )	The numeric value of N/A.

Index

Companion Discs

COMPANION DISCS are available for most computer books written by the same author(s) and published by BERNARD BABANI (publishing) LTD, as listed at the front of this book (except for those marked with an asterisk). These books contain many pages of file/program listings. There is no reason why you should spend hours typing them into your computer, unless you wish to do so, or need the practice.

ORDERING INSTRUCTIONS

To obtain companion discs, fill in the order form below, or a copy of it, enclose a cheque (payable to **P.R.M. Oliver**) or a postal order, and send it to the address given below. **Make sure you fill in your name and address** and specify the book number and title in your order.

Book No.	Book Name	Unit Price	Total Price
BP		£3.50	
BP		£3.50	
BP		£3.50	
Name .... Address		Sub-total	£.............
		P & P (@ 45p/disc)	£.............
		Total Due	£.............
Send to: P.R.M. Oliver, West Trevarth House, West Trevarth, Nr Redruth, Cornwall, TR16 5TJ			

PLEASE NOTE

The author(s) are fully responsible for providing this Companion Disc service. The publishers of this book accept no responsibility for the supply, quality, or magnetic contents of the disc, or in respect of any damage, or injury that might be suffered or caused by its use.